KENNETH FRIEDENREICH

OREGON WINE COUNTRY STORIES

Decoding THE Grape

AMERICAN PALATE

Published by American Palate
A Division of The History Press
Charleston, SC
www.historypress.com

Front cover image courtesy of Willamette Valley Vineyards. Back cover images courtesy of Analema Wines.

First published 2018

Manufactured in the United States

ISBN 9781625858757

Library of Congress Control Number: 2017963229

Notice: The information in this book is true and complete to the best of our knowledge. It is offered without guarantee on the part of the author or The History Press. The author and The History Press disclaim all liability in connection with the use of this book.

With thanks to the muses, Barbara, Ellen, Margo and Sharon.

Don't wait up for me, but I have the corkscrew.

Nothing else is so irritating as impartiality.

Every harvest is a miracle of the Earth and a whim of the Sky.

—*Will Durant,* The Reformation, *vol. 6 of* The Story of Civilization

Fifty-four forty or fight!

—*campaign motto on the disputed Oregon Territory regarding claims by Britain and the United States of America in the 1840s*

Was Gott tut ist wohlgetan.

—*Johann Sebastian Bach, Cantatas 99 and 100*

CONTENTS

CONTENTS

PREFACE

The origin of this book dates to 1984. Ironically, that year was a "harvest from hell" in the Willamette Valley, and few winemakers or consumers in Oregon have not repressed their recall of that time. The years prior and following, on the other hand, were very good for Oregon wine, as much as was available. The industry was tiny: labels like Bon Merde and Henry's Rhubarb Wine flew under the radar of regulations. If California vintners were styling, Oregon winemakers were feisty and a bit scruffy.

In the dog year of '84, I visited Portland for the first time as a corporate consultant and trainer in the radiology field. On my bucket list was a meal at Jake's Famous Crawfish, located on the corner of Stark and Southwest Twelfth Avenue, a landmark place that had operated since 1907. When I wanted some wine to accompany my salmon on a plank, the server sent me the wine steward. Well, in a universe of correspondences, this wine guy turned out to be a party to this book more than thirty years later, after I finally told the Doc Wilson story in the *Oregon Wine Press* in December 2014 (see the Appendix). So now we're here.

I guess I'm a slow learner; life conspired to bring me to Oregon. In the time after my first visit to the Rose City, I drank in more of the Oregon wine culture thanks to my proximity to both the restaurant industry and the media as a writer and producer. One incredible afternoon, a *contigu* to the plaza before the Metropolitan Opera at Lincoln Center, I waded through scads of wonderful Oregon wine. Then, too, my friend John Ortega, a hospitable high roller, introduced me to some favorite Pinot Noir from the Pacific Northwest, especially from Ponzi Vineyards and WillaKenzie Estate. (Alas, this latter property has been digested by the California gold of Kendall-Jackson. Claims to the contrary notwithstanding, the wine won't be the same.)

I enjoyed wines that expressed attributes other than California bigness and duly took note, far more as consumer than wine writer, although I qualified on both counts. The wines were a bit hard to track; for thirty-four years, I lived in Orange County, home to Disneyland and shopping malls—if not the happiest place on earth then a fast-paced, diverse community nonetheless. For many of those years, I was happily inundated by California wines. California remains the eight-hundred-pound gorilla in the domestic wine trade. Thus, it remains no anomaly that even at this writing many people are surprised to discover that wines also originate in forty-nine other states and many more postal codes. In 2013, as I stood in a Beverly Hills checkout line holding a bottle of Willamette Valley Chardonnay, the woman behind me was astonished to discover that this grape wasn't grown only in California. This moment is one in a chain of experiences big and small that led to this book.

From the outset, place and timing matter. Oregon is currently fourth in America for wine production, trailing California, Washington and New York while leading Texas and the other forty-five. When I started writing in 2012–13, the state already claimed more than 450 wine properties. It has 720 at this count, as well as 1,046 vineyards. This book accounts, in its own quirky way, for how this growth goes on. And here is the tail to wag the dog: I write the story of my own learning about Oregon wine as the means to celebrate the stories told to me by winemakers and, by inference, the wines they make.

When Eric Asimov claimed in his "Pour" column for the July 14, 2017 *New York Times* that Oregon was the most exciting wine territory on planet Earth at this time, he missed one detail that makes his assessment even more remarkable. Of the top five domestic producer states, Oregon is barely one-twelfth the size of California, about one-eighth that of Texas, one-seventh of New York State and about half as populous as Washington State. This suggests that many people living about the nation and in Oregon itself remain blinkered about Oregon wine as agricultural product or its significance to the state's perception of itself. What is more troubling is the way successful winemaking has attracted big money from outside with attitudes resting on bragging rights and celebrity rather than what actually comes out of the land and wineries by those who make them. Time, not money, is the serpent in the wine industry here.

Having thus fought far above its weight as a viticultural champ relative to size, we must wonder whether Oregon will retain the stamina and independence that makes its wines so compelling. As the generations succeed in the vineyard, the two-minute bell is about to sound.

This is a memoir, a panegyric to drink as commercial and social ecology, laden with some lore and describing transitions from modern founders to their heirs and successors. The book is more meditation than buying guide, more observation than how-to, but these elements are necessary as they are both useful reminders and fun to write about.

Throughout I have monitored the balance of entertaining narratives with the how-to practices in developing one's taste memory so that wine

Eddie, the Erath labradoodle, consults his human, Dick Erath, about the Poodle Rating System for wine. *Courtesy of Dick Erath.*

This bottle of wine, like this book, is intended to be taken into the field. *Courtesy of Naked Winery.*

and place reinforce each other. Largely brief chapters allow readers to use the book for learnable steps as well as good tales. It is a book you can carry with you into Oregon wine lands, emulating the fine sensibilities of Lewis and Clark as they trod west to the mouth of the Columbia River. It's still a thrilling journey of discovery.

I consider what comes in the following pages a snapshot of Oregon's wine industry as it appears between penning my narrative and its publication. I recall an episode in Joseph Kanon's *Leaving Berlin* when the hero sorts out the contact sheets of a photographer who was gunned down. Outside the cropped images, more is revealed than what one sees before one's eyes. This also holds true in film or television production. The most accurate rendering is always part illusory and incomplete. So, I'd wager that my take on Oregon wines reveals more by what sits just outside the frame. In appreciating wines, much of the good stuff is also just beyond what you think you know.

If by the close you have not poured yourself a glass of wine in a nice stem, it is not my fault. Read the book again.

ACKNOWLEDGEMENTS

Oops! Okay, so a survey of this kind that doubles as a kind of brief on behalf of Oregon wine trade and is also a memoir will omit some joys and bungle a few others. I apologize before readers' "gotcha" glands go to work. Use your secretions instead to enjoy the wines and their narratives. Thus disposed, come along with me—run softly, sweet rivers, until I end my song.

Books may originate with a writer or two. However, no man or woman is an island or, for our purposes, a single block in a vineyard. A good deal of care and feeding go into making an author's notions palpable and sensible.

At the top of my list are Jonathan Potkin, my friend of over sixty years, and Doc Wilson, the "Kevin Bacon of Oregon Wine," both of whom contributed mightily to the logistics and arranging many of the appointments that created the subject matter of *Oregon Wine Country Stories*.

Others deserve a substantial measure of my gratitude. The list begins with my column publishers, Jay Beeler and Susan McFadden in southern California, and a number of commercial importers and wholesalers, including Ciro Cirillo of Mission Wine Company; Patrick Ruzgerian, most recently of Wine Warehouse; Pilar Lemma of Lemma Wine Company; and Tim Hirota of Southern Wine and Spirits, to mention those most prominent. As the book neared completion, I hooked up as well with Gene Cameron of Awesome Wines Company in Silverton and the late Dave Fry, who bought the company from Gene.

Acknowledgements

I have been fortunate to establish working relationships with Hilary Berg, editor of *Oregon Wine Press*, and Rachael Woody and Rich Schmidt of the Oregon Wine History Project and its archive located at Linfield College in McMinnville, where among other things the Spruce Goose nested after many years in Long Beach, California. I add to this mix Rachel Ritchie, who is the chief editor at *Portland Monthly*, for which I wrote a piece on gin. The following pages owe much to these associations and other iterations of the material. On the other hand, I thank for myriad reasons Gordon DeBoer and Sid and Julie Gall, as well as, for his Road 31 Pinot Noir, Kent Fortner and his pithy newsletter. All are fine folks.

In the bacon-preserved department, I owe much to Frank Trowt, although at the moment I owe him no money. For a lifetime of support, service to our country and a bent sense of humor, I acknowledge my paternal uncle, Gilbert Friedenreich. Although indifferent to wine, he condescends to drink it with me. Also, I must thank the unrelated Doyles: the late Ed and the still mortally coiled Brian, one my co-editor of hotel book dining annuals and the other my attorney. To these Irish-sounding friends I add Paul M. Bryant for his pinot noir enthusiasms, John Ortega for turning me on to Oregon wines in general and the Richardson brothers, Todd and Kevin—one invested my money to good effect and the other spent a little of it. Alex and Eleanor Schub actually left LA to confirm on site what I advertised about Oregon wine. Kenneth E. Grubbs kindly assigned me op-ed excursions prior to sending me to Santiago, Chile, to see the Andes up close and visit vineyards for *World Trade Magazine*.

I could go on with barkeeps and winemakers, but the whole book has been a celebration of drinking customs, habits, rituals and thankfulness for making life more interesting. I greet and thank all vintners and winery proprietors for their continued willingness to share lore and wine.

Others, like David Gene White and Ryan Csanky at Bull Run Distilling Company and his Aria Portland Gin, invented related wine and spirits opportunities.

I am grateful to oeno-friends like Dr. Mark Lindau, Judy Erdman, Dick Stinson, Craig and Karen Mills, Dr. John Maggiano, Larry Walters and the amiable host of people who shared their wines with me. This applies especially to Bill Brown for both wine and wit and to Dewey Faulkner and John W. Halperin for the latter. The Good Old Boys, a monthly aggregate of wine geeks, pioneers and other malefactors, deserve to a man my good will and thanks. This holds true for various grower and wine associations such as Columbia Gorge, Southern Oregon and Walla Walla. The chamber of commerce in our coastal Newport has invited me more than once to its annual February Wine and Seafood Festival, with splendid hostelry at Hallmark Resort at Nye Beach.

Other thanks I extend to the Astoria Seafood and Wine Fest and, in particular, to Morgen McLaughlin, executive director of the Willamette Valley Wineries Association, its North Willamette Valley association counterpart and the PDX Urban Winery group, as well as the enthusiasts who hosted me and Potkin at Walla Walla.

My friend Dr. Joanna Dovalis and Kurt Fritzler, veteran barkeep (ret.) of Seratto Trattoria, are in the rare company of those who turn me on to modern fiction as well as good pours.

I owe more than can be expressed to the Braille Men's Group in Anaheim, California, where I would go to "catch" my particular case of legal blindness, and to the Oregon Commission for the Blind in Portland. "See better, Lear," the loyal Kent says to the foolish, testy king. These two groups allowed me to see better, my foolhardiness notwithstanding.

I started my vision vicissitudes in a clinical polka at the Stein Eye Center at UCLA in 2000, picking up new dance partners at the Casey Eye Institute at Oregon Health Sciences University under care of Mark Panesi, MD, which will at least ameliorate some of my vision issues if not getting me to swat a two-seamer or read a wine label at sixty feet, six inches. One can hope.

Susan Sokol Blosser appears in pages ahead as author and winemaker. I owe to her the short detour that brought Anne Horowitz of Brooklyn into my orbit as editor for grumpy columnists, as well as acquisitions editor Ben Gibson and project editor Ryan Finn of The History Press and Carl Giavanti, a fine fellow who knows his wine marketing and media.

Last, there are the men of the Vortex, a movable sewing circle of bar experts (or at least they maintain this assertion), from Geno (aka Eugene Brady, who moved to the nineteenth hole) to Chuck Boggus, the Honorable Bill McCormick, Dennis O'Connor, Les Osborne, Tom Kallas and John Walling. Thank you.

Wine indeed is the toy we willingly share with others. Still, a glass in hand in a private moment is a kind of communion for which no prayers are mandatory. Although wine is sociable, it offers moments of solitary discoveries. My gratitude balances on a fulcrum of social intercourse and "eureka!" moments in solitude needing no audience or occasion. The following pages encourage readers to take to wine in both modes of experience and recall. My compass better finds True North thanks to the Sunday gatherings of the *Confrerie ves vignerons de Saint Vincent Macon*, Oregon chapter. The company and the cuisine only serve to reinforce our continuing education about wine both local and coming from afar.

A Mexican proverb avers that a fish dies by its mouth. Let's give the lie to that piscatory knowledge in the work to follow. Speaking of good fishing places, the maps within come courtesy of the Oregon Wine Board. So thank you to Michelle Kaufmann, its prior communications director, and to Sally Murdoch, who followed on and faced a baptism of fire, figuratively, with the 2017 Eagle Creek and many other incendiary events across the state often caused by the Nimrods our race seems destined to suffer among their betters.

California Wine Institute based at San Francisco has been an excellent source of industry data as well as contributing to my research by absorbing some costs on my behalf for a sequel that covers Southern California. My sincere best wishes to Gladys Horiuchi, the institute's communication director, for keen insights and timely cooperation. I like people who answer the telephone.

I owe thanks to my Cape Cod cousin E.I. Ravetz for trenchant observations and general encouragement with no conditions—a rarity in my family—and to Dick Erath, wine pioneer, for allowing this writer to create a kind of publication symmetry involving his mighty contribution to Oregon wine. Dick kindly read the book in manuscript, pointed out some errors and clarified some valuable points from his own experience. In Oregon wine lore, it is akin to having Sir Isaac Newton polish your apple.

There is also Ray Wyman, who a decade ago shared with me the inspiration of decoding grapes for a long-defunct wine magazine. You never fully predict what sticks. I also enjoyed the hospitality of Charlotte and Harry Boxer as I began this project in earnest.

Sergio Ortiz provided a pin-up of the Portland Streetcar that serves as one of the indispensable metaphors I use near the close. And the end matter in general owes much to Michael Higgins, busker and database designer, for the wine listing, the index and eyes sharper than mine for proofreading. Thanks to Carl Giavanti, Mr. Higgins performs the little onerous tasks for my website, www.decodingthegrape.com.

In the course of writing my book, some friends have left life's casino and will no longer share wine and stories with me. They are Ed Doyle, Dave Fry, John Halperin and Jim Moo. They will be missed when we pop a cork or two.

Cheers! He drinks from the cup. (*Hamlet*, Act V.)

CHRISTMAS SEASON AT THE CLOSE OF THE TWENTIETH CENTURY

A YETI AND A JEW WALK INTO A BAR: A FABLE OF PERFECT TIMING

Readers may think this is one of those "A Jewish guy and a Yeti walk into a bar" stories, but I demur. This really happened to me. Now you're going to know of it too.

In 1999, as was my custom, I spent my idle hours at the bar and table of Gustaf Anders, a famous Southern California eatery that began its life in La Jolla and ended its run in Orange County. Every year, chef Ulf Anders Strandberg put forth a smorgasbord for the more than twelve days of Christmas that had the color and richness of a cinematic spread. His partner, Bill Magnuson, would always gripe about his fellow Swedes, native or otherwise, who spent money only on special occasions and left this exceptional dining room all but empty most of the year entire. No matter the asides, six kinds of herring brought me to this feast every year—several times.

On this night, I was sipping a Bombay Sapphire when I saw "Buster" (that wasn't his name), who came over with his wife to say hello. Buster looked a bit like Theodore Bikel in his pre-beard days. He was a serious, bearish kind of man, and from behind his horn rims he arbitrated the area dining scene for the *Los Angeles Times*. He wore his pomposity with some charm, however.

Making a point at the Winderlea tasting room. *Courtesy of Jonathan Potkin.*

We knew each other from the dining review wars, as I worked for a hotel magazine and television station, where I invented an advertorial product called Savoir Fare with an outsized woman who had a radio voice and face to equal it.

"Hey, Ken," Buster said, "come to our table for a drink. We are leaving for Las Vegas, big city magazine gig." Although I know not what came of that intended move, I knew enough good manners to accept the invitation. And so I sat.

And then the fable began to spin. Buster's bride was from Nepal, a mountaintop land of insanely thin air sandwiched between those behemoths of billions, China and India. Although it was simply a matter of cruel convenience, and even more because I couldn't pronounce her name, I thought of Ms. Buster as the Yeti. I imagined her as a speck moving on the white face of glacial mountain majesty, yak in tow. Indeed, she was a pleasant and intelligent person, but that would ruin the fable.

So, we did the pleasantry waltz, and I heard all about Las Vegas, a place I cared little for. When it got to my latest work assignment as we went around the table—a miscasting in a pharmaceutical company—the Yeti inquired of my origins, for which I answered the Bronx, New York City.

She said, "New York City. I wonder if you know my brother-in-law."

Then Buster said, "Yeti, don't be foolish. There are 19 million people in that metropolitan area."

Her: "Well, maybe he does."

Him: "You are being ridiculous."

By this time, I was having a second aquavit (I had switched drinking partners). And still they went to and fro on the imposing figure of the absent brother-in-law, who loomed like the Commendatore, just offstage, in *Don Giovanni*. Buster rolled his eyes, cast a condescending frown and insisted that the matter posed was all but impossible. And then it happened. It was possible.

Gradually, without betraying the certainty I knew not a jot, I knew the outcome. It was visceral, like the prelude to a climax. From the toes to the loins and through the thorax to the febrile imaginings to the hair standing on end—something electric.

You see, the iron gears of the World Clock were enmeshed with a perfect alignment of planets and stars. The cosmos was of me and in me, and I knew it. I throttled an impulse to burst out laughing.

Buster: "Enough, enough. Ask him." Exasperation was a trick he could summon at will.

Yeti: "Do you know _____?"

The gears struck the universal hour of time past and present and future. "Yes," said I. "I graduated from Great Neck South Senior High School with him." My classmate had married the Yeti's sister and lived in Nepal, where they operated a hotel.

After Buster recovered, he said, "Just think. A little old lady in the Himalayas must be wondering how both her daughters married Jewish guys from the East Coast."

I have always considered this incident the most perfect example of Jewish Geography, as when everyone at the medical school at Duke once dated the same woman from Wantagh, Long Island. The story is rich and strange enough, but it is the rightness of that moment that has remained so crucial to the narration of this shaggy yak tale.

And why tell it now? Because my sense of moment is all over the food and wine of Oregon. Oregon's wine country did not receive an official American Viticultural Area (AVA) designation until 1984. That same year, I covered the Napa Valley Wine Auction for *Orange County Magazine*; one of those tony trust fund couples from the city described the event as "just a bunch of rich people having fun."

It was already becoming too late to experience Napa and Sonoma as I had first done in 1973, more as a casual tourist than as a serious student of the wine industry in California, which is a demerit since I worked in the spirits and wine industry at the time. But yet I experienced firsthand in those years the handiwork of winemakers Mike Grgich, Robert Mondavi and Charlie Wagner, when they loosed their contemporary energies to show that French varietals could indeed produce great wine in California. This was the time when New World wines asserted their right to sit at table with the Old. It was a great moment in the life of Napa and Sonoma Counties.

In less than a generation, Napa was evolving in the mid-'80s from rural grape country to mega Japanese tourist attraction, then Chinese tourist attraction and so forth until the natives showed up in droves on tour buses, wine coaches and hot air balloons. In other words, the human scale of California's most noted AVA had been devoured by conglomerates, developers, public relations flaks, wedding planners and Lord knows what else since. The tasting room fee at many wineries sailed well above $45 or more per person. And you can't even use your food stamp card! Bring your balance sheet. To wit: the glorious Joseph Phelps Winery, home of the great Insignia red blend (aka "meritage"), can set you back between $75 to $140 for a tasting flight of five wines.

The wines are often wonderful, though. Nonetheless, some wineries and their output have gone Hollywood—more affected than pleasing.

I wrote about a return to the earlier Napa story in 2008. What amenities! What restaurants! What spas! It affects the châteaux of Bordeaux with better plumbing and more ATMs. Napa has also become a victim of its own success; most years, Napa ranks with Disneyland as the state's largest tourist destination. So many hotel beds to fill and so many sheep to shear.

I am repeating some of what I expressed elsewhere then and as recently as the summer of 2016 because even advocates of California's wine industry like Gladys Horiuchi, director of communications for the California Wine Institute (a trade organization), acknowledged that it was "about time" consumers get beyond numbers to see how small producers have much to say in their wines made in the less-traveled AVAs in the state, a kind of corrective to flashing scores all about. The number fetish tends to obliterate distinctions in wines and does little for the efforts of those making them except to spur unnecessary competitive gestures that cloud the scene.

The net damage is oversimplification of wine language and overcompensation for differences in the wines themselves. This sorcery conjures an international style of wine made uniformly to win points. It has yielded the funny fruit reminiscent of a passage in Alison Lurie's 2006 novel *Truth and Consequences*, in which the narrator describes a certain kind of Southern California woman as "noisy, frantic, self-centered, and overdecorated." I think this happened to much California wine over time, and we will look at the consequences in the coming pages.

The Oregon wine country is nothing if not rural. I describe it as being behind the curve of the inevitable corporate plunder to happen in several generations. If Napa has become Babylon, Willamette and beyond still have intimations of Eden and the pastoral. Get to it before it goes away.

And so, the purpose of the book: to wean readers off California wines, less because of their dominance in the imagination of casual wine drinkers than because I wish to show wine adventurers and novices that there are other, often comparable (even at times better) bottles produced in other places—wines coming out of Oregon, for example. To make this volume more than a geek's report, I interleave the useful information within the larger narratives of the vintners and the wines.

In his 1993 biography of James Beard, Robert Clark closes the account of this most enlarged and famous American foodie with a comment on changing fashions. He observes that after about a decade of intense food and wine consumption and celebrity chef worship, many people moved on. They had less budget and leisure to make dining a big deal. He laments that people no longer huddled around the warm stove or the well-laden table, and with that change of habit, they lost the "tales told" by both stove and table.

When you're finished, you will know what matters and will further know I am playing Virgil to your Dante. When you regard a wine in your glass, when you swirl it around there and then sip it, you are the big show. The wine writer is not. The larger-than-life James Beard, dean of American cooking, saw it coming.

For his subject, Beard, who so championed the American cuisines, especially of his native Pacific Northwest, the loss of taste memory would be tragic indeed. I add this sentiment to my own well-honed sense of place and taste, as recollection is often an act of loving re-creation. And I want readers to take from these pages more than just my impressions. I want them to engage the spirit and the sport of re-creation.

For indeed the crux remains what pleases you. And it remains that recall of the narrative helps steer you to satisfactory and, at times, extraordinary wine decisions.

"Memory is hunger," Ernest Hemingway wrote once—a man who knew how to empty a carafe or a fifth of gin or a flagon. Actually, what he might better have said is, "Memory is thirst." Learn to savor wine in the moment without somebody else's hazy numbers shaping your anticipation.

We need to inoculate ourselves from the tendency to allow ratings to predispose us to any wine no matter its place of origin.

Author's Note: The items throughout this work that I call "PERSPECTIVES" represent several kinds of additional comment and illustration. I address the notion of numerical scores throughout the book because they limit one's expectations about wine and betoken a decline of sensibility. Spend a few pages with my friend Nimrod Persiflage and you will become inoculated to wines by scoresheet. A composite of several wine critics, the actual Nimrod reveals himself in chapter 1. How he became the Alpha Critic is part of my story about Oregon wine.

PERSPECTIVES: MEET NIMROD PERSIFLAGE, OR, WHAT IS A WINE CRITIC?

Everyone needs an imaginary friend. My sister had one called Johnny years ago, prompting Mother to consult experts. At the end of her run, our mother herself lived only among imaginary friends. It is the way things go.

Never having such a friend then, now occasionally I will summon one to help solve a problem of content or tone in my writing; sometimes the wraith joins me in staging a private Punch and Judy show. It's the way things go.

Let me acquaint you with my imaginary friend. Nimrod Persiflage is "the man with the trillion dollar nose," the "Bane of Burgundy." He is, arguably, the emperor of the world of wine. Like Caligula or Nero at the Coliseum, his thumb brings triumph or ignominy to the gladiators of the grape. One elite Brahmin monthly, *The Atlantic*, printed that Nimrod was the most influential critic of any field in the world. No spokesperson rushed to deny the claim on his behalf. Fame is tough.

Nimrod Persiflage needs no new emperor's wardrobe. That's because he, to an uncomfortable degree, is us. A May 2015 item in the paper of record called into question how so much concentrated opinion power ruined the joys of wine for millions of consumers. Persiflage popularized the esteem of individual wines by number, like a score on a fourth-grade spelling quiz.

The numbers racket for wine consumers provides a good instance of unintended consequences. Persiflage started a numerical system in part to assess the qualities of wine. Instead, it dumbed down wine assessments to a kind of *American Idol* audition. Wine seems to be made with the score in mind, and the resulting wine arrives as something reasonably made and with little individuality.

Worse, the Persiflage Pronouncement pushed the prices of wine skyward. Yes, I know it's de rigueur to blame the hikes on Chinese demand, but that's too pat. The price rose as a consequence of watching the scoreboard and turning the pleasures of wine drinking into a high-five jockstrap locker room event. To compete in the marketplace becomes a drive to win at any cost. The consumer pays for the winespeak, which includes words and phrases such as "hand-crafted," "artisanal" and made by people of "passion" driven to "excellence." Gimme a break!

Readers ought to consider whether their wine preferences have been shaped by encounters with wines of naturally similar character or determined by the numbers. I compare this foolishness to the color-by-number faux watercolors we made with the Venus Paradise Pencil Kit, depositing wax onto corresponding spaces on a grid. The outcome was predetermined, and it proved more puzzle-solving than art. That is why, despite the wine score hype, I prefer to trust my more cost-efficient palate and taste memory.

How have we arrived at this sorry pass? I'm identified as a "wine editor" for a shelter magazine; this elastic title allows me to write as reporter and reviewer (i.e., about what happened or what impression I took away with me).

A critical role is more intended to set parameters—not para-metrics—and realizable standards to broaden appreciation of something by expanding our knowledge of it. Criticism, alas, is for most people who even consider it as a kind of fault-finding scavenger hunt. The reach of the critic is as much informed by fear than admiration.

This distortion merits for me as much space in wine writing as a petri dish filled with *phylloxera* bugs introduced to a spring planting. Airing concerns about the "critic" helps to clarify what does work in tasting many wines and writing about them. Issues become magnified because our wine scene is global and much of what is produced is good.

Northrop Frye published *Anatomy of Criticism* about sixty years ago. Many years removed, I returned to it because having finished this book you now hold about Oregon wine, I started to consider what I am doing when I write about wine. Am I a critic?

Rather, as writer, evaluation comes into play, but it remains a matter where I don't take the critical slice of cheese as the whole enchilada. Persiflage started okay, but his pronouncements became the message and he became the point. This has little use, despite the automatic reply that we need the numbers. This is not merely nonsense; it is a dodge. We need words—not ad-speak or buzz words or look-how-clever words. We require descriptive, non-technical words that convey an impression of savvy and skill applied.

The responses made thus expand our taste memories, bringing more to the consideration and experience of, as here, Oregon wines than leaving a number, masking subjective reactions as phony objectivity.

When searching for what passes for my readable prose, I invoke the spirit of Mark Twain. He avers that the difference "between the right word and the wrong word is the difference between lightning and lightning bug."

A critic or reviewer who holds the door open for readers deserves our gratitude, but when the same person blocks the doorway, no service to the reader, the winemaker or trade occurs. Push said obstacle from your path.

———— ✴ ————

CHAPTER 1

THE CORVAIR, THE CRITIC
AND THE OVERPASS

Suetonius recalled an episode that occurred in the reign of the Emperor Vespasian (AD 69–79). A community organizer—a person without a real job except that of inciting complaints on behalf of "the folks," whose outrage said organizer represented by self-appointment—approached the emperor regarding the fees charged to visitors to Rome's public urinals. The Roman Empire, whatever its flaws, did administer a capital with running water. As the agitator babbled on, even the emperor's son and successor, Titus, chimed in about the unseemliness of the tax. Vespasian opened his purse, withdrew a fistful of coins, shoved his hand under his son's nose and demanded, "Now son, tell me if this money smells." Although the tax derived from urinals, the money itself smelled like coin. Its collection helped maintain public cleanliness and a little public order.

Will Durant, who related this anecdote in *Caesar and Christ*, the third volume of his *Story of Civilization*, also noted that every imperial citizen—man, woman and child—accounted for fifty gallons per capita wine consumption per annum. Thus the need for public urinals is self-evident.

Ralph Nader's "urinal" was the Chevrolet Corvair, an innovative compact car with a rear-mounted, air-cooled engine. When Nader published *Unsafe at Any Speed* in 1965, both wine critic Robert M. Parker Jr. (aka the Alpha Critic) and your author were approaching our majority. Nader's book and its dubious claims made their way through the talk show gulag. Only in the hindsight of a half century can we say that the science used to defend the auto design was no more nor less selectively employed by the rich, complacent General Motors brass than Nader's use of similar "facts." But this matters not much today.

GM initially stonewalled. This gave Nader's assertion about a little car that fishtailed more credence. It's hard to resist becoming David when a clumsy Goliath is also in the room.

What matters is how the defeat of the Corvair concept design set back the American automotive industry's interest in smaller, efficient cars by at least a generation. Yes, share prices factored into the lassitude, but the consumer turned offshore. Americans lost jobs, and the term "Rust Belt" no longer referred to a fashion accessory.

This tale of two community organizers gains import here only because Nader, who became a consumer advocate and perennial presidential candidate, inspired Parker, the Alpha Critic, to do to the producers of Bordeaux wines what his idol did to GM. Is it a surprise that he called his wine newsletter the *Wine Advocate*? Has the quixotic mission in its own way damaged the wine market for American consumers as did Nader's crusade against a vehicle that was fun to drive? More important, were the negative consequences of each act of urinal fetish accidental? When *Wealth* magazine celebrates holding wines for appreciation comparable to precious metals, are we far from the vineyard, even farther away than from our youthful car fantasies?

Karl Popper's law of unintended consequences or outcomes is a motif that recurs here and later in the book.

"Decoding grapes" does not begin with Vespasian or Nader or even Parker. It begins in the vineyard with the nurturing of vines to produce healthy grapes and the practical magics of the artisan, who turns these into enjoyable wine.

Readers baffled by wine arithmetic may ask first, "Who is Parker?" Answer: Robert M. Parker Jr. is an attorney who practiced in Maryland and discovered wine as a collectible in the 1970s. He developed a one-hundred-point rating system that has influenced countless wine buyers and critics since.

Parker likes fruit-forward, big wines, and his *Wine Advocate* scores are handy, provided one doesn't take them as holy writ. Because life isn't fair, Parker had a total command of his newsletter from 1977 to 2012; at this point, he sold the *Advocate* to Singapore hedge fund game boys. It seems appropriate that the creation of the man who put so many wine prices out of reach ended up with people who make money by gaming the system.

If you have come by this book because you know wines you like to drink and wish to explore Oregon, or you're curious and just trying to demystify wine, then it is wise to know how Parker is evidence of how someone out to do good does the opposite.

As a writer seeking the right words to extol the virtues of wines produced in Oregon, I aim to follow the advice regarding Twain's lightning bug, previously noted. Sheridan Baker, author of a college textbook on composition, put the matter most eloquently. "Writing is discovery," he said, and in writing over decades about wine and food, no number ever tells an "end user" what is going to happen or what is going on. A number only "suggests" what self-important experts demand you discover. I think such wisdom goes nowhere.

We need wine words, not ad copy, buzz words or look-how-smart-I-am words. If adventure, ambition and experience go into producing good wine with "chops," should not we also strive to describe its qualities without a number crutch? Indeed, without a prosthetic?

The public toilet tale and the faltering of the Corvair only point out that all too soon, and often by premeditation, a cause is advanced, a position staked, that engenders damning consequences.

Insofar as I have staked my own claim, this is a significant moment in the brief history of Oregon wine—and places us at a Rubicon. The overpass noted in the chapter heading—the Newburg-Dundee Bypass under construction on Oregon Route SR99—is not only a bridge but also a totem of transition made inevitable by the very success of the wine coming out of the state. Conditions today exist for a spiritual meltdown in wine fancy even as the industry matures.

The Alpha Critic's exaggerated importance determines not so many jeremiads as a distortion of what, by observation, drew me to Oregon both to live and to write this book.

What Parker did was inexcusable. He takes himself seriously, and by believing his press, even when justified, he calls attention away from what the wine expresses about its place of origin, its fruit and its character. A shortcut, like a numerical rating, tells nothing about the *genius loci* or the sheer exuberance in that glass.

To reiterate this claim installs Parker as a oenologic ultra-montanist; it misplaces the authority of the wine under the searchlight, not to mention the winemakers' labors.

Bunkum. Here is the real skinny. We grew up with Top 40 songs on *American Bandstand*. We took standardized tests like the SAT or LSAT to compete in races to college classrooms and law schools. We are a generation addicted to list making and rank pulling. The List-o-Mania that the Alpha Critic's ratings spawned affected cellar auctions, wine allocations and what restaurants put on their lists and helped to set prices and even determine what vines were planted. In other words, Parker and his acolytes mistake the sidelines, in Garrison Keillor's words, for the goal posts; they want to know what a thing costs as opposed to what it is worth.

The man atop this pyramid scheme only wanted, with his febrile lawyer's mind, to understand and express what he liked in wine. He was its advocate pleading its merits to a relative court of opinion. The summation always came down to a number. And in the Alpha Critic's *weltanschauung*, the numbers aspire to one hundred. Parker thus marketed the bogus illusion that a wine could be perfect. Nothing as finicky as wine grapes can express perfection with a straight face—for by that sin fell the angels. A one-hundred-point wine does not need to be written about; it does not require being uncorked. It does not require humans, for we are flawed critters. An eighty-nine or ninety-point wine will do just fine. A one-hundred-point wine, like a unicorn, does not exist—not now, not ever.

The consequence of the Alpha Critic's successful advocacy is the diminution of the less precise language of poetics that responds to the impressions a wine makes on us. It is wine by the numbers, and all major wine geek publications rely on like systems to sell wine.

Parker and I also grew into manhood with the help of CliffsNotes, the bumble-colored black-and-yellow crib sheets. I suggest that the Alpha Critic system has devolved into a version of such cheat sheets. Had you come upon an early Reagan-era copy of the *Wine Advocate*, you would less find the actuary Parker became than the fellow who studied history and art history in college. In what the *Wine Advocate* became you can see the sweet revenge of unintended consequences. In trying to codify wine experience for Bordeaux wines, the Alpha Critic accomplished something else: his scoring system drove down intelligent comment and helped to drive the consumer costs of wine through the ceiling. Between 1977 and 2012, when the *Wine Advocate* was sold to those hedge fund bandits, Parker set new standards for self-inflation. No false modesty here, just a succession of bulls and anathemas. He should have written in Latin.

I began this chapter noting the per capita wine drinking in imperial Rome, although the wine was watered down often, by local custom. The drinking expressed a kind of demotic truth. Wine was in reach of all people, and surviving records describe a means of refreshment and social lubrication, made not to produce scores but pleasure. After all, a number simply regurgitates a subjective response that itself is a nexus of sensory, real-time experience.

On his way to becoming rich, famous and feared, Robert M. Parker became the tool of those he planned to expose. His famed independence made him an accomplice in the wild overestimate of esteem for Bordeaux and California wines from Napa Valley, a variation on the French snooty caricature that seems to limit pleasure of wine by presenting it as arcane, out of reach and restricted to cognoscenti. I am not taking the Alpha Critic to task for being too influential, although such influence doesn't impress me. I am impressed by the taste memory Parker cultivated and his aesthetic inclinations to explain what he likes. Rather, though, thanks to his undue sway, he has helped to create massive dysfunction in wine reviews. Symptoms include:

- The rush to be first. By jumping ahead, the Alpha Critic makes his opinion more anticipated and more important-sounding. Imitators prefer to be first rather than accurate.
- The big pronouncement. The pronouncement is like a fatwa or a papal bull. It apes authority so as to bury other points of view and stifle dissent.
- The 33 percent solution to price. The well-documented price spikes bear little relation to what is in a bottle, but much to its perceived worth. So, hospitality and retail sellers are often marking up wines to obscene premiums because people with too much money rarely insist on a cost-to-value correlation. They are out to impress by spending $1,200 or more for a bottle of wine with a big rating. In all fairness, however, many eateries offer better prices than expected in order to please good wine customers and maintain inventory. *Caveat emptor.*
- Dumbing down winespeak by relying on numbers. Parker's claims to authority derive from a rating system even he admits is really subjective. The categories have a truth, but

the numbers are phony markers. People lose any vocabulary to describe a wine because a like/dislike is easy. If this sounds like the gibberish on Facebook, you're getting warm. Reading someone else's scores obviates the need to actually make an effort to describe what pleases or displeases your take on the wine. Don't be so lazy, pardner.

- Turning a style of winemaking into statute. The "international style" of a Parker red is a perfectly acceptable expression of certain varietal qualities. But it is also a funhouse mirror. And, alas, the path out of this funhouse is obscure. So the style becomes a statute, discouraging further exploration of wine. Parker as young idealist advocating a path of liberation in turn put up a barricade of insider snottiness where a good critic gets out of the way.

I have no doubt the Alpha Critic believes he has done good over the long haul. He has surely done well for himself. And he is partner in an Oregon winery, Beaux Frères, since 1993. It is almost too funny that this imperious wine arbiter has ended in the Northwest rather than in the tony trails of California, where his words still thunder like storm clouds over Mount Shasta.

As Oliver Cromwell told the Long Parliament, "For whatever good you have done, you have sat too long. Now in God's name, please go." We will close the door after you depart.

In June 2015, the online wine newsletter *Snooth* published an encomium to Lodi, a long-established "industrial wine" growing area in the Sacramento region. It turned five editorial staff members loose in the vineyards, and they were wowed. And why not? Everyone assumes that Lodi means Zinfandel, but it means far more in the viticultural orbit of California wine lore. But because of Parker, few deign to let it register in the Gospel of Cabernet orthodoxy.

The Alpha Critic ceased to be the messenger. He became the celebrity message. It almost appears that he is comfortable in this role. Read his bio on the Beaux Frères website. It screams with self-importance and notes that the man in the photo never reviews his own wines. Poor us. (We have noted the sale of Beau Frères to a French company announced in 2017. The clock ticks on.)

The tale has a moral, and this book will end on an unresolved cadence. The objective assessment of wine by numerical scores is like trying to tell time with a cotton swab or the beard of a billy goat. The wow factor is beyond the reach of words and surely as well of arithmetic. I pay little attention to the Alpha Critic–inspired scores; however, I think he would concur that the more interesting pleasures are revealed in wines scored between eighty-eight and ninety-four than the Empyrean bottles occupying the highest steps on the ladder. It's shorthand, not a destination. The Alpha Critic is wealthy; he is respected and reviled. That does him credit despite the awful mess he created.

"We came this close," Oregon wine pioneer David Adelsheim told me, holding out one hand and separating his thumb and forefinger by a tiny margin, "to having no wine culture in this country at all."

President of Adelsheim Vineyard, which he founded in 1971, David added winemaking to an eclectic Portland origin that still finds him building, as well as playing, harpsichords. Imagine Bach making wine.

Adelsheim and I spoke over one of his Rieslings. He said the American wine palate is both challenged and intimidated. "Look at our history. We have traveled across a great continent planting vines where it seemed suited. But the migration was interrupted by a civil war, a number of panics in the economy, two world wars, a decade-long Depression and, to cap the mess, fourteen-plus years of Prohibition."

After a sip, he added, "Then take the experts who insist on showing how smart they are, and the consumer approaches ordering wine at dinner or shopping for it like making a dive off a high board into a tank full of hungry sharks."

Well, I could hardly say it better myself. Winemakers and wine drinkers may aspire to one hundred points, but let us remember that when we reach the top rung of this ranking ladder, we are standing on the scaffold. And here's another punchline: Adelsheim sold to his longtime Belgian investors in 2017. The parade passes.

The new flyover on Route SR99 past Dundee center betokens doom. Contrary to claims that it will provide a bypass to speed people to the coast, the overpass actually is a means to develop wine property into something else. As you drive under it, think of Moose Malloy on Central Avenue in *Farewell, My Lovely*, who, Raymond Chandler wrote, looks "about as inconspicuous as a tarantula on a slice of angel food." Rather than alleviate transit, this "improvement" southwest of the Dundee Hills AVA will bring more cars, more noise and less tranquility to the lands where the vines still soldier on and people in the rows tend to grapes with affection and respect.

As you head through Dundee center, remember that real estate moguls are funding not construction and development but destruction and envelopment of land graced by nature and enhanced by the men and women working in the wineries and amid the vines. The moral of the story? Rewind to ancient Rome and our friend Suetonius. If you use a public urinal, bring correct change. And stay on the lookout for shady characters. These will not be registered sex offenders; rather, they'll be wine critics.

———— ✳ ————

PERSPECTIVES: A WALK IN THE CLOUDS

My case doesn't take the Alpha Critic to task for being the Alpha Critic; it serves to present a superior method to share wine preferences. In a dumbed-down, hyperlinked world peppered with social media, my point comes down to this. Numbers are best used to identify vintages and cost; the exuberance, on the other hand, is of a higher order. We might say, "priceless."

———— ✳ ————

CHAPTER 2

FOUNDING FAMILIES TAKE A VICTORY STROLL BY THE PARK, MAY 3, 2015

Interviewing winemakers for my book about Oregon wine has produced some bumper comments. One winemaker I saw in early 2014, Jim Prosser, owner of J.K. Carriere Wines, observed, after setting aside his chainsaw, that at best his stewardship of his property would last about thirty-five to forty years—"just about the length of a typical working career. That is about as much a chance we have to run things." Only when I recall this comment does the chainsaw seem a powerful prop for an image of remorseless time shaving the years away like so many spent vines.

Prosser was planning to add some vines, though. He and his small crew, assisted by a couple of bounding dogs, were felling fir and pine stands to add a little more acreage for wine production. Small clutches of trees gave way to vines, becoming timber as they metamorphosed from just another part of the forest to an element of Willamette Valley's viticulture scene.

The stand of tall trees remained dense despite Prosser's machinations, as he staked a claim for grape clusters rather than pine needles. This is what happens in the course of one man's winemaking life: nature pushes one way and mankind pushes another. But this action bears little resemblance to denuding the Amazon or plowing under productive farmland to make room for yet another Walmart. Prosser was rather adjusting the delicate balance between nature and wine commerce. The air was full of fresh wood, whirring saws and the conversations of canines and probably not a few squirrels. When eventually the new vines themselves give way on that hilltop, the forests will reclaim some of the land again. That is likely because

The Willamette Founding Families. *From left to right*: Susan Sokol Blosser, Adelsheim winemaker David Paige, Elizabeth Adelsheim, Joe Campbell, Nancy Ponzi, Dick Ponzi, Pat Campbell and Diana Lett. *Courtesy of Doc Wilson.*

Oregon had the foresight, encouraged by pioneer winemakers and slow-growth proponents, to define land use. Development for commercial and residential use may appear as "progress" to Babbitt boosters, but flurries of construction activities against the forest fence are really a big spasm of consumption. The new communities and their amenities take up space, and in time, their novelty and utility fade. To reclaim nature takes more than a few pinecones or thinning out some trees.

Something more than mindless expansion of sprawl is going on. And one notices that in Oregon the energy seems put to a little bit better use than elsewhere. So, to come up to Oregon from other wine places and put the vines next to filberts and plums took some daring and temerity. Would it work?

The answer was provided in part by a group of five families who made the leap, families who converted long-in-the-tooth farms and their rickety barns into vibrant wine country—a ferment of grapes and people, farmers and tourists, restaurant owners, adventurers and dreamers. On May 3, 2015, wine lovers celebrated this complex outcome with a simple event. As self-congratulatory events go, this one proved tame. It was no Grammy grab bag or Oscar night overdrive. Hey, there were only a

Dick and Nancy Ponzi test the wine in one of their barrels to ensure that the process is proceeding successfully. *Ponzi Vineyards Collection, Jerald R. Nicholson Library, Linfield College, McMinnville, Oregon. Donated by Dick and Nancy Ponzi, 2012.*

few sports jackets. The event was in celebration of people who came here more than half a century ago, and here they remain. Time's chainsaw may run on, but so do the farm enterprises these families established. And thus the party had a theme: the "Grapes of Place."

So much more remarkable seems a half century in the vineyards. That sunny spring afternoon, five Willamette Valley pioneer families took their bows before an appreciative throng at the Portland Art Museum. The fifty-dollar admittance (the equivalent of a small-production, single-block bottle of the Grape of the Half-Century—Pinot Noir) attracted the anticipated 250 enthusiasts of Oregon wine, and they were well treated. In addition to featuring starter wines, the event concluded with a panoply of library wines and recent releases from the main attractions—the roster was as familiar as it was enduring.

On hand were Adelsheim, Ponzi Vineyards, Sokol Blosser, Elk Cove and the Eyrie Vineyards. All have morphed from winemaking in an underutilized garage or shed to destination visitor centers showcasing both their respective wines and stories describing the making of them. At the heart of these stories is the varietal—Pinot Noir—and the can-do persistence to create world-class wine despite more than a little advice suggesting that it couldn't be done.

Early sipping and mingling segued into a showing of the Oregon Public Broadcasting hour-long documentary *Grapes of Place* (shades of John Steinbeck), produced in 2011 by Nadine Jenling, who was on hand to introduce it and moderate the panel following.

Jenling began her project without having heard about, let alone consumed, Pinot Noir: "At first I figured I would be traveling the whole state for material.

Then I realized the major story was close by in the Willamette Valley." And with that, down came the lights and the big picture rolled.

Of course, the big picture was a record of the small but determined steps taken by those whose adventures the movie distills into an encomium to the grape and the place it grows, best tended when left alone to express its unique characteristics. Thus the story is as much about how men and women emerging from the self-induced campus turmoil of the later 1960s became farmers and stewards of the land.

In the telling, one senses that memories have been embellished. The film pays tribute to Richard Sommer, who founded HillCrest Vineyard after first planting several varietals, including Pinot Noir, in the Umpqua Valley in 1961. Another UC-Davis contrarian, Charles Coury, advocated the important notion that certain Pinot Noir clones were better suited for certain places than others in a state where climate and growing conditions seem to vary by the foot.

The founders in their comments tended to portray themselves as running away from conventional careers. David Lett, who founded the Eyrie Vineyards with his bride, gave up the sirens' song of dentistry to pursue growing Pinot Noir grapes on forty acres in the northwestern Willamette Valley. Referring to the effervescent energy at the beginning of Oregon's modern wine industry, Diana Lett told the audience, "We'd say, 'There was Paris in the '20s and McMinnville in the '70s.'" Each night for the next forty years, from the time the first seedlings hit the rows, the Letts walked their forty acres to check that their waking dream was still where they'd left it the evening before.

Susan Sokol Blosser said, "We all had the idea of doing something different. Wine seemed a cool thing to do, and although we had empathy for the environment, we invented sustainability farming just by doing things that suddenly made perfect sense." As an example, she recalled a Salmon-Safe advocate who came up to her to sell her on the concept. "The salmon swim upstream, not uphill," the advocate said. "But your run-off goes downhill." And that was that.

The hard work, the day jobs needed to hold down the fort (Dick Ponzi happily taught school for years), the guest workers camping in the living room or in outbuildings—all went to supporting a kind of whimsical, damn-the-torpedoes pluck in meeting challenges and crises associated with both commerce and nature. What kept the beat was collaboration.

From the time he left California's Monterey AVA, Adelsheim winemaker Dave Paige told the group, he was amazed at the annual retreat in

Above: David Lett works on the young vines at the Eyrie Vineyards in Dundee, Oregon, with the help of his eldest son, Jim Lett. *Courtesy of the Eyrie Vineyards and Jason Lett.*

Left: David R. Lett christens the first planting at the Eyrie Vineyards in the Willamette Valley. *Courtesy of the Eyrie Vineyards and Jason Lett.*

Steamboat down south, where winemakers met to debrief one another. "What went wrong?" they asked. "How am I supposed to fix this?" And someone always posed a solution. All through the vine year, informal get-togethers provided needed relief and connection with the other vintners over the next hill. The spirit of collaboration runs deep and has since the first rows were planted.

Sokol Blosser said, "We were liberal arts graduates. We knew how to work in teams. Imagine if we were all MBAs…." She trailed off, leaving the audience to imagine amped-up execs farming in Rolexes with stilettos on hand to overcome the competitors.

The reality is a little different. Many of the pioneers were left-brainers. Dick Ponzi was an engineer at Disney's Imagineering Studios. Joe Campbell of Elk Cove was and remains a practicing physician. Dick Erath was an engineer in high-tech manufacturing. Harry Peterson-Nedry of Chehalem owns an undergraduate degree in English literature but is professionally trained as a chemical engineer. Bill Blosser cut his teeth in urban planning in and around Berkeley and Oakland. And as mentioned, David Lett turned away from dentistry. Readers need to recall that the founding men and women were on the verge of living more compartmentalized middle-class lives when they literally took to the up-country. They were not buying a lifestyle. They did not cash out of Silicon Valley. They were following a

Diana Lett and the author. *Courtesy of Doc Wilson.*

considered but risky inspiration. Today, that is cause for content reflection on the relatively recent past.

In the mid-'70s and again in 1985—a great vintage year—Parisian wine mavens discovered these Oregon winemakers. The vagaries of winemaking in Burgundy spanned a millennium at least of popes, barbarians, Frankish thugs and nature's whim, only for the French to discover, a New World away, people getting it right without all those centuries of blood and chaos.

Indeed. French wine producer Joseph Drouhin's great-granddaughter Véronique, interning at Adelsheim, was instrumental in prompting her family's entry into the Willamette Valley with Domaine Drouhin in 1987. Suddenly, the parallels of Burgundy and Willamette Valley were no longer abstractions. There was dirt with a deed in the county recorder's office.

"At once, we weren't those hippie guys from up north," recalled Pat Campbell of Elk Cove. She remembered her baby-on-board Volvo, which doubled as a delivery truck for the winery. As in most start-ups and new businesses that actually make things, titles and organizational charts meant less than getting the job done. These producers are farmers who make wine from what they plant and grow. It is essential to keep in mind the ideal of a family farm as a sustainable business rather than a

Left: Dick Erath stands next to barrels of wine at his winery. *Erath Winery Collection, Jereld R. Nicholson Library, Linfield College, McMinnville, Oregon. Donated by Dick Erath, 2012.*

Right: Dick Erath crushes Sauvignon Blanc grapes in Walnut Creek, California, in 1966. Erath's first crush occurred the previous year. *Erath Winery Collection, Jereld R. Nicholson Library, Linfield College, McMinnville, Oregon. Donated by Dick Erath, 2012.*

get-rich-flip of property. Although land for vineyard farming is far more "spendy" than it once was, Oregon real estate is only now aspiring to California volatility and then only in small, well-known parcels. This is buy-and-hold country. The winemakers may change, the old tasting shed may be replaced by something more amenable to human comfort and the parking lot may even boast white lines, but the feel of nature in harmony with the purposes to which man puts it remains less precarious than elsewhere. No one had to build an Aswan Dam to make Oregon wine country work. The scale and the megalomania remain in proportion. Not to say this is not a delicate balance.

As Dave Paige of Adelsheim noted, "I cannot imagine those here who charted every hilltop in the Willamette Valley being able to push through the legislation successfully in 1973 even five years later." Success has a way of ruining success.

As readers explore Oregon wine country, I recommend they consider not only its beauties but also its quirks. The terrain and terroir rarely stay the same over miles of countryside. There are too many rivers and streams in some places. Elsewhere, the mountains shelter arid and warm places from others brimming with air that has worked its way from the Pacific Ocean or snow-capped Rocky Mountain peaks. The layer cake of soils gives the growing regions fecundity and variety. This challenged the early winemakers.

Dick Erath recalled planting thirty-one varietals to see what might work and then running into an early frost. "I had visions of going back to California to become an engineer again," he told me over pulled pork pizza at the Ponzi family bistro in Dundee. "We were in a new land, and we had to try everything." When I suggested it was like scoring a piece of music, Erath said, "I think it's more like being the conductor trying to keep all of these different musicians on the beat."

After selling his winery operations in 2006, Erath, present in name only that festive May Sunday, bought vineyard property in Arizona, which he recently sold. Of his buyer he told me, "Now he can learn about farming."

And indeed the farm and land remain profound components of the wineries—even more than the wines produced and sold. This helps to explain the continued spirit of cooperation in Oregon wine lands. It begins with the fruit on the vines. So it extends the import of the land as idea and object. The pioneers, to their credit, have not lost sight of their particular commercial ecology. The collegial nature of the industry contributed to the almost sacred regard for the land. It was property, of course, but it also was a calling.

As Dick Ponzi remembered, when the family winery was growing, the equipment salesmen would arrive with labor-saving machines. "We tried a stemmer," he told me, "and it made an improvement in the wear and tear on labor. But it didn't handle the grapes with quite the same care handwork could provide. So we returned to the old way."

The relatively small outputs of Oregon wineries make possible a continuing effort to be less aggressive in manipulating fruit in the growing and winemaking process than elsewhere. So many Oregon wine people came out of California with the notion that they could do things a little better. The streak of iconoclasm persists and shows no inclination of abating anytime soon.

In our celeb-centric fifteen-minutes-of-fame culture, events like the one at the Portland Art Museum can devolve into self-congratulation fests. What matters most remains this fact: when this writer was taking driver's

Janie Brooks, owner of Brooks winery at Salem, at the International Pinot Noir Celebration, held annually at Linfield College each July. *Courtesy of Doc Wilson, private collection.*

ed, there was no Oregon wine industry. Yes, there was Honeywood and then HillCrest. And for the rest, no wine culture existed. A world guide to wine didn't know where Oregon was, and no wine book spent a squib of ink on Oregon wine. These men and women changed all that. Today, bankers stock their cellars with Oregon wines grown on land their forebears wouldn't finance and for which no business model existed.

Imagine sitting in a talk session where Jesus or Einstein or Louis Armstrong were up there reminiscing about some nifty idea to try out. In this combustible and indifferent world, here come some of the good guys.

Where does it go from here in, say, another fifty years? "I know where I'll be," said one panelist, who must have also remembered the dude with the chainsaw.

More happily, Joe Campbell said, "At first you think you're building a winery for your children. But it's our grandchildren who will enjoy the best of it." The still-on-call physician added, "And we have eleven. We did our job."

The overarching theme is survival borne on the wings of cooperation and innovation. It is easy to look back to the days when the Sokol Blossers camped out in a VW bus and David Adelsheim strung six hundred feet of garden hose to irrigate grapes from a spigot on the side of his home. The iconoclast theme plays easily on the keys of recall. But all the ad hoc efforts made California refugees into land barons, wine royalty and millionaires.

There is a little diffidence in the successful Oregon winemaker. The impulse was not contrary for its own sake. The Buddhists have a proverb: "The work will show you how to do it." I would say Oregon's wines more than not express the veracity of this saying. And it makes a difference.

Again, it is not the wine that separates the good wine from the ordinary; it is an ethos past the terroir. Visitors will sense a non-attitude attitude. Much wine subculture reminds me less of the Food Network than ESPN highlights—you know, something akin to jockstrap mentality. High fives

Allan Ingram and others plant ten thousand nursery cuttings in March and April 1984 at Elton Vineyards in Salem, Oregon. Shown are Allan Ingram, an unidentified woman and unidentified man. *Elton Vineyards Collection, Jereld R. Nicholson Library, Linfield College, McMinnville, Oregon. Courtesy of Dick and Betty O'Brien, 2015.*

find the monkeys in the skyboxes aping the gorillas on the Game of the Week. It is a sporting gesture, but it does not add to a pleasurable encounter with wine from a particular place. Thus, sporting metaphors have a different place in our hierarchies of value, but it doesn't translate easily to an appreciation of a varietal. And though I've noted the cosmic affinities of baseball campaigns with the vineyard season, it's an analogy, not catechism (see *Oregon Wine Press* 5:14).

One must celebrate what has been achieved without playing overmuch the footlights. The fiftieth anniversary celebration is no endgame but a starting point for the next generation. In this the freight carries more than cases or tonnage. It defines place. And that was how Ms. Jenling approached her commemorative documentary subject.

As Ken Wright of Ken Wright Cellars in Carlton put it, "Winemaking is pretty easy. Farming is hard." He sipped one of his pre-release 2012 Chardonnays and added, "It is all in the grape." Well said.

Joe and Pat Campbell think they did what was necessary among the founders to build a Willamette wine legacy. So, indeed, did they all.

Since mine is a cautionary story, let me tell you about a man I met who made a fortune in another business, enough to pay for five children to reach college and purchase tony vineyard property between the Rex Hill and Chehalem vineyards at Pear Mountain. He scarfed up about three bills worth of Pinot Noir at Oregon Wines on Broadway and told me he planned his entry to vineyard tending so as to "participate in a community of good people." In other words, he is buying a lifestyle. Call the sheriff.

ON YOUR DIME

Purchase a bottle of wine, especially a bottle of Oregon wine. Varietal does not matter, but it should be purchased from a bottle shop or a grocery store with volume enough to keep inventory moving. Price should be relevant to your drinking budget.

Now, here comes the really hard part: open the wine and pour it into a wine stem. The intermezzi that follow *inter alia* in this book will provide some ways to contemplate key elements of the wine you have poured. For the moment, however, the whole exercise is to come to the wine without anything greater than your experience.

Pour generously, but this isn't Coke or Pepsi—leave plenty of room for air in the barrel of the glass. Now take a sip or two. Then, as an ancillary to whatever else you're doing at the time, drink most of the wine in the bottle, leaving enough for a glass tomorrow when you re-cap it.

Make the kind of one-word instant responses a psychologist might ask of you in a free-association test. They usually want to determine if your responses indicate a Napoleon complex. Here we may discover that the wine is complex, but without the psycho-speak.

Once you've jotted down your immediate responses over the hour or so it takes to empty the bottle save one glass, put the paper in a drawer so you can retrieve it later. That's all. It's a pretty cool exercise.

Extra credit: uncork the retained wine the next day. Take a new piece of paper. Do as before. Anything different you might notice? Better? Worse? There are no wrong answers. It is your body at the heart of this exercise. The soul will come along in time shortly.

A coda: Bill Fuller, Tualatin wine pioneer, began his winery in the Willamette Valley in 1973, nine years before the place had an AVA identification. He sold his property in 2006 to Willamette Valley Vineyards of Turner, Oregon. As I write in 2017, he has returned to make some single-barrel vintages for WVV.

Likewise, at the same time, the thirty-five-acre Prince Hill Vineyard surrounding Dick Erath's Dundee Hills home has gone quietly to the owners of Silver Oak winery of Napa Valley. It's a free country; you can sell your vines to anyone, even to Californians.

Being an Oregon wine pioneer does have its benefits, even after cashing out some prime vineyard property. Dick and Suzie, farmers and garage vintners both, can go a few hundred yards to see what Mo Ayoub is up to at his property, where the inside kitchen door leads into the room where the tanks and hoses reside. Across the way, Tom Fitzpatrick, GM and winemaker at Alloro, also tends to five acres of neat and closely planted Pinot Noir vines for his own brand, Elevee, 550 feet above sea level—thus the name. His motto: "Land. Time. People." So, if Dick Erath and the other pioneers want to consider how the time flew as they were inventing a new kind of Oregon, they need only look to their neighbors.

PERSPECTIVES: WHERE IS JIM MARESH?

The oldest operating wineries in Oregon can be dated to 1934 (Honeywood Winery in Salem) and 1961 (HillCrest Vineyard in Roseburg, home of the state's first commercially viable Pinot Noir). HillCrest founder Richard Sommer passed away in 2009, and Mary Reinke, who for many years piloted Honeywood, passed away in early 2015 at age ninety-five. Charles Coury, founder of what became David Hill Vineyards, passed in 2004 and David Lett of the Eyrie Vineyards in 2008, survived by his wife, Diana, and their son, Jason, who did not become a dentist but is today Eyrie's winemaker. Another pioneer, Dick Erath, sold his operations to Washington-based Chateau Ste. Michelle Winery in 2006, started vine farming in Arizona, sold that and as recently as the production of the centerpiece film still makes wine at his hilltop home.

Maresh Red Barn is now the tasting room for his family winery and vines now guarded by a trust dividing the assets sixfold. As so often is the case in stories of etiolgy, the Worden Hill Road landmark in the Dundee Hills was, according to neighbor Erath, a site for indicator plantings—that is, a varietal helping to size up ripening times in one place for different varietals such as Chardonnay, Pinot Noir or Riesling. At age ninety-plus, Maresh tells it differently. So what? The vineyard crew tore out these purposeful grapes, and Erath and Maresh tell somewhat disparate tales.

Erath credited Maresh for becoming the first grower to plant new vines for wine production in 1969. Cuttings from Livermore grower Karl Wente came the following year, indicator vines notwithstanding. It is less a who's-on-first routine than the relative emphases made in recall. The fact is these fellows did it.

Likewise, despite the Hillcrest claim on Pinot Noir in Oregon, *sud* Sommer was successful with Cabernet and Riesling. So, reader, let the stuff planted tell its tale. Memory is a glorious trickster.

Back in the chaw-and-spit days—really 2012—Jim Maresh found some of the pioneers at his Dundee Hills cherry orchard. "Grow some grapes," they said. And Maresh, nobody's fool, said he wondered why his cherry customers dyed the fruit red. Well, no one dyes his vines or the fruit coming from them. This Wisconsin native can still be found on his tractor with his Red Barn label and his vines. So, reader, at this writing, you know where to find Jim Maresh.

CHAPTER 3

WINE AND THE HISTORICAL MEMORY

I was reading in Oz Clarke's 2003 *New Encyclopedia of Wine* and encountered the term *plonk*. It is colloquial British for cheap wine. It almost rhymes and shares consonance with words such as *junk*, *punk*, *skunk* or *stunk*—you get the drift. I cannot recall hearing the term even while visiting the UK in the '70s, but we were sipping whiskeys.

I like to say the world contains very few great wines, but it surely has an abundance of very good wines to consume.

We live in a worldwide wine region that has all but ceased to produce plonk wine. When I began work in the wine and spirits import business, we had brands of high regard in the latter category. With the exception of Piper-Heidsieck champagnes, though, our wine portfolio was the oenological analogue to a 1957 Nash Rambler. It was plonk all the way. We imported nonentities from northeast Italy such as Bardolino and Valpolicella—serviceable at table and not worth writing home about, although since then some producers do these utility reds credit.

So, as the Oregon pioneers were keeping their fingers crossed, the imperatives of the global marketplace had begun to assert themselves, and in languages other than French. At this writing, the Veneto wine region of northeastern Italy produces 8.75 million bottles of Amarone. At the time we shipped Amarone in the USA, it was known better for the Igor twist in its bottle neck than as the great wine we know it to be today. Rapidity is the speed of the wine industry since 1970. Thus, the opportunities and pratfalls that we can witness firsthand are symptomatic of global reach and resource, though often in the face of market conditions that also conflict.

Our Amarone and Chianti Classico were pretty nice to drink. In particular, the Amarone, bottled as late as 1968–70, was bold and unique, allowing me to acquire a taste for a certain winning style of wine production that remains with me.

Taste and historical memory are a cuvée of place and vintage wed to winemaking skill. The Italian wines we handled during the early '70s saw a confluence of events. Most Oregon plantings of Chardonnay and Pinot Noir were still very young, and the big varietals of Napa and Sonoma, commercially further along, were testing the implications and nuances of significant changes in winemaking styles. The year I met the wines of our Italian portfolio was the year Italy seriously, through statute, set out to regulate its wine industry in a meaningful way. Yes, great wines appeared heretofore, but the globalization of wine began in earnest at the time. We were fortunate to be present on the cusp of major changes in drinking habits.

We trace the origins of agriculture to about ten thousand years ago. Viticulture has its origins tracked to Shiraz in modern Iran and dates to about 5000 BC. Of course, the present theocracy in that nation does not commemorate this event now. Wine grapes, however, relatively easy to set to farm, migrated west and north along river valleys and in time made their way to the end of the Eurasian peninsula. By the time of the Caesars, people knew the value of Bordeaux real estate for wine. Roman infrastructure allowed reasonable transport of goods, including wine. I suspect that most viticulture remained local, and when it moved regionally, it moved as well at a measured pace.

Wine in the New World followed a migration north thanks to the descendant friars of the conquistadores and also west from the middle Atlantic colonies until it crossed the plains and the mountains to reach the Pacific Ocean in an oenological rendition of Manifest Destiny. Like humans driven by conquest from place to place, so wine growing was a constituent of settled agriculture that succeeded the chaos of wars and various persecutions. It's an interesting and varied tale, but it remains a topic for another time.

Suffice it to say, the global reach of winemaking and viticulture is today an established fact where pack mules and caravans have been superseded by cooled container ships and big-rig trucks. Local is everywhere and, alas, nowhere, given the demand for approachable wine made in a way to make the rough places plain.

Ubiquity and uniformity ensure easy access to myriad wine from many places; Oregon producers contribute to these conditions but have, for my money, retained a bit of individual personality. Thus, Oregon takes its place among the most singular growing areas on the planet. But again, I call attention to the relative novelty of standards applied to winemaking and wine marketing.

For all their experience, it was not until 1855 that the French classified wines with terms like "grand cru" that distinguished one great châteaux from another. In other words, humans were making, selling and tapping wine for thousands of years before anyone really thought about classifying them.

In fact, other than closely managed Areas of Control that specified things such as minimum alcohol, yields and such, most French wine, *vin du pays*, was relegated to bulk production where the varietals of the first order—including Cabernet Sauvignon, Chardonnay, Merlot, Pinot Noir and Sauvignon Blanc—were strangers to regulations governing appellation, vintage and constituent varietals that we oft like to know as we shop for specific wines. The habits of many centuries have changed only in the past forty or so years. When the change came, it came from the places old European powers sought to colonize elsewhere.

As the New World lands welcomed settlers, viticultural practices as they were also came ashore. So the local wine, often produced with cuttings from the old country, was made as before. But there was a real difference. The climate differed, the soil differed, the pests differed—the wine differed. What remained true to the old ways was, indeed, the old ways. Wine produced in the North American hills and valleys might aspire to the best of the old-world wine practices, but it was different. It was humble. And often it was plonk.

Vineyards were not new to the New World, and in the United States, gentlemen farmers like Thomas Jefferson had an unproductive run trying to cultivate Bordeaux varietals. (Maybe his slaves weren't interested.) Nonetheless, sustained viticulture found welcome climes in the Mexican west, where Franciscan monks, moving north, planted vines starting in 1769. Over the next century and then some, wine production improved, and some Gilded Age Bay Area dwellers could enjoy some reputable wine.

When the *phylloxera* epidemic decimated the plantings, it took well into the early twentieth century to return to a semblance of quality. The Great War came next. It made America rich. But the wine industry took another jolt—the Noble Experiment of temperance and prohibition.

Wine produced both before the unfortunate arrival of Prohibition and following its repeal too often retained the signature of wine in a barrel, although bottling was hardly a new way to store, sell and transport it. Yet much of it still had the signature of wine without ambition; it often proved too acidic or rough or simply so out of balance it had vertigo. So often the wine that came to dinner was oxidized; whites looked jaundiced and reds looked like they had rusted. Taste was aftertaste and not pretty. Even as distribution became more automated, too much juice just went from barrel to jug or to a cache on a bar. People did not compare releases. They did not line up for futures. Wine brought down to town last Tuesday was the Tuesday vintage.

It was very simple. It was, one hoped, potent enough to overcome the casual sanitary conditions in which it arrived from the harvest and finally ended up in the barrel. I am, of course, overstating the case, but there was good reason people liked fruit wine or sweet wine when they strayed from the hooch. Residual sugar and rocket-launching ethyl power combined to cover a multitude of defects.

Prohibition ended in the teeth of economic depression that was, in turn, relieved by another world war more miserable than the first one. Even as Georges de Latour had begun to address seriously the great potential foreseen in using French varietals during the 1930s, his efforts were overwhelmed by the rush of history.

As children of the baby boom, my generation represented perhaps the fourth successive American generation unaccustomed, for the most part, to fine wine. That was fifty years ago. Without subsequent visionaries willing to get dirt under their fingernails, it is quite possible the wine boom that began in the 1970s would have had less impact. We came mighty close to becoming a haphazard oeno-system. Talk about the poet's "road not taken"!

Not until the 1970s did the market for wine drinking leave the metaphorical paper sack and the jug. The 1976 surprise at Paris with Chateau Montelena's triumph among Bordeaux and Burgundy tasters announced that it was possible to produce good wine in a place where nobody spoke French.

Cooling and stainless steel fermentation tanks were postwar innovations whose introduction widened the potential for making wine worldwide—that is, wherever vines could survive.

We might pause for a moment to look at our doomed social-engineering project called the Volstead Act. As of January 1920, when Prohibition took effect, the war on domestic drinking habits started with a sneer. It pitted the settled white Protestant church ladies against waves of recently minted immigrant citizens whose wine drinking was a matter of tradition, no matter how coarse the stuff they produced.

Alicante Bouschet (pronounced "beau-shay") was a formidable varietal that produced dense clusters, which in turn produced a dark-red elixir. The varietal is still around; it is not a leading varietal, but it is found in some New World blends. A few vines even remain in the old country, Italy.

The restrictions of Prohibition caused many farmers who grew wine grapes commercially to switch gears and plant other cash crops. This, in turn, was followed by migrations of farm families who had failed because of bad luck, bad weather and poor common sense to cities or to pockets that could use their cheap labor. And this war on the vineyards, followed by the slow urban migration in the next decade, paradoxically helped to set the stage for the cultivation of the wine industry that was to occur from the late 1960s onward, when California produced 95 percent of all the wine grapes in the country.

If the good ladies helped to quash many local vintners, the Second World War did the rest. German occupation of France's cru cradles set off a race for booty. The abstemious Hitler, it was discovered by American soldiers, owned a nice store of first growths at his Berchtesgaden retreat. The war began in a bad year for Bordeaux and Burgundy, but when it ended in 1945, the vineyards left so under-attended miraculously produced one of the five finest vintages of the twentieth century. The god of wine has a sense of humor.

I divert the traffic in order to suggest that that great vintage is generally regarded as the last fine vintage of the nineteenth century because it also marked the end of many traditions followed by generations of vintners and their heirs, many of whom, like the Rothschilds, were lucky to have survived.

Europe was in ruins. The "economic miracle" of West Germany and the other combatants and neutrals like Italy, Portugal, Spain and the Balkans did not translate into modern winemaking. That is why so many nonstandard French wines—and indeed so many wines from Italy and elsewhere we prize today—were so miserable. They lagged in the recovery because quaffers from afar who sampled them had few signposts. Much was lost in translation, and this, in turn, created a race of condescending sommeliers who caused the very people who liberated Europe to freeze in terror when confronted with a wine like "Musigny" or "Médoc." I once heard a customer at a nearby table at a well-known Manhattan restaurant complain, "They should translate all this French so I can tell what I'm drinking." *C'est ce bon...*

Embrace the time. This is the era when taste and wine technology intersect; when quality assurance, commitment and knowledge extend the old traditions and reconstitute them in ways individual and varied, as rich and strange as each wine sets itself off from the next. This is a magical time borne on wings of expertise and practice.

Allowed free rein, grapes would do their own thing. Winemakers today have the most advantages to cultivate their grapes so that when they show up in your glass, they express the best the grapes of that moment can. If you love wine, you arrived on earth at the best time in its history.

The moment began in earnest for Oregon in about 1960. Richard Sommer came to the state with a determination to plant Pinot Noir and Chardonnay cuttings near Roseburg in the Applegate Valley; a few years later, dental school refugee David Lett planted the same grapes farther north. On 150 acres outside Forest Grove, Lett's friend Charles Coury planted Alsatian varietals and Pinot Noir. Disney engineer Dick Ponzi and another engineer, Dick Erath, followed suit. At this writing, the vines here span back as long as the present history of Oregon wine's pioneering days (see chapter 2).

Jim Maresh Sr. was likely atop his tractor in a fruit orchard in 1969 when several of his Dundee Hills neighbors convinced him to replace plums and cherries with wine grapes. That was a leap of great faith, for the state had a settled agriculture that included largely German varietals like Riesling, brought by way of California and also via westward migrations. Comparatively speaking, California's wine industry, as noted, was far more developed and vast. Prior to the Second World War, producers like Georges de Latour had planted Bordeaux-like vines in the Napa Valley. California wine's commercial potential was already in a Renaissance when Oregon wine left the Iron Age. Mary Reinke of Honeywood Winery in Salem only acquired a bottling machine in 1955. The Golden State was already able to capitalize on the improvements in manufacture to its dominant benefit in American viticulture and wine sales.

When the Sokol Blossers arrived in Willamette Valley, inhabiting a red-from-Berkeley VW camper, they visited a real estate office in Newberg. "We are looking for acreage to plant wine grapes," said they. The realtor looked over his desk, wondering if these folks were serious or just another pair of Bay Area whackadoodles. "I never heard of people wanting to grow grapes in these parts." This anecdote reminds us how personal initiative and vision, married to market demand, can change an entire region in a nanosecond of geological time.

However, as we ramp up to the point where we might say the modern clock was wound and set, we start in the prehistory, down the road, when the Prohibition restrictions fell away and when even a good five-cent cigar or nickel beer was all but out of reach in the teeth of a great economic depression. Some Oregonians were ready to produce something they could call wine, but plonk-ish humility would persist until a few people looked at a map and decided that Oregon could be like Burgundy, even when everyone else knew Oregon could be, well, like Oregon.

I have deliberately recast some of the story related earlier in this book to impress upon readers that a few intrepid families made a huge difference. It is furthermore to recall David Adelsheim's comment about the close call for viticulture—that this country "came this close" to having none at all. Wine knowledge and its commercial potential were ill defined for most American consumers. The past, novelist William Faulkner offered in this bromide, is always present. But he added, "The past isn't even past."

Historical memory is defined by places, like Gettysburg or Iwo Jima or Normandy. It is defined by actions like driving the Golden Spike or opening the Great Bridge between the cities of Brooklyn and New York in 1883. It is summed up by Bobby Thomson's homer in 1951. Places resonate.

So do vineyards. The business card for the WillaKenzie Estate winery states, "Dirt matters." Yes, indeed, but so does taste memory. Adelsheim's cautionary comment reminds us that America ran the risk of an oeno-lobotomy. Memory of taste in relation to place is what I consider the heart of commercial ecology about wine. We are lucky that in America, it was the lobotomist's day off.

PERSPECTIVES...AND A CODA

By 1859, in the town of Jacksonville, in the future Applegate Valley AVA, Peter Britt had established the first commercial winery in the Oregon territory, called Valley View. Trailblazers brought vine cuttings to the land they opened, although we have few accounts that detail these first plantings. An Oregonian named Ernst Reuter won a silver medal at the St. Louis Exposition of 1904, during Theodore Roosevelt's presidency. The medal winner was a Riesling, the predominant varietal planted in Oregon until the Pinot Noir Gold Rush began in the 1980s and '90s.

The first two decades of the new century witnessed what was to that time the highest alcohol per capita consumption in our history, albeit the population was roughly one-third its present size.

Although I consider Prohibition a monumental failure of social engineering, as bungled as was the Reconstruction of the Confederate South in the late 1860s and early '70s, it nonetheless had the effect of reducing per capita alcohol consumption by about one-third. Whatever such moderation achieved, it came at a great cost. I point my readers to Paul Johnson's *A History of the American People* for a concise summary of the experiment and its unintended effects.

Here are some considerations and inferences I draw from Johnson's book. The ban on booze provided the market and the capital to fund organized crime. It made scofflaws of ordinary citizens who continued to imbibe. It wasted federal money on highly visible soft targets while simultaneously providing all incentive for bribery of judicial and law enforcement officials. And it was unpopular!

The residue of this moralistic nanny movement can be found in the sport of binge drinking by young people who have not been acculturated to the rituals of the table, which also include the enjoyment of spirits and/or wine. "Adult" restrictions only make the temptation to break or mask them more enticing to the young; in turn, the appreciation of the labor and output from the soil is lost on them.

Somewhere along the line, the Puritan ethic—a society, by the way, with a healthy appreciation for its spirits—became abstemious and also faultfinding. The "carding" of American young people is one of the surviving damages of unsupervised enjoyments, and it is another component of today's underground market for false documentation. We need not blame identity theft on the spirit of moral improvement carried out in the name of the Volstead Act, but the surviving restrictions have, in our time, made scofflaws of many young people just wanting, as the song goes, to have fun. If you think this is pushing it too hard, ask any proprietor of a package store or bar who is cited for selling wine or spirits, even without volition, to a minor with good fake identification.

The baby boom children who participated in the raucous and disrespectful confusions of antiwar, anticapitalist and social justice causes also celebrated in their popular song of the day a freewheeling attitude toward drugs and sex—or, as Emmylou

Harris recalls in a particular boozy night, "Feeling Single, Seeing Double." It ought to come as no shock that numerous participants in the famous 1969 Woodstock event were dead of substance abuse before they were out of their twenties. Of course, of 79 million baby boomers, about half will tell you they were there.

It fell with considerable irony often lost on this Least Generation that their rebellion against their middle-class upbringings included a rejection of the cocktail and the discovery of bulk wine as a substitute. The taste stuck, though, through all of the pot smoke in the air, and their maturation—if we want to call it so—came at the same time the wine industry in America shifted into high gear.

At this time, Oregon had seven wineries. In the year of Watergate, 1972, Napa Valley–based Sutter Home made a two-hundred-case experiment with a blush called White Zinfandel. This not only saved older vines that were historically part of the winemaking in the Golden State, but it also made drinking this pleasant and innocuous varietal an alternative to jug wine and overlarge soft drinks for a generation raised on beverages cool and mildly sweet on the palate.

Without any scientific specifics to sustain my observation, I will nonetheless assert that the enormous commercial success of Sutter Home's wine accustomed many millions to the pleasure of wine as a beverage of choice just as the timing, as in my opening geographical story, was perfect and inevitable.

Another anecdote: as this writing came down to the wire, Oregon's marijuana law went into force. The owners of my Willamette River apartment building sent a letter to tenants to point out that although one could theoretically smoke a joint, the building was nonsmoking. The next paragraph added that although the state's feel-good voter block was going to turn on, federal law prohibited lighting up and turning on no matter what the Oregon electorate wanted to decriminalize.

This contradiction of enforcement jurisdiction comes nearly one hundred years after Prohibition took effect. The contradiction then put enforcement of anti-drinking laws in the hands of federal tax agents as opposed to local law enforcement. This allowed those "untouchable" agents—immune to graft—to do their duty, while local, state and jurisprudence could wink at

French investment in Oregon: Jacques Lardiere of Louis Jadot and Resonance Vingeyard of Oregon. *Courtesy of Doc Wilson, private collection.*

the laws people did not obey and pocket the graft and influence payments peddled by the newly enriched criminal enterprises providing the bootleg beer, spirits and bubbly to those who could afford it.

We shall see how the latest bifurcation of authority and purpose plays out on the sinister streets of Portland and Gaston and Elkton and Bend. The lesson of this tour? Despots and cranks notwithstanding, viticulture has rejuvenated countless generations of the inhabitants of Planet Wine.

As an envoi to this story of migrations and sudden exits, I wish to cite the International Pinot Noir Celebration, nearing its fortieth year and held at McMinnville. At this moment, months ahead of the annual July event, the nabobs of *Food and Wine* intend to tour acolytes through Oregon Chardonnay producers. At least five of these are scions of Burgundy vintners. In other words, these winemakers from Burgundy have cast their lots in the Northwest, asserting the primacy of this relatively young wine region to augment their pedigrees of repute developed long ago and far away. They bring their history and traditions. But they'll be making Oregon wine. And who are these Gallic adventurers?

- Véronique Boss-Drouhin | Domaine Drouhin Oregon, Dundee Hills AVA
- Dominique Lafon | Lingua Franca, Eola-Amity Hills AVA

- Jacques Lardière | Résonance, Yamhill-Carlton AVA
- Jean-Nicolas Méo | Domaine Nicolas-Jay, Yamhill-Carlton AVA
- Alexandrine Roy | Phelps Creek Vineyards, Columbia Gorge AVA

CODA: THE OCEANIC EXCHANGE AND THE ROMANCE OF IT ALL

One of the favors the New World did for the Old, among many others, focused on rootstock. In the last decades of the nineteenth century, France's prime wine country, Bordeaux, was stricken by *phylloxera*, carried along in aphid infestations. They like roots. In a short time, they can destroy a vineyard. The problem called for a solution provided by Napa Valley farmers before the place became chic. Grafts of native rootstock, itself an evolved plant material that already came west, was introduced to French land, thus solving the problem. Yay us! We remain on patrol for *phylloxera* anywhere wine grapes take hold. Re-plantings are not uncommon in a world more mobile than ever, so pests and threats move with the footfalls and the cargo.

There's a second cadence to this coda. Although I consider enough of my New York origins preserved in amber, some of it leaks like a caustic. Still, there is plenty of the *plein aire* painter's admiration and regard for these collected anecdotes and wine stories, thus explaining why I urge readers to graduate from the applause meter numbers. Its reductive Pavlovian barks and sniffs only spawn arrogance and cynicism.

The historical moment contains markers of place and people and varietals. But it also encourages reaching into past transformations of landscapes cultivated while staying afloat on the rapids of commerce, fashion and individual preferences. For all the hype and me-firsts, the dirt and the tended vines exude romance, spirit and a tradition.

For my purpose, it points always to that imagined doorway through which the white noise doesn't penetrate, the passageway to your own private Oregon wine story.

CHAPTER 4

WHY DATE MATTERS

E ach year, the grapes come off the vine and are trundled swiftly away to begin the winemaking process. What kind of year was it? Vintage, as an organizing concept, helps bring a semblance of continuity to an annual cycle that progresses unseen in dead winter, emerges as blossoms in late spring and then challenges the vintner with bundles of grapes we hope are not too amped up by warm weather or drenched by squalls that come up seemingly out of nowhere when they're ready to harvest in the autumn.

Above all, vintage is continuity. Collectors of wines prize verticals that stack one winemaker's handiwork by varietal year upon year. Some others may prefer a horizontal continuity of different wines of the same vintage and then compare this in turn to another like vertical stack of an array of wines from several places made at the same time. It is labyrinthine the way collectors amuse themselves.

Yet continuity is in a way the story itself. I often cite as examples of continuity the royal lines of British monarchs from the time of William's 1066 conquest. Or take account of the 266 popes or the 45 U.S. presidents. Each line bubbles over with maniacs, martyrs, saints, sinners, the arrogant, the clueless, the geniuses and the innovators. It provides a context for how things became what they became.

A wine vintage tells a similar story where the end result, the wine in your glass, belongs to its own temporal emergence and also looks back to the past. It is not necessarily a march of progress, but it does shake up an Oregon cocktail of winemakers' response to the pitches Mother Nature brings to the plate. The stem with its nearly royal hue here or golden gleam there manifests all of that improvisation, ingenuity, labor and luck; it is the epic sweep of endeavor reduced to a pleasing mouthful of wine. And it is a measure of commercial success as well.

Let us not delude. Not all vintages come out equal. The year 1976 produced a show-stopping Eyrie Pinot Noir that wowed the French. In 1984, the Oregon wine industry had its own version of the Day After, but sandwiched between two stellar vintages. More recently, the 2006 and 2009 vintages produced wine full of brightness, character and depth. But 2007 and 2008, to put it calmly, posed challenges in the vineyards. The yields were austere, and the wine made reflected as much. The years 2012 and 2014–16 were abundant, producing hypertrophied yields with excellent results in Willamette Valley across the boards. The 2014s are prized and luscious.

And the missing '13? Try Helioterra, Ann Haubach's take on what some think a sketchy vintage. These Bjornsen Ranch wines are typical of the vintage year—a bit more austere, even closed-in, but they reveal wonderful structure and reticent layers as they mature.

Where vintages came from is as relevant in today's Oregon wine landscape as it was when wine producers first paid serious attention to the year, the place and the price. The '07 has some marvelous surprises; we tasted one proprietary Pinot Noir from Ken Wright Cellars of Carlton that drank beautifully in 2015. I made a purchase of '08 Chardonnay from Kramer Vineyards in Gaston at a closeout price and ended up purchasing three cases in all between 2010 and 2012. The '08 wines that were made to outlast the vicissitudes of that vintage year are rewarding patience at this writing in summer 2015. The "off" years can outlive me-first fatwas by the experts—a disappointing year condemned to mediocrity shows up later, showing up the gurus. The years 2007–8 and 2010–11 have shed ugly duckling smears to emerge later with class and dignity, doing justice to Oregon growers and winemakers.

Oenophiles may drink Coke or Pepsi and expect it to be the same year in and out. But wine seasons differ, and thus, wines put aside for a spell do also.

I was very partial to 1999, 2006, 2009 and 2012 Oregon Pinot Noir, as they had big fruit-o-licious properties. Then my palate and taste memory improved. I think 2011 and especially 2013 vintages sing beautiful music. Poco Collina, the "little hill" at Cheshire Vineyard near Eugene, strikes me as a lovely expression of the varietal, and its price is nearly just as pleasing. Experience and a healthy dose of skepticism can lead you to wines that the experts and the general public pass to their peril, missing some wonderful drinking and cellaring opportunities.

Far be it from me to warn you, dear reader, not to believe everything you encounter in print. Just remember the Marx Brothers' challenge: "Who are you going to believe, me or your own eyes?"

H.L. Hunt, a famous oil billionaire, said that money was just a way of keeping score. Vintage is perhaps another. Some people go into a wine shop or retail outlet and exercise so much due diligence one might think they were filing a flight plan. Others, like my one-time friend Joanna, buy books and wines because they like the dust jacket or the label. It doesn't matter to store managers, who want to move inventory. They may help supply information, but rationalizing is the provenance of the self. I like Sara N. Dipity as well as the other fellow, so uncovering a surprise wine provides the double pleasure of describing the hunt nearly as much as sharing the wine itself.

Still, vintages do help us make sense of it all. How often does a casual consumer pick up a great bottle of wine only to forget not merely its vintage but who made it? To know the value of vintage can add or subtract from one's holdings or shape the anticipated experience of a particular wine.

These points justify what follows. The Wine Cellar Insider website publishes a chart of all Bordeaux vintages since 1959, one of two years in my lifetime the Chicago White Sox made it to the World Series. I use Bordeaux because they were first to classify by market worth what their vintages could fetch and offered a method to classify the wines we interpolate and use still with modifications.

This system is important for New World wines and other viticultural areas too. A standard works when it guides; it works when it sets a foundation for appreciation. It does not work like ice-skating competitions, where everyone is already in the bag flashing a number card in the air. Wine, said Oz Clarke among many others, is for pleasure. No number-crunching substitutes for the mouth epiphany wines can inspire. Although the Alpha Critic's initial thrust intended to make the Bordeaux producers more consumer-friendly, I took exception to him because his scoring system ultimately obscured its stated objectives, making matters worse for collectors and consumers.

I consider the vintage characteristics and the abstract aspect of the numbers themselves as interstate exit signs. They indicate past direction and anticipate in the present some ultimate destination. In such a regard, vintage is an imposing metaphor. In fact, however, the predominant varietals in much of the dirt on planet Earth are Cabernet Sauvignon and Merlot, the red wine staples of Bordeaux, just as Chardonnay and Pinot Noir dominate the wines from Burgundy.

Long ago, the acolyte winemakers beyond Gaul who planted these vines learned soon enough that the names might be the same but the results differed. New lands recast the story the vines express. It is good to recall that we are on an international highway made of memory and taste. We can view the vintage map to provide but a unique frame of reference and not a slavish imperator. Even when the vintage designation is not much more than a notice of time, it grounds us to a starting place.

So how did the Wine Cellar Insiders come up with their number rating? Here is exactly what they said:

> *Rankings and scores in the Bordeaux vintage chart are not awarded for a mathematical average of scores. The years in the Bordeaux vintage chart are scored using a rough average based on your chance of randomly purchasing a bottle of Bordeaux wine from the vintage of your choice and have it offer a reasonably good, wine tasting experience. This is the purpose of the Bordeaux vintage chart. Of course there are always some good and even great wines produced in moderate years. But one good wine, or even a few good wines does not make a great vintage.*

So, it is a number, but it's not. Because these web pages are so useful with weather conditions, grape yields and tasting notes on so many wines and the prices they fetch by property, the values are almost shorthand for all of this joyous labor. Whether everything went into a Cuisinart is less important than that the chronology is accurate and the assessments fair. Finally, the ad hoc shopper described earlier leaves room for what some call serendipity, as noted, or what someone else calls dumb luck. In either case, it serves.

Readers ought to apply, at least in theory, an analogous view of vintages in Oregon, with eighteen AVAs and hundreds of wineries to consider. A highly touted vintage year in the Willamette Valley AVA might not necessarily hold for Rogue River AVA wines produced in the same year, and vice versa. Some place in a so-so year you'll find compelling wines. The discovery is almost as much a pleasure as the drinking.

The Wine Cellar Insider proffers this trinity about wine purchase, storage and quality quaffing:

1. Buy today
2. Drink now
3. Hold

These simple imperative verbs speak great wine wisdom, and one need not collect or taste maniacally to grasp these simple concepts. A British scholar of note once wrote about a play manuscript by Christopher Marlowe that, unlike an apple, it "did not rot in a drawer." A wine, however, is more like an apple than a writing desk. It can mature and express all those qualities of the varietal and the handiwork that comes with it. But it shall, sooner or later, come to a tipping point where its manifold virtues begin to fade.

BUY

Wine is a promise of future enjoyment, and people pay dearly for the privilege. A wine in a uniformly acclaimed vintage offers little to resist the impulse. Purchase what you are able to afford; taste whenever you can. Pop one cork from your new treasure hoard to enjoy it even when your experience differs from the sales tag or what you have read in the wine press. You may not ably predict the nuances of future maturation, but at least you have entered the lanes of memory and taste.

If you invest in commodities and like to intelligently roll the dice, remember that like hog bellies and oranges, wine is a commodity and a cash crop. A future that you acquire also means that when the wine is released, you go to the front of the line. The only better experience of similar pleasure happens when you go to the DMV or the passport desk and nobody stands in your way.

If your future friends know of your good fortune, you will have plenty of friends and opportunity to sell or trade some of it—or not. Just keep it and share it later. Maybe…

Not all vintages are equal. The Bordeaux wines after the great success of 1961 (though matched again in 1982, 2000, 2001 and 2010) are best forgotten, although I have had more than one memorable surprise from two first growths of that general time. There are bad patches on the road to the one-hundred-point years in every wine-producing area. Wine is like neither gin nor Pepsi, where millions are spent to ensure no variable intrudes. It is pure coincidence that the Chicago White Sox made their two trips to the Fall Classic in wave-the-flag years for Bordeaux, 1959 and 2005. Causality has naught to do with it.

Overall, one has to investigate further. Since we're drinking wine, this is not exactly work. In some vintage years, one finds right bank wines doing far better than the left or vice versa. It is very important to know your right from your left and how to look at the map. Some good years find Saint-Emilion doing worse than others in the Haut-Médoc (upstream in Bordeaux). So it takes reading, conversing and asking questions of disinterested parties who are making the same judgments.

Just as a sailor knows the conditions of waters he sails over and over, I recommend getting the lay of the land—that is, know the outcropping, river bends, tree lines and changes of elevation. You need not become Lewis and Clark, but their keen observations of place are a very good way to travel Oregon's wine trails, time of year noted. The sense of place, once you have experienced it firsthand, should make your wine choices more reliable.

Location matters as in all real estate. Just remember, however, that a nice view of the vineyard is less important than the view from within it.

The main waterway in Bordeaux is the Gironde estuary. Upriver lands are where wines do best; downriver lands do not always share the cachet, but these are real vintners who have been at it for two thousand years. Trust your taste buds and your investment advisor.

I would further add that sometimes a wine of no repute because of the vintage emerges from the obscurity to which it has been consigned. I brokered about $37,000 worth of wine for a restaurateur whose display was far better than his storage conditions. I had a Château Latour from the dog days of 1978. This soldier lacked most of its label—no dog tags. However, it was splendid.

More dramatically, the godawful 1973 vintage offered up four cases of Mouton Rothschild, a first growth with a label executed by Pablo Picasso. It was like hiring Rembrandt to paint your car. Well, I sold at least thirty-six bottles for about $210 apiece and kept one for myself that I opened in the late 1990s long after Picasso picked up his paint box, and the very bad vintage was best not spoken of by persons with decent manners. It was beautiful. A swan! A princess! Probably a mistake! But it was a gorgeous and supple wine whose reputation only prepared me—set me up—for my astonishment.

The moral is this: go by what you learn but keep a sense of awe and wonder on hand.

A mixed-case purchase in a good year is often a great way to part with some serious dough, but it also offers you over time a chance to taste and evaluate the relative characteristics of each wine, both to compare prior vintages of the same producer and also to stack the earlier years in relation to one another.

The antonym of to buy is to sell. If you hold too much of a good thing that you cannot conceivably consume in a timely way, look to sell it through wine channels or trade these soldiers for others.

If budget allows, I recommend acquiring a "vintage suite," akin to a musical revue. See how each wine struts on the stage. If you can acquire, say, two cases you intend to drink over time, I would recommend purchasing cases with three or four of each wine from that year. Make a note after auditioning one of them and keep going around, revisiting at discrete intervals or as third-party information you trust reaches you.

DRINK NOW

This means open the bottle and share it now. The reason is a function of two particulars: the wine is regarded as being at its peak, or the wine is now in decline and your last memory of it will probably be better than now, if albeit just a little.

Many Bordeaux will express fruit and a pleasing aroma after having been cellared five to eight years. Many a Burgundy will after five years be full of bright cherry supple elegance. But these wines are made to balance the fruit essence of vines appealing to our senses. Then, after a longer spell— twelve to twenty years—they begin to express structural subtlety that almost justifies the sticker shock these wines cause in the sellers' market.

As to take the propositions here and turn them on their ears, readers should think about the body in the library no one wants to acknowledge. There are bulk bottled and boxed wines made on the cheap, termed "white label" wines. Madeline Puckett on her *Wine Folly* blog discourses on this topic, which points out that people in general prefer cheap wines to more costly ones. Robin Goldstein in *The Wine Trials* (2008) made a study of this based on 501 consumers. For contrarians, the matter comes down to residual sugar. Net sugar (brix) and high alcohol mask defects, producing tasty grape juices with two buzz instigators. It's not surprising that four-year-olds run to the candy counter and not to the tins of anchovies. About 92 percent of wines purchased are consumed within a few days. White label wines reflect that fact. They want you to take them to the dance *now*.

So, we might say that taste memory and preference evolve from accrued experience encountering the knowledge, occasion and practices of people producing wine and integrating these variables into a dynamic taste memory.

The epiphany happens like opening the cottage front door in *The Wizard of Oz*. The earlier characteristics remain but have been transfigured. You will know what has occurred when you experience it for the first time.

Remember, too, what you read about how staying power represents a sliding scale, like the background in a Bruegel painting. It seems close enough, but it really recedes. Time also marches on! Wine is a living thing and, unlike a can of sweet peas, so packaged to make it stable, even inert—the wine in a bottle goes on to mature or slip-slide away. Vintages generally accepted as being superior not only hold their value but actually increase. But if your only motivation is to make money as the primal pleasure, maybe you should collect animal figures or postage stamps or antique cars or old watches. Using French wine to elaborate the matter of dates is no slight to my native wines. The French have a tradition long established; we are still fashioning one in the Northwest.

PERSPECTIVES: A FEW KIND WORDS

Although the subject will come up again elsewhere in this book, I might here put some words about age concerning Oregon wines. I have been drinking Oregon wines for a bit more than three decades. I cellar perhaps ten to fifteen cases of all wine, including Oregonians, most of the time. Oregon wines, like their Burgundian antecedents, please me more with a little age on them. But I am speaking of the whites. If a Kramer Chardonnay from 2006 can intensify its appearance in the glass to burnished gold from brighter white gold after six years, I am all for it. The fruit doesn't sparkle but retains a reassuring presence. Lemon and lemongrass notes recede and reappear in wisps of light mineral scent, dried green apple with whispers of citrus. An Eyrie 1989 Reserve Chardonnay was characteristic of later vintages, but in appearance and flavor it resembled a comparably aged twenty-year-old bottle from the Beaune commune.

Domaine Drouhin augmented its serious Burgundy reputation by coming to the Dundee Hills in 1987–88. Perhaps that most Burgundian of Oregon Pinot Noirs, the peak seems at its tipping point between six or seven years. Over a two-year interval, I acquired four magnums of their 2006 vintage and found each one delicious without impediment to fruit or structure, although each of these qualities took the lead in this dance of life by an alternating beauty worthy of Fred and Ginger in those great MGM films of the '30s. Several 750ml versions of this same vintage held but five years also showed very well.

Generally, I like to hold Oregon wines three to five years as a rule and believe that at this point in their collective history, Oregon Pinot Noir will continue to show best maturity and grace in the four- to five-year window, with another year added for good measure. If a very pronounced fruit appears early on, I would like to see whether it becomes more subtle later and able to sustain structure and a layered texture. Your experience might cause you to assent or demur. There is no accounting for my taste.

I might point out that 2009 Cerulean, produced out of Hood River and sourced in the Columbia Gorge without any oak time, elicited from my wine-drinking friend Billy Bob one comment: "This is frog wine"—meaning, in his inimitable way, that this bottle captured something serious of Burgundy in its expression of the Chardonnay varietal. The years 2010 and 2011 had some oak barrel age on them, but the 2011 appeared to achieve a better balance overall. Cerulean owner Jeff Miller, when told of Billy Bob's encomium, responded, "Good. That's what we meant to do."

The message in this is twofold. One is this wine will be most memorable if you drink it after eighteen months and wait no longer than twenty-four. What is more telling comes back to the vintage exercise. In a wine-growing region without a long history, everything is news. Traditions, as they exist, have novelty and daring; inasmuch as one sips and contemplates wine, its narrative is still evolving.

As most visitors to Oregon tour wine country in summer, anticipate much rosé. Often made from Pinot Blanc or Pinot Noir, and sometimes conjured from other varietals that stayed on looking for attention, these tend to be calendar wines—if they're more than a year old, no matter. They refresh and go well with many light foods and patio furniture. They are oft terrific, with their effects more appealing than a small price and summer breezes. Drink now and often.

———— ✷ ————

HOLD

Hold means just that. Keep the wine in good storage and note when you laid it up. "Forget about it" largely proves correct. But in your dining, reading and travels, keep an ear to the ground or lip to rim. See what restaurants have in their libraries. See what comparable wines your geek collectors pull from the caves of possession to share with you. Check prices as published in retail outlets and websites. They will have cellar notes and point you in the direction of holding or serving your racked inventory.

As the Marx Brothers say, "Who are you going to believe?"

Drink the good wine today; life is brief. Believe in your own responses to your wine acquisitions. And remember, about 92 percent of all wine purchased domestically is going to be gone in nine or ten weeks, starting tonight. I imagine much wine purchased has a home-cellaring duration comparable to a Slurpee on a hot day—about a half hour.

Some underrated vintages might not please the purists, but you like it for reasons of your own. If it matters to you because you cellar several more of the same, make notes about the circumstances—the hours, the meal, how you were feeling physically—as such variables might affect your impression of the wine you then sip. The objective of knowing why dates matter is, alas, subjective.

You may wonder why I have taken some pages to discuss vintages in the most intelligently managed viticultural area in the world (France) in the context of New World wines, including those of the American West. I love history. Wine travels on every brigantine or galleon, along every trading route, over mountains and along arid stretches of sand. It is not solely a marker of a vintage obscured by centuries; it is also a marker of conviviality, enterprise and, let's face it, imperial designs. Above all, wine is durable, as are we. So, vintages attest to staying power, good seasons or ill, with the promise that good times will come again. Raise a glass to the shadows of the past.

The value of trying to latch Oregon wines, especially Pinot Noir and Chardonnay, to a vintage stacking system is, in one sense, a fool's errand. There is not enough history. On the other hand, in recognizing that the Oregon Chardonnay and Pinot Noir are analogous to but not in most respects just like the great grapes of Burgundy, an object lesson remains.

That is why I pose the exercise here. Vintage matters because it yields perspective, and the best way to fashion wine and drink wine from the current year's crop brings perspective to the whole. And if wine is going to tell a story, it must have its "once upon a time."

ON YOUR DIME

This is catechism. If you have some wine laid up, classify as:

1, Drink now.
2. Buy and hold.
3. Lose it, gift it or trade it. Also—drink it.

This exercise works best if you own more than one bottle half-finished stored in your refrigerator. Over a week or two, check your vintages to determine whether they are around peak (1), best put away (2) or pop it so as to be put to reasonable use.

PERSPECTIVES: A POSTSCRIPT TO THE 2006 KRAMER CHARDONNAY

The 2006 Chardonnay produced by Kramer Vineyards tells a unique story that asserts my impression, as told to me by proprietor Trudy Kramer.

The vintage was the last of the Chardonnay until 2010. The 2006 harvest was a good one, and the Kramers decided to experiment with the maceration. After stemming and crushing, they put the juice in vats for twenty-four hours with dry ice. Dry ice is used for cold storage of transplant body parts and on the sets of Universal Pictures horror movies made in the 1930s and 1940s to simulate vampire mist. And Dracula doesn't even drink wine.

The dry ice came as a result of research, and its use with Chardonnay varietals comes from a practice certain vintners used in Italy with the idea that an overnight stay of this kind would improve the flavor profile of the Chardonnay.

Trudy Kramer said, "Our experiment made no difference in the flavor profile once the wine was in the bottle. But once it aged, we noticed how complex and interesting its texture had become." That is what gave it its Burgundian semblance and made the bottles I cellared for more than three years so interesting.

Until I heard the tale directly from the vineyard owner, I never imagined dry ice having to do with things Italian except perhaps for gelato. We drink and learn.

In an e-mail to this author, Kim Kramer, the winemaker at the vineyard who is also Trudi's daughter, recalled having this wine late in the year 2012: "I had a similar experience with the '06 Chardonnay. I always liked it, but we opened a bottle at Thanksgiving, and it really blew me away. It was quite unexpected for me, especially since I don't expect the wines from warmer vintages to age so gracefully. Wines such as this make me question what I think I know about Oregon wine!"

If the winemaker is surprised, we who appreciate the effort have nothing to fear.

Finally, the Kramers' attitude to winemaking suggests both the paradigm for the singular nature of wine made here and, in addition to the dogs on the property, what makes Kramer my favorite winery in the state: good humor and good wine.

And now, please, check sommelier Doc Wilson's take on Oregon vintages. Doc has been instrumental in bringing winemakers to my attention and their wines to my acquaintance. He has been near the industry since 1982, so his take resonates for me both as complement to my notions and as confirmation of my instincts. Since I was familiar with Oregon wine prior to meeting the wizard, we have enjoyed a rapport on baseball and especially food and wine. Our tastes are complementary, our palates long in the tooth if not taste memory, and we are not above telling wine stories. I trust the importance of character and differences in vintage years will stand you, the reader, in good stead.

---※---

CHAPTER 5

THE CONSCIENCE OF THE CALENDAR

CONTRIBUTED BY JAMES "DOC" WILSON

In our modern technological age, most commodities are measured and evaluated. In recent years, our national pastime, baseball, keeps hordes of statisticians in business. In the early days of baseball, it was just ERA, BA and RBIs. Now everything is measured: OBP, GIDP, RISP and so on and so forth! Following this line of thought, we find an interesting fact: the fruit grown in the largest quantities in the United States is the grape! Wine grapes are responsible for the latest round of statistical analysis.

We have to start with the mystical origins of fine wine, and thus we cast an eye to history and the country of France. Any country that foists a generalized term such as "*gout de terroir*" on a worldwide population of hopeless oenophiles deserves recognition! The term simply means the natural environment of a viticultural site. The major components include soil, local topography, climate (temperature and rainfall) and sunlight energy.

As you can see, the statistical groupies will have a (pardon the pun) field day with these measurements. If you want to be "Francophilian" specific, you could say that a viticultural site will exhibit certain characteristics in the finished product (wine) from each vintage to the next, more pronounced in a good year than a bad year. That raises the question of how good years and bad years are defined.

With a similar latitude as Burgundy in France, Oregon has discovered that it has a cooler climate with a variety of soils conducive to producing quality in varieties like Riesling, Pinot Gris and Pinot Noir. The wine writer Matt Kramer said it best: "Finesse is an attribute, where the wine does the

This photograph shows crates of Riesling grapes being loaded onto a truck by Andy Humphrey and an unidentified person. *Weber Vineyard Collection, Jereld R. Nicholson Library, Linfield College, McMinnville, Oregon. Donated by Vivian Weber, 2012.*

work, as it serves to effortlessly deliver all the forces present in the wine to the winemaker. Acidity is the key to finesse. With these soils and a cool climate, Oregon delivers wine with uncommon finesse."

This is where vintage in Oregon becomes more important. With the success of the 1983 and 1985 vintages, Pinot Noir became Oregon's signature grape. With notable quality in '98 and '02, 2003 became a "teaching moment" for Oregon winemakers. Around the world, 2003 was for most winemakers the hottest year in memory, and Oregon was no exception. The thin-skinned Pinot Noir grape suffered, along with other cool-climate varieties. Winemakers tried everything from harvesting early to dropping fruit and keeping canopy cover to protect the grapes. Some veteran winemakers said that they didn't make a particularly good wine in 2003. But the lessons learned from that hot year helped them when the 2006 and 2009 vintages came with excessive heat at harvest. Some great wines were made with the acquired knowledge of past "hot" years.

It was apropos that the vintage of 2007 reflected the flip-side of Oregon's climate. Rain at harvest made this one of our most difficult vintages. When to

John Paul, owner and winemaker of Cameron Winery in the Dundee Hills AVA, and Doc. *Courtesy of Doc Wilson.*

pick? Before the rain or after? Some waited while others didn't. Ken Wright echoed the credo of most Oregon winemakers: "You pick when the flavors are right." In this vintage, the best and more experienced vintners made the best wine.

And then, bingo! The 2008 harvest came along, with longer hang times and an Indian summer in October. The grapes ripened slowly, with great complexity. Harvest in that month was accompanied by smiles from most of the winemakers and, later on, great appeal from the major publications. The aforementioned 2009 was a hot year and was handled well by the veterans of '03 and '06. These lessons were passed on to newer and a growing number of second-generation winemakers.

Then came the "Alfred Hitchcock year" of 2010, so called because the grapes took a long time to mature and the ripening coincided with the arrival of migratory robins and starlings. Great clouds of ravenous birds pounced on the grapes like ants to a picnic! Some wineries had netting, others had sonic cannons going off at different intervals and others had "sound boxes" that emitted sounds of raptors like hawks and falcons. The birds were smart enough to circumvent most of these determents, including diving through holes in the netting. In the case of one vineyard that forgot to close off the ends of the rows, the birds joyously gorged themselves at each end. Many wineries lost 30 to 50 percent of their crop!

So, just when you think you've experienced everything, 2011 came slowly with its own digression. The coldest year in the vineyards produced the latest-ripening vintage ever. Cold, damp weather kept the grapes from maturing. The birds came and flew on and the crush started in late October and went all the way into November, with some sites still harvesting on Thanksgiving weekend! The emerging adage in the '10 and '11 vintages was that the best winemakers made the best wine.

After two somewhat scrambling years, 2012 was a hotter year with perfect fruit set, veraison and a bounty of fruit. With great responses, the 2012s are drinking well now and will last eight to twelve years for maximum pleasure.

The 2013 vintage started out like the '06 and '09 years. The hot weather in August prompted some wineries to leave canopy cover on certain sections of Pinot Noir in the vineyards to protect the thin-skinned grapes. Then, in September, monsoon-like rains dropped two to six inches in a three-day period. As the hot weather returned after the rain, it was necessary to remove the canopy cover to guard against mold and mildew. The lessons of 2007 and 2011 proved valuable in bringing the 2013 to fruition. Many fine wines made from this harvest are in the market and showing well today.

The recent 2014 and 2015 were mostly hot years, with an abundance of fruit in 2014 and an exceptionally hot harvest in 2015 (like 2003). As noted, a new and second generation of winemakers is taking over in Oregon, with documented expertise and a new batch of technological data that will handle anything Mother Nature can throw at them. With these weapons at their disposal, Oregon vintners are moving into a renaissance for their product. This recent era has produced interest in Oregon wine from investors in France, Germany and California. The future holds great promise for this and future generations here in Oregon.

Many winemakers feel there were higher acids in the 2014 and more heat degree days in the 2015s. Then came the 2016 vintage, which some producers compared with the 2012. It was also a hot year, with a bounty of fruit and optimum conditions for fruit set and veraison. Of course, with the 2016s "the proof is in the pudding"! Or, in this case, the bottle. Some will be released in 2018, and some will need another eight to twelve months of bottle age.

The year 2017 was again hot with harvest, starting in mid-September and continuing through an Indian summer in October with warm days and cool nights. Longer hang time could mean higher sugars, but with a longer ripening window, complexity and quality could be on the rise. The 2017 vintage, however, is "still up in the air" (literally) from smoke particles from 600,000 acres of fires burning in Oregon's forests. Fires put a light dusting of ash in some of the Willamette Valley vineyards, which produces 70 percent of Oregon's output. It was a different story in southern valleys, where the fires were vast and more outreaching and could affect the vintage there. It seems that smoke particles can adhere to grape skins in tiny quantities that can't be detected by the naked eye or touch. For imbibers of smoke-tainted wine, they can have an ash or petrol nose and harsher earthy, leathery flavors on the palate. The southern vineyards, which produce 20 percent of the yearly crop, were helped by a healthy rain just before harvest. For now, winemakers are optimistic about 2017. Earlier it was a cold, wet year and there was a lot of soil moisture. However, there was consistent flowering and a good fruit set, and then it got warm and stayed dry. It looks like a fairly large crop with very good fruit.

Just like in baseball, there's a new generation of statistical groupies here in Oregon. It used to be tons/acre, gals/ton and plants/acre. Now it's %berry wgt/sugar, farm cost/ton and %berry wgt/acid. With all these statistics and figures, the old question is always asked: "What is a good wine?" For Oregon winemakers today, that's a no-brainer. A good wine starts and ends with a smile.

As with the cheesy asterisk appended to Roger Maris's sixty-one home run record set during the regular 1961 season, the 2017 vintage in Oregon as elsewhere up and down I-5 will have to account for the fires. It will be an asterisk vintage. (See also my article about the fires in the *Oregon Wine Press*.)

PERSPECTIVES

Winemaker Ed Fus of Angel Vine and Urban Crush in Portland remarked how abundant and high quality the vintages since 2012 have arrived—"right down the fairway," he says, mixing baseball with golf. He sees the challenge as handling abundant good fruit and making wines with focus and structure where such a bounty could tempt some to phone in their wines, as every producer can release good wine almost at will. So, a highly regarded and abundant season may, as in recent warm years, release wines lacking startling exceptions. Success is sometimes very tricky, indeed. Fus also told this writer after the fires that he hopes fellow growers and winemakers can identify and carry out steps to mitigate the damage caused by disasters so responses are better coordinated. These procedures have yet to be fully articulated.

Harry Peterson Nedry, proprietor and co-winemaker of Cheehalem in Newberg, told Doc Wilson that Oregon was becoming the "canary in the mine" (i.e., the indicator of climate changes in the Northwest). For how long this canary sings remains to be heard.

And now we return to our regularly scheduled program.

CHAPTER 6

WINE WORDS AND THE EXPLODING MAX HEADROOM

You might remember a cartoonish mesomorph called Max Headroom, from British TV in the 1980s. He had blond hair styled runway flat. The cut of his jaw looked like he had been imprisoned for weeks at a dental implant clinic. When I think of decoding winespeak, I often recall Max, as it does take maximal cranial area to process how bright people describe wine and how their descriptions differ from what they appear to want to convey about the experience of a wine they taste for the first or nth time.

It taxes my RAM, and thus one feels that Max is mad again and that his angular ferocity is about to splatter onto my monitor. So I thank the Snooth sleuth (snooth.com) for an exercise about wine words and for having a website advanced enough so that readers can post comments on the comments about wine commentary. If you are looking for cheese in this maze, keep reading.

Decoding the Grape grew out of a linguistic exercise that I return to at various times and in various magazines: Just how do we describe the expression or explosions of wine as we engage it with our senses?

I like to scrub opaque terms so they become clear, like Isaiah's prophecy about making the crooked straight and the rough places plain (or plane?). I contend that wine consumers are often put off by myriad wine nomenclature, including descriptors found in reviews and tasting notes, in marketing palaver, in sales pitches and in varietal viticultural jargon. Nonetheless, many terms work, and it would do wine lovers a disservice to make them unfashionable, just as it would be obnoxious to insist on recycled cardboard containers to drink from on the grounds that glass breaks.

So, here are just a few we can live without and a few we should hold dear. As we go along in our narrative, winespeak words come into play often. Some are technical, like "brix," and others describe one step in some wine production, like "carbonic maceration."

ON YOUR DIME

Following is a sequence of wine words, both formal and informal, commonly used and appearing in many books, lists of wines by the glass and in-store tags used to promote a bottle for sale. Open two Chardonnays to start, one from a California producer and one from an Oregon producer. Use appropriate stemware that allows you to swirl and sniff. Sample the wines simultaneously and mark or note the terms that best describe each at first impression and then perhaps a quarter hour later.

- acid
- aromatic
- bold
- bright
- citrus
- color
- complexity
- easy drinking
- finish
- floral
- grapefruit
- green apple
- green as in grass
- mineral
- nutmeg
- pineapple
- smooth
- sweet
- tart
- vanilla
- well-rounded

Since there's no single right answer, you will likely discover that some of these terms do not really apply at all and some terms apply to one but not the other in degree or kind. Do the wines meet your conception about what a Chardonnay tastes like given your prior experience?

This is less a word lesson than a trusting lesson. Trust yourself and add other words to the list if they better help you to describe what you tasted. This is an exercise best done with three other people, so you each ultimately quaff about twelve ounces of the wines. See whether you see camels and your companions see whales or squirrels or abominable snowmen.

This exercise can also be tried in a *ménage à trois* with a white burgundy to offset the California or Oregon representative wine. If you wish to do this blind, put the bottles in secure paper bags so you're not influenced by the origin and vintage and brand name before conducting this little experiment.

A Gloss on Max: In reviewing this prose for the nth time, I prepared a smoothie composed of fresh honeycrisp apple, apple juice, fresh carrots, organic beets and kale, plus parsley and a sliver of fresh ginger. Well, I liked this *mélange*. But beet does dominate, and the flavor reminded me of what I like in Pinot Noir, more as inference than half-time marching band—dirt—with a sweet song playing on the Eternal Radio somewhere beyond the barn. Beet is not a taste component of wine *per se*, but I believe it can do a walk-on to good effect. Anyhow, a beet is better than "state of the art."

PERSPECTIVES

A brief trek on Highway 99W or 26W from Portland center will get you to Rex Hill's tasting room. Before striding to the bar, visitors confront a wheel that poses thirty-six distinct aromas emitted by grapes made into wine. Visitors owe to their nascent taste memories a pass through this wonderful exercise. It opens the mind and helps each person to find the lightning in Mark Twain's right words to describe wine.

The *Wine Folly* post for January 24, 2014, has a nice overview of useful winespeak. It ends with the following wisdom about the power of suggestion. Roll over, Polonius.

Someone says something like "carnauba wax" when describing a Chardonnay and suddenly that's all you can smell. Now you've been unwillingly transformed to your last visit to the auto detailer. How do you move past the power of suggestion?

A TRICK FROM MASTER SOMMELIER TIM GAISER

In order to pass the rigorous blind tasting exams, Tim Gaiser has recommended that sommeliers practice overcoming the power of suggestion with a visualization technique. Identify the most obvious flavor and imagine putting it on a sheet of paper. When you imagine setting the paper aside, suddenly you can smell new flavors. This powerful memory training technique is referred to as "the palace of memory." You'll be surprised how well it works when you try it yourself.

The last bit of serendipitous gloss on Max Headroom's glossary comes from the Snooth wine website in a post dated October 6, 2017. The editors asked wine bloggers to write about describing what wine smells and tastes like—indeed, the inspiration for the book you're holding in your hands (and for which you paid full retail).

The bloggers write competently but with a veneer slapped on of self-regard like a second coat of paint on a dreary wall. "To thine own self be true," writes one, comically missing the point that this advice has been offered by Polonius, a time-serving bag of wind killed during Act 3 by Hamlet, the star of the show. Indeed, Hamlet's camels and whales in cloud shapes mocks Polonius shortly prior to being skewered. You need context to use brainy or famous quotes effectively. The best comment by one blogger concerns Merlot. She describes its feel and flavor as "velvet rope." You know, like Radio City Music Hall uses to separate the swells from the tourists. I wish I came up with that one.

PERSPECTIVES: BRIX AND BEAUJOLAIS

Since I bring them up, I won't send you to the bookshelf or computer. The first term is the measure of the sugar in fermenting grapes. Yeast converts sugars in grapes into alcohol. The process stops on its own or when the winemaker stops the fermentation to achieve a particular characteristic of the juice that is indeed, technically, wine at this stage. The net sugar content is expressed in degrees, and this measure is called brix. If juice is twelve degrees bx, it is going to be less sweet than when the residual sugar is eighteen degrees bx.

The second term describes a process. In Beaujolais, the most noted wine to use this method, gamy grapes come off the vine and into a barrel without going through a crusher to remove the skins and juice and all those good grapy things. The weight of the grapes above crushes their neighbors to the bottom, and as they, in turn, release their grapy things, they foment fermentation upward. The fruity pale red Beaujolais Nouveau is what arrives by November 16 to celebrate the recent harvest, and everybody drinks a lot. It is Burgundian ritual, so don't be surprised when this same process occurs in Pinot Noir places elsewhere—as in Oregon. Gamay shows up in certain runs from time to time. It isn't the Gamay of California jug wines that were around forty years ago, and it translates the French wine idea into plain English. It's an appealing and uncomplicated wine with enough bright notes to light a small patio. I like its fresh flavors.

Do I really need a "chunky" white wine? I would say that high acidity finely tuned, coupled with little or light oak ageing and a flinty or stark sense of minerality—all supporting an essence of fruit—makes more sense than "chunky." Rocks go well in gardens but not in my stems.

And what shall we say about "supportive" tannins? The Snooth editor, though not Samuel Johnson, makes a good joke about psychotherapy here and I agree. Tannins help wine age, ripen and set the stage for what we experience in tasting the wine. In a figurative sense, tannins do support the overall structure of the wine. But they are not "supportive" like people in support groups. It seems an unnecessary qualifier to me, whereas "fine tannins" suggests these acids balance and harmonize the expression of the winemaker's effort when all cylinders click.

Wine writers may use pencils still, but I doubt when they compose their columns. "Pencil shavings" are often picked up in certain well-aged Cabernet varietals or based blends from Bordeaux to Beringer Knights Valley, especially when they have some age. If you recall your first algebra class, summon up the ghost of that pencil sharpener mounted on the desk or blackboard frame. A freshly sharpened pencil always evokes my math teacher Mr. Lauber, who was nice enough to give me a D in ninth grade when I should have better repeated the class. But academic defeats aside, that recall contains a nutty aroma suggesting iron and slate. When this algebra shows up in the wine, it reassures us that our senses engage a wine of many layers. The nut essence comes from the oak used in fermentation and aging; the illusion of graphite comes from the soil content at the vineyard. Will this quality sharpen your wit? I leave that to you.

Also related to the preceding are adjectives like "cedar," "cigar," "leather" and "tobacco." The best way to experience what these describe is to buy a box of premium cigars and, leaning into it, lift the lid. The rush of aromas contains at least three of these four sensations. We should note these flavors do not come from grapes imitating Davidoff smokes, but from the aging and the barrels.

The cedar nexus seems to lead some commentators to juniper and pine notes; what matters is that in the maturation of the wine, the interaction of the original oak used before bottling is transfigured, once in the bottle, to suggest the other aromas as well. Like the pencil shavings and the cigar box, the leather can be distilled, in this case by walking into a shoemaker's shop where they don't sniff that glue. The leather or "saddle" in the wine is a component of the mature flavor of big and intense reds.

Oak itself is the major wood used to age wine; laying up the wine from three to twenty-four months after it's fermented allows for the spice, tannin and vanilla in the molecular stew of the wood to interact with the wine. Tannin produces the astringent puckers that novices may not appreciate, but in time they soften, allowing the wine to keep longer and mature.

Although their behemoth varietals of Cabernet and Chardonnay have slimmed down in the last decade, Napa's Far Niente was traditionally a champion of oak, so much so that its wines probably also contained antique roll-top desks. When vintners wish to keep the oak touch light or avoid it altogether, they age the wine in stainless steel or cement tanks, both inert materials; this allows them to bring the wines to market more quickly. If one is producing a small lot of, say, Chardonnay or Pinot Gris and wants to emphasize the natural characteristics of the varietals, the lack of oak does the trick. Bulk producers such as E & J Gallo have millions of gallons held in tanks for its mass-market wines, stored underground behind its headquarters in Modesto, California.

Although we have strayed a little out of the way, this excursion should remind us that labors we love are loved better with a net profit from operations. Finally, polyurethane containers for storing wines post fermentation, as you can see when visiting Vidon Winery (Chehalem AVA), offer the benefits of neutrality and cleaning ease. Just think of the oven in your first off-campus apartment.

Although the Snooth fellows castigate "round" as a descriptor, I am less put off. "Roundness" makes a balance impression, where fullness of the wine in the mouth doesn't lead us too far astray from an overall impression of something pleasant to behold. It is not quite "balance" because that term inspires an entirely more serene confidence. Drink a premier Cru Burgundy when you have the good fortune—you will need a small fortune just to play—in order to see what balance is.

Another contested term is "approachable." This applies to some wine and to some people, but not precisely in the same way. In winespeak, it means the wine is ready to enjoy from the first pour. It will change in the air, but the alterations will be neither dramatic nor surprising. In this respect, perhaps, it is like the nice girl your mother wanted to fix you up with whose aunt was in her canasta group.

On the other hand, I demur when it comes to "terroir." Romance language origins notwithstanding, this term accurately expresses a characteristic of wines I prefer to drink. It does, indeed, refer to the soil and the weather, in the way music may state a theme in C major and then the same thing in the relative key of a minor. In either passage, the *there* is there. And this is true for terroir. We therefore take into account other variables: the elevation, the axis of the vines in relationship to the path of the sun, the depth of rootstock and the skill of the winemaker in realizing the challenge the fruit poses based on cluster size, harvest time and maceration to begin. "Terroir" does more than describe. It asserts. It argues for something. And that is good enough for me.

For the French producer, terroir is mystical and at the center of the entire approach to farming wine grapes; it remains for me the spiritual nexus of any fine wine made anywhere vineyards flourish.

Then, in a tangential way, the term "barnyard" comes up in a tenuous relation to terroir. Popular winespeak, "barnyard" connotes everything from chicken pellets to tractors leaking some effluence. It means dirt. It means earthy. It means rustic. And it means, I think, that you watch where you step. It's kind of like a word you think of that illuminates your impression of a wine's flavor at the moment it slides past your anticipation. Hey, watch your—*splat!*

Is the barnyard part of the terroir? I think certainly. The aroma and the attitude are not fetid but rustic in many top Burgundy varietals, and the barnyard seems, in the air in the stem, to breathe into something more luscious and yet still willing to admit its salt-of-the-earth aspect even as it ascends to heavenly beauty.

The best advice given about tasting wine is indeed to taste it and respond to it with whatever words come to mind. The vocabulary comes with more tasting, and like words acquired in school through reading, the vernacular of wine tasting will in time expand the descriptors you use when tasting it. My vocabulary seems to refine itself as I experience new wine.

Sometimes I feel as if I am in the scene in *Hamlet* in which the prince of Denmark mocks the old busybody court advisor Polonius. They see a cloud, and Hamlet says it looks like a camel. Polonius agrees. Then he changes his mind, and Polonius changes his mind, too, as the cloud now looks like a weasel—and then like a whale. Polonius never gets it, although he does get it a while later when Hamlet kills him by mistake. The lesson: form your own impressions and the wine will not kill you (unless you're one of the victims in the final act of Shakespeare's play). Wine words are useful in trying to describe by metaphor and simile an experience of an entirely different set of sensory impressions. At its best, trying to describe wine is like trying to separate the dancer from the dance.

The more different wines you explore, the more you will expand your appreciation of the differences in even the same varietals from around the world. Thus, wine drinking elevates your knowledge and your vocabulary. Believe yourself—it's your mouth.

Since I began this chapter in other guises before I moved to Oregon, I think it meet to comment on some words Max Headroom would zap with his lantern jaw.

These include "handmade," aka "hand-crafted." Please, enough sleep-away camp artifacts! If Hesiod means anything, the work of the land is the work of hands, so why be so redundant? A grower and winemaker walk into a row, move aside the canopy of leaf and pluck a little fruit to assess ripeness or other characteristics. That is handiwork enough for me, and it remains time-tested.

Although "craft" implies a skill set, I find this term, like its Mr. Potato Head variant "hand-cut" (as in French fries), completely over the top and therefore unnecessary. Use a machine. God gave us the gift of mechanical invention. If you wish to use your hands, pick up the fries.

Another weasel or two seem to imply scarcity and superiority of goods. These are "small production" wines from "boutique" wineries. The former all but screams, "Short inventory!" in order to prompt action at an artificially inflated price. "Small lots" are attractive because they allow us to infer that the winemaker could pay better attention to his art, like the small classes teachers' unions insist will produce higher student test results. I believe neither claim is infallible. A "boutique" winery is also going to feature "wines of limited output." A "boutique" shop caters primarily to carriage trade ladies who were written of derisively by Edith Wharton. These small shops have a loyal following and will not sell to "just anybody." This means their rightful customer is you.

The veneer of exclusivity translates to wineries that can parlay their handmade scarcity into consumer demand and higher prices per bottle or case. I think boutiques belong on Rodeo Drive and Worth Avenue, but not among vintners or their wineries. Low output may presage a very enjoyable bottle of wine, but the correlation is not automatically positive.

Similarly, "award-winning" is overused. There are plenty of ways to recognize good wine. First, of course, is to drink some. Wine competition is more a way to obtain a read on the results of one's labors and also is a great way to conduct informal competitive analysis. Sampling wines in the context of other like wines is very instructive. When wine critics and merchants beat the drum too much, we grow tone deaf. That is why I look past the chintzy medal to what's in the glass.

Finally, there is the numeric score. Some might contend that given the vagaries of winespeak the reduction to a score may be preferable. We need not excoriate Robert M. Parker Jr. again to point out that this is nonsense—just as a one-hundred-point Alpha Critic rating is fatuous or even flatulent.

Believe what you drink and not what I, or another author or expert or blogger, advise you what to think.

CHAPTER 7

OREGON AVAS

A BRIEF DESCRIPTION

DEFINING AN AVA

An American Viticultural Area is a designation of place where wine grapes grow. Each AVA is distinguished by its unique characteristics of geological formations and soil, elevation and microclimates that distinguish one particular viticultural area from another. These natural traits supersede old appellation names that are formed around place as defined by political boundaries, such as a county or town.

The assignments of AVAs are the purview of the Bureau of Alcohol, Tobacco and Firearms (BATF), which has been re-christened as the Alcohol and Tobacco Tax and Trade Bureau, or TTB for short. Firearms, practically and perhaps regrettably, has been shunted elsewhere in the federal system. It is a sign of the times. Both BATF and TTB operate out of the Treasury Department of the United States. Thus there exists a uniformity of compliance and descriptions for AVAs, despite the state and local restrictions pertaining to the licensing, production and sale of beer, spirits and wine.

The first AVA in the nation, covering four states and twenty-nine thousand square miles in the middle of the continental United States, was established in 1980. Oregon's first AVA, as previously noted, is Willamette Valley (1984). Large AVAs contain smaller ones, like boxes of Chinese puzzles. Prior to the AVA regulations, a winemaker could slap "Willamette Valley Red Blend" on a bottle, even if half the fruit was purchased from some other place. The new designations, and most stringently in Oregon, restrict the assignment of place to the pedigree of grapes starting with their place of origin. This means that a Willamette County Chardonnay is the produce of vines in Willamette Valley and not Hackensack, New Jersey. It is one of the best things to occur in the classifications of wine and their marketing despite some exceptions, as noted in this chapter.

Let us begin with a curiosity. An American Viticultural Area refers to grapes, not to spas, tony resorts or tasting rooms. In Oregon, noted Nicholas Doughty of Portland's Elephants Delicatessen, the AVAs represent the fruit produced rather than the marketing concepts used in selling wine: "In California, where I grew up, the AVA is driven by wine sales. In Oregon, the AVAs are established to represent what we grow. The vineyards drive the process." A sound observation, and it may help you, the reader, put the varied landscapes into perspective.

We must also remember that, as Edward Bernays once said of the public and its opinions, these are part of a passing parade, not standing armies. Thus, the AVA count changes. There are 138 in California and now 18 in Oregon, 2 more than when I began writing this chapter.

If the AVA designation provides a lever to lift wine sales, it approaches the unique aspects of the designation from its ultimate output. This can help the consumer set some expectations. When the grapes do the talking, the output describes elemental facets of distinctions in the air, the climate and the soil. We stand in relation not to seasonal buying habits, for instance, but to geologic time. Each perspective has merit; nonetheless, it does seem that commercial considerations may obscure genuine viticultural distinctions or, worse, obscure a relative lack of differences in order to print an appellation on a label so it stands out on a real or virtual shelf in the wine department of the mind.

What follows here seeks to express the elemental differences; that, after all, is where the experience of wine begins. It also helps to explain how an AVA, such as the Snake River AVA, has commercial growers but not commercial wineries. All this can change. Humans are prolific and mobile. Where once a valley or hillock dominated a view, now stands a community college or a bed-and-breakfast or a visitors' center. Seize the moment. What you see is ever in flux, and it's moving away.

Although a reader can browse the internet and poke into myriad lists of American Viticultural Areas, including Oregon's, readers will find here a short description of them as consolidated from various sources, as well as my visits and tasting.

Aerial view of Willamette Valley and Vineyards. *Courtesy of Willamette Valley Vineyards.*

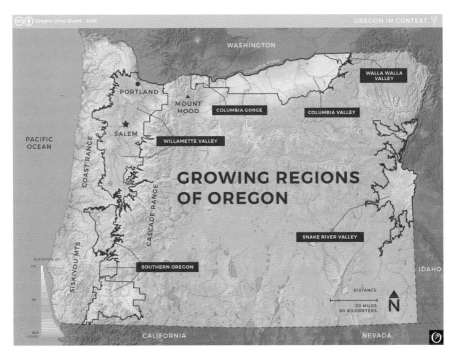

Oregon wine state map. *Courtesy of Oregon Wine Board and Oregon Wine Research Studio.*

The reader ought to know that each AVA is approved by the federal government. This arm of revenue collection parallels state and regional bureaucracies that, in turn, assess fees and taxes. Growers and vintners likely will originate AVA applications.

To wit: the late Robert Mondavi and I shared a dinner table at a wine event in 1988. This avatar of America's wine respectability advised me, "Wine is also food. It is not typically consumed in multiple six-packs, causing drivers to run school buses over the side of a mountain road"—alluding to one such accident that occurred in that same year somewhere in the Deep South. For a man who started out working in Minnesota mines, this seems a little snooty. However, he had formulated an idea that led him onward.

His point was that wine would be better regulated by the Food and Drug Administration, as this would allow producers to be subject to a different set of standards than those that regulate spirits. I tend to agree; however, both wines and spirits are usually distributed through state or private wholesale channels. Oregonians are accustomed to state-owned stores for spirits, and as my friends at Bull Run Distilling Company pointed out, they like the state-run channel because it eliminates a layer of expense and makes the compliance process more transparent. In the instance of wine, its sheer multiplicity probably makes selling in "control states" easier than trying to jockey for distribution in wholesale states. As a point of comparison, E & J Gallo completely integrated its viticulture straight through the bottling, marketing and sales functions at an opportune time decades ago, making the company a permanent power in the industry, with farm sources in numerous California AVAs. Most Oregon wineries operate on a more modest scale, often taking five thousand cases or fewer to market.

In the end, I suggest the BATF's (and its successor TTB's) oversight of wine is a holdover from the days of Carrie Nation and the Eighteenth Amendment, but in a scheme of fiduciary rather than criminal compliance. Mondavi's mission was serious. He saw the success of his wines and those of other American producers as part of the food revolution that coalesced during the 1970s and '80s. It caused far more wonderful dinners than traffic accidents, he said, and education would ensure greater pleasure and also encourage a more responsible attitude to drinking itself. As we shall see later, the foodie revolution had better effects on the quality of American life than the hidebound, nativist repressions of G-men and frigid farm women with hatchets.

Mondavi's commitment to FDA oversight notwithstanding, I believe winemakers are habituated to a BATF process of obtaining licenses to produce wines for commercial purposes. Were the industry subject to an entirely new bureaucracy, it would inundate vintners in an ocean of many drugs and foods, leaving consumers even more tentative about varietals and vintages. Mondavi could wax about food because he sold gallons upon gallons of wine—savvy marketing, indeed.

Consumers benefit from AVA certification because it guarantees that for all varietals the grapes that end up in the bottle come from the areas specified according to specific percentages. Were wines handled by the FDA like canned peas or tortilla chips, would all of the sexy language on some reverse wine labels be more like that on a container of grape juice? Although the BATF regulates wine through its licensing process and approves new AVAs, states are free to specify what it takes to make wine a Columbia Gorge Nebbiolo or an Eola–Amity Hills Pinot Noir.

I expect to see further AVA designations in Oregon as producers lobby for greater distinction for marketing and firm standards for production. With 720 wineries in the state, it is desirable to manage the clutter, whether one produces or consumes wine purchased at the winery or supermarket.

Portland's urban wineries banded together in 2012 to create a trade organization; it may be the first step toward another AVA, complete with streetcars. After all, the San Francisco Bay AVA includes seven counties. The idea is that a city known for food and wine would make a good marketing hook for winemakers. Why shouldn't Portland do the same thing?

AVAs are less rigid than the French *Appellation d'Origine Contrôlée* (AOC). While the Paris Exposition of 1855 created the standard for Bordeaux's great estates, the French had actually toyed with some kinds of regulation as early as the late fifteenth century. However, just two months before the United States fell under its Prohibition laws, the AOC took effect in November 1919. Thus the attempt to certify the place where the wine is produced remains the preeminent qualifier.

Contemplating what many regard as France's finest wine, Château Petrus, one sees the logo—the letter *P* on a field of red—on the left; the top-center of the label dominated by the name Petrus; and beneath that the place of origin, Pomerol, in letters scaled to the regulatory millimeter. Then we read *"Grand Vin"* (great wine) as well as the vintage year. What are not on the label are its varietals. Petrus is always almost entirely Merlot and is tempered with Cabernet Franc. You won't see this on the label anywhere, even at $2,500 per bottle. In explaining AOC, less is apparently more.

Like its Haut-Médoc neighbors, Petrus is situated at the top of a rise,

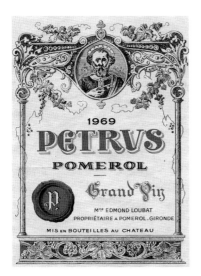

Petrus label. *Courtesy of Wikimedia Commons.*

perhaps 1,200 feet above sea level. Its soil contains much clay, and its exposure to the sun makes it ideally suited for its superb Merlot output. As one moves east, the soil becomes more composed of limestone gravel and light sand, which makes for stellar Cabernet varietals. The *Grand Vin* classification is less baroque than the classification of Cabernet-based wines of Bordeaux or Burgundy Pinot Noir, which is at first glance even more arcane. Other departments such as Languedoc, the Loire Valley and wines of the upper and lower Rhône Valley (i.e., Loire River) have their own variations on these practices.

The Petrus appellation does, however, indicate that the grapes used come from this single place, a forty-nine-acre site.

Small output and high quality make for big demand and sticker shock. What remains unsaid in print, though, is the magic of the terroir—that combination of climate, elevation, soil and sun that are the core of this oenological magic and the traditions guarded almost as fiercely as the *magus alembic* formula to turn lead into gold. As wines go, Petrus is red gold.

Whereas Rioja, the first certified area in Spain, more or less tips its hat to France in its certifications, Italy is characteristically lyrical and musical and a little insane. The classifications are not crazy but are also relatively recent. Classifications were first introduced in 1963 and significantly upgraded for one class in 1992.

Four classes exist. The broadest category is *Vino da Tavola* (VdT), or table wines, and the second is *Indicazione Geografica Tipica* (IGT), or wine that's typical of a particular region. The former is widely sourced in Italy from any region. The IGT classification—the one introduced in 1992—narrows the distinction to a specific region like Umbria or the Veneto. The wine does not come from one producer's vineyards but from several producers in that region. But these are also table wines.

The real fun concerns the two upper tiers. Even if place, the *genius loci*, is of greatest importance, a Tuscan Brunello del Montepulcino is made exclusively of Sangiovese varietal, the most abundant in the country. But you don't see the varietal on the label.

Likewise a Barolo, one of my favorite wines, will show the name of the producer, then the wine designation and then the vintage. What you do not find is the actual varietal, Nebbiolo, the glorious grape of Piedmont. The best known of Tuscan wines is Chianti. And perhaps ten folks out of a dozen do not think of Chianti as a place but even now as a bottle in a straw basket.

Italy's *Denominazione di Origine Controllata e Garantita* (DOCG) is for the most superior wines, and the next tier, *Denominazione di Origine Controllata* (DOC), is for wines meeting many of the same conditions for quality but with wider scope. The French appellation is very narrow by contrast and is rooted in a very conservative set of standards. Italy produces so many varietals that its labeling begins to read like Dante or the screenplay of a Fellini film. The Bolgheri region earned its own DOCG for Sassicaia, the first Super Tuscan, more than twenty years after its introduction. Oregon, too, has AVAs inside other ones.

Mosel, the benchmark region in Germany, emulates French certification, though in a perfectly Germanic way (its label descriptions are more detailed than the plans for the V-2 rocket). So we are fortunate that Austro-German varietals planted in Oregon (and for many years the leading varietals by acres planted), such as Grüner Veltliner, Gewürztraminer, Müller-Thurgau and Riesling, mercifully display the label information we also find on other Oregon wine bottles: producer, area, varietal, vineyard designation and vintage. When Oregon wine pioneer Ernst Reuter won his medal in 1904 at St. Louis, he had Riesling to show and very few details that an AVA designation would require.

In one sense, I have presented these contrasting classification systems so my own understanding improves. Let me illustrate by way of an analogy. Over time one becomes accustomed to look for the designations. One might say that in the 1960s and '70s national television news in America had but three dominant networks: ABC, CBS and NBC. With the launch first of CNN, Fox and then later hyper-local news channels and "cable access" (known as the "ghetto"), the threshold of what became news on television lowered. It became, in a sense, more democratic. When the AOC and its regimen of blind tastings per annum and all other practices became the standard, what constituted a wine worthy of a classification really meant Bordeaux and Burgundy. The system, of course, extended elsewhere.

Now and for decades before, other producing countries have taken their own unique form. Note label differences on new-world venues—Argentina, Australia, Chile, New Zealand, Portugal, South Africa and Spain. If you visit a good wine department or a bottle shop, you can browse the wines from all of these places, including our own states, to see what is important to them. It will help demystify the wine terminology and you begin to see the form replicated on other bottles. Even "generic" wines have a look and feel. This is all about democracy.

What I should like at last to note once more is how recently systems have been applied to the plethora of vines in the world. Italy's main reforms center about the early 1960s to early '70s, with further clarification in 1992, when the IGT category was introduced. All this despite viticulture on the peninsula for three thousand years. Though more venerable, French standards take familiar shape only in the time Franklin Pierce, no stranger to the bottle, was president of the United States.

Before I return to the topic of Oregon, I am pleased to note that the lower Rhone—where the now eighteen varietals are grown that are associated with Châteauneuf-du-Pape, one of the planet's greatest wines—is by local statute protected from incursions from space aliens. You are prohibited both from landing a flying saucer and from taking off from the village of Châteauneuf-du-Pape. This, according to the Wikipedia entry on Châteauneuf-du-Pape AOC, seems worth citing, even if not correct or true, for its patent wackiness.

Habemus Papam ("We have a pope," as the rite proscribes) has become "We have an extraterrestrial"—please phone home. (For this great wine, minus the starship, we can thank Pope John XXII, who died in 1334.)

If your eyes haven't glazed over, we can look at Oregon proper, the whole point of this chapter, and its AVA distribution across fifty-five thousand square miles. As of the spring of 2015, Oregon counts eighteen different AVAs. For ease of mapping the continued adjustments and growth of the wine industry, the date of its appellation accompanies the place name.

The first iteration of the AVA listing should be easy to recall. Grapes, despite their individual characteristics and indigenous qualities caused as a result of environment, do share certain common characteristics. Wine roots run deep in order to find nutrients and water. If ground water is scarce, expect to see irrigation systems. You will not see this in Willamette, but you will in Walla Walla or the Snake River.

All grapes used for wine also need sunshine, and vine placement in relation to Phoebus's run affects the term from bud to harvest, the sugar content and taste, as well as yield. Canopy management is all about the sun. In warmer territory, big acidic as in tannins and precocious fruit grapes will probably become the cash crop. In these warmer climes (especially on valley floors), you can expect to find the Cabernet varietals, Merlot, Petit Sirah, Sangiovese, Syrah and Tempranillo, among many others. Oregon today plants seventy-two different varietals. Because of their durable nature, expect to see Chardonnay and other white varietals like Pinot Blanc, Pinot Gris, Sauvignon Blanc and Viognier showing up within some of the warmer growing regions. The cooler climes encourage Pinot Noir and the other Pinot grapes. When you see Pinot Meunier on the vine, expect eventually to also see sparkling wine.

Many varietals are planted in places conventional wisdom eschews. Sometimes conventional wisdom prevails; at other times it doesn't. Australia's Hunter Valley, at first glance, did not appear to be vine-friendly. It is a killer viticultural area today because a few intrepid souls defied the pessimistic view.

A single-varietal wine, like Willamette Pinot Noir, is produced by vintners working within the conditions and requirements of the AVA. One can grow and produce a Pinot Noir in the Umpqua Valley AVA, but its character will be quite different, even if you recognize the main tune as the Pinot Noir varietal.

If you intend to enjoy the stories the wines tell, I recommend also knowing where they created the tale.

Table. AVAs by Name and Date Approved

Applegate Valley, 2000
Chehalem Mountains, 2006
Columbia Gorge, 2004
Columbia Valley, 1984
Dundee Hills, 2004
Elkton, 2013
Eola-Amity Hills, 2006
McMinnville, 2005
Red Hill Douglas County, 2005
Ribbon Ridge, 2005
The Rocks, 2015*
Rogue Valley, 2005
Snake River, 2007
Southern Oregon, 2004
Umpqua, 1984
Walla Walla, 1984/2001**
Willamette, 1984
Yamhill-Carlton, 2004

* Sub-appellation Walla-Walla subsumed in Columbia Valley AVA.
** The second date amended the original assignment to include Oregon.

The table here demonstrates the relative youth, but thirty years, of the classifications in Oregon. When three AVAs were established by the Bureau of Alcohol and Tobacco in 1984, they brought a broad certification to Oregon in two large areas and one even larger in Washington State. In both instances since, these large AVAs have become umbrellas for smaller ones. Apple, Elkton, Red Hill Douglas Country, Rogue Valley and Umpqua Valley all are wholly contained in the Southern Oregon AVA. Elkton, like Mendocino in California, has the distinction of being its state's tiniest AVA.

On the other hand, the Columbia Valley AVA has more than 1.5 million acres to contend with and more than forty thousand acres for vines. Seventeen thousand acres are planted with all manner of varietals red and white. Snake River's relative handfuls of vines produce by comparison only few different varietals.

To the other side of the state, Willamette Valley runs over 150 miles from south of Eugene to Portland, where the Willamette River soon merges with the Columbia River. Within its green shade are contained smaller AVAs including the Chehalem Mountains, Dundee Hills, Eola-Amity, McMinnville, Ribbon Ridge and Yamhill-Carlton.

As viticulture expands, the need to better qualify output tends to specificity, and so for producers, this means increased attention to management practices based on the habits of behavior in these microclimates. For the consumer, this means more options.

The Columbia Gorge is another, if different tale. Its town center is Hood River in the eponymous Oregon County. Nonetheless, it straddles two states over the river, Oregon and Washington. Its growing area is small, but its personality is large. It is not contained in either umbrella AVA, and its stretch over forty miles along the river is one of the most imposing viticultural scenes, with its peaks, its waterfalls and its wide rolling river. I think its time as a wine power is yet to arrive.

Americans are famous for having little knowledge of world or even local geography. (I once had a very bright student look at a jeweler's advertisement in *Los Angeles Magazine* in which an elegant couple in formal wear were superimposed on a photo of the Doge's Palace on the Grand Canal in Venice. She understood the snob appeal in the display, but one thing puzzled her: "Why are these fancy people shown in front of a slum tenement?" That is pretty scary). Lacking the geographic sense and the spirit of a wine region is like showering in a raincoat. To make the most of any investment of cash and time visiting wineries, learn about the region; the experience will improve much when you know where you are. The "Great Out There," as I call it, takes you out of a foggle (fog plus muddle) of self and into a zone where you can encounter awe and wonder. Wine is part of the Great Out There, and appreciation of the wine will be more palpable and satisfying when you know where Venice—even the beachfront in southern California—might be. You can always trust the Marx Brothers, but even he would suggest in the end you trust yourself.

It is not difficult to find literature or online resources to locate Oregon's wine regions. The difficulty resides not merely in abundance of information but also its relevance. So much of it reassures you of having so good a time that the informational value is either buried or elsewhere. Some vintner associations seem mirrors for those who fund them. I am all for knowing where to dine, tryst, sleep and wake. Many businesses prosper because of wine tourism. I support this but always remain wary of Babbittry. Self-funded guides stuffed into backpacks snatched on the fly from metal racks will give you some information, but be wary of the boosterism. Remember what lies outside the frame.

Still, I have benefited from resources that include the *Oregon Wine Press*, the Oregon Wine Board and the Oregon Wine History Project at Linfield College at McMinnville, as well as many wine trade people. I think in topics such as this, where current issues do not intrude on presentation of basic information, Wikipedia is an indispensable resource, even for those of us who, like this writer, have limited vision but great enthusiasm. The wine moment for Oregon is a continuing story, and this is as fine a time as any to join the rest of us around the campfire, glass in hand.

I have culled from my research just enough comment and information to pique your interest in the following display. Drink it in. An *envoi*: insofar as we are about to consolidate disparate and useful information for wine fans and wannabe wine fans, I do want to add something about wine websites. I like a handful of them and use them as I need to learn more of their offerings. But that is but one part of the story.

I ought to add a caveat about too many wine websites. They're of the halt and the lame, and I don't mean they are tannic beasties. The people who design websites are, if not taking illicit chemicals, then at least not sensitive to the needs of the visually impaired. When conformity leads to slavish imitation, the functionality of websites for wineries withers as if *phylloxera* attacked them. I will give you two instances just from one site and its link to another. The navigation bar on the Applegate Wine Trail site is dark gray, and its lettering is black. Within the bar are these words: "Cannot read this. Can you?"

Once I circumnavigated this hazard and went to the links for the eighteen individual businesses posted, where some links had no links, I chose "Red Lily" and the site popped up right away with a lovely MP3 tune on acoustic guitar (synthesized?) on a warm red PMS 69, almost the hue of the Tempranillo wines that justly earn repute throughout the West. But getting more affect than substance, I was frustrated by navigation one might use to learn of the wines made. Well, the winery has apparently re-thought its online presence, so its present iteration excites visitors to want to sample the wine.

A good functional website more likely induces sales and visits than a flashy one or one designed by someone's nephew on the cheap. The web has great potential for educating people and informing them about what's available and helps mitigate the damage that public schools have done over decades concerning geography and history. Winemaking and vineyard tending are products of migration, conquest and settlement; they betoken human enterprise and ingenuity that describe a more intelligent use and enjoyment of nature's opportunities. The Internet can reflect these things, but feet on the ground amid the rows of grapes brooks no substitute for the real thing. That makes AVA distinctions very helpful.

As postscript to this chapter, we might comment on the newest AVA, the Rocks, approved as recently as February 2015. The baseball-sized basalt composition of the dirt in this stretch of the Columbia Valley makes its viticultural profile unique. There is no place in the domestic geology like this little slice of Milton-Freewater, Oregon, the only AVA in the country whose boundaries are determined by the soil type. In other words, we have an AVA inside another AVA (Walla Walla), which, in turn, is inside the Columbia River AVA, which includes land in Oregon and Washington State.

The fruit is all Oregon, therefore, but the wines that have garnered critical attention are Syrah crafted in Washington. So, who renders unto Caesar has an Oregon license plate. The peculiarity of federal labeling regulations makes it possible for a winemaker doing business inside Portland city limits to use the Rocks appellation on a wine sourced miles away, whereas a vintner on the opposite side of Columbia from the new AVA cannot do so.

Thus, the accident of the basalt prompts wine-geek concern to the extent that *Wine Spectator*, famed for using endless lists of point scores to sustain alternately turgid and brilliant wine writing, has gone on record opposing the AVA designation. Well, the force of the unique geologic properties trumped editorial pique. Readers will find wineries sourcing Cabernet, Tempranillo, Cabernet Franc and other varietals in addition to Syrah from the Rocks. I look forward to diving in.

CHAPTER 8

A FRAME TALE

OREGON VITICULTURAL DETAILS

A reader may find the following snapshots a little mechanical; the point is not to overstate the amenities of Oregon's AVAs or their appeal to visitors but to provide some generally acknowledged appreciations of their characteristics and output. I make no apology for my sources or for my experience in describing these unique aspects, even though these certainly repeat a bit from one place to the next. Were I to give my sense of the whole, it would read thus: Oregon is a medley of geologic wonders and climatic dissimilarities. As in all producing regions of the globe, Oregon exhibits often in modest detail how one or several features dominate its winemaking and its viticulture. To state the obvious—that it's cool here and warm there; that this AVA gets considerable rain and this other one gets very little—only hints at the whole story.

We do not necessarily see the variety of life teeming beneath the sea; likewise, we do not perceive the difference of vines as they roll away from our vantage upriver or toward the distant hills. But the life is there, and it becomes expressed in the making of wines. Consider these descriptions a frame tale to the larger story compacted in the glass. As each culture has its lore, so too will wine grape growing areas. The secret is to listen to their stories and follow your palate.

The maps that follow in this chapter are courtesy of the Oregon Wine Board and Oregon Wine Research Studio.

APPLEGATE VALLEY

You know you are not in Beverly Hills with wineries named Cowhorn and Cricket Hill in the neighborhood. At current count (according to www.applegatewinetrail.com), there now operate eighteen vineyards and wineries in this AVA subsumed within the Rogue Valley AVA, itself subsumed in the Southern Oregon AVA. The promo on the website announces "big wines from little wineries." What growers like here is not merely the dry, warm growing days but the altitudes above sea level of 1,000 to 1,500 feet. These conditions auger well not only for Cabernet Sauvignon and Merlot, the bumper crop varietals, but also for Chardonnay and Zinfandel, each sympathetic to the area weather, which produces assertive versions of these wines. It was in what became this AVA that Peter Britt founded Valley View, the first commercial winery in Oregon before 1859. It has been restored and operates again.

CHEHALEM MOUNTAINS

Do not be overly surprised if wines produced in this appellation call up the wraiths of cherry orchards, plums and nuts. Located entirely within the Willamette Valley AVA, these mountains run parallel to vineyards following the course of the sun. We can thank David Adelsheim for advocating this heavy-soil terroir its AVA status. It runs about twenty miles through Clackamas, Columbia and Yamhill Counties, and its output from 1,600 acres is largely Chardonnay, Pinot Blanc, Pinot Gris, Pinot Noir and Riesling. Plum Hill Vineyards is owned and operated by RJ Lint, a man of many stories, as befits a person of Falstaffian proportions, with a good humor that seems needed on this property, a joyful work in progress. The tiny ocean uplifts sediment-rich Ribbon Ridge AVA, wholly contained within the Chehalem Mountains, continuing the Chinese-puzzle distribution of Oregon's wine appellations. The Chehalem Mountains produce lustrous Pinot Noir, the kind that calls out for good food. At this writing, thirty-one vineyards and wineries operate in this AVA. Among its outstanding producers are Ayres, Chehalem and Vidon. There are many others.

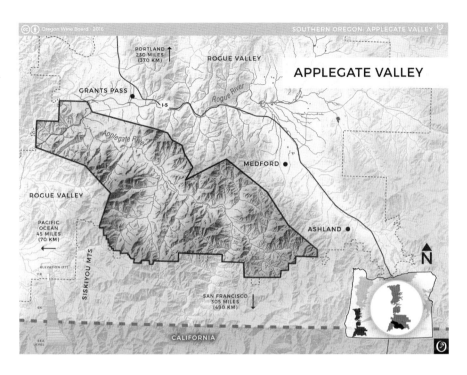

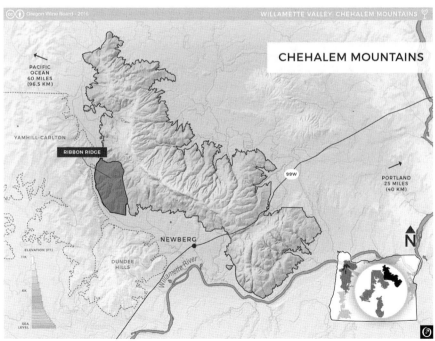

COLUMBIA GORGE

If memory serves me, sooner or later Interstate 84 will take you to Idaho and Utah as it follows the original trail of Lewis and Clark. But sixty miles east of Portland, past myriad cascades and falls and Mount Hood, the interstate enters Hood River County, where the eponymous city on the Oregon side of the grand Columbia River traces the shoreline. Oak Street is the town's main drag, and despite its affected rusticity, Hood River is smarter than it lets on. The gorge runs forty miles upriver; Washington's peaks and vineyards straddle the north shore, Oregon's the south. The AVA is not subsumed by another AVA, although it took some amending to distinguish the Oregon side upstream from the Columbia Valley.

The Columbia Gorge is a wind farm. This narrow channel, first explored by Lewis and Clark, has in effect two valves. Mount Hood is the western side— beyond its rain shadow is far more moist air, courtesy of the Pacific Ocean. Mount Adams is the eastern valve that leads into the continental high desert. Warm, dry air moves toward the west, and the tensions of these two air masses make this AVA a veritable Dagwood sandwich of microclimates.

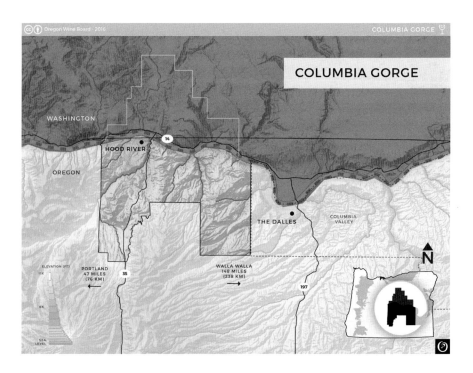

Author explores Nebbolio at Cascade Cliffs wine tasting room in Hood River. *Courtesy of Jonathan Potkin.*

Tasting room at Cascade Cliffs at Hood River in the Columbia Gorge. *Courtesy of Jonathan Potkin.*

The mighty mountains are reformed volcanoes, so the legacy of their once-active condition has left its mark on the soil, the ash, elements and minerals mixed with river silt and the effects of earthquakes, floods and glaciers. Its geological history opens this narrow strip of wine heaven to many growing opportunities. The first wine grapes started to replace some of the area's apple orchards in the 1970s, and winemakers soon took notice. Alma Terra Winery produces especially Syrah and Viognier; Cascade Cliffs Vineyard proved long ago that Piedmont wines like Barbaresco, Nebbiolo and Tuscan Sangiovese work in this splendid environment; Domaine Pouillon Winery specializes in Rhone varietals; and so it goes. There are more than thirty different established vineyards and wineries here, growing near the banks and high atop the basalt cliffs that make Columbia Gorge a singular and spectacular prospect, made even better when seen through the gilded aura of a local Chardonnay or Pinot Gris. I hate the term *unique*, as it has been so overworked. But the Columbia Gorge is a unique AVA.

COLUMBIA VALLEY

John Quincy Adams was in the middle of his presidency when Hudson's Bay Company planted the first wine grapes in this territory in the year 1826. The valley is situated between the forty-sixth and forty-seventh degrees latitude, making it the most proximate to Bordeaux and Burgundy among all AVAs, with the caveat that Columbia Valley is not the Gironde estuary any more than *pommes frites* are like a sockeye salmon caught and pan-seared on the shores of the Rogue River. The gorge and the river give way to 11 million acres in the Columbia Valley. Here seventeen thousand acres are planted in Washington's largest-producing area containing in its umbrella eight other AVAs, including Red Mountain, Walla Walla and Yakima. The valley has long been regarded for its white varietals, but it also cultivates many red varietals that flourish in this dry, vast and warm growing place. Rainfall is sparse, six to eight inches per annum, so irrigation is a must. More than thirty varietals come out of the AVAs in this spread, from Barbera to Mourvèdre to Viognier. The area is prized for its Cabernet Sauvignon. Its Riesling varietals, however, have long been a sustainable crop. Oregon is mightily represented in the umbrella AVA of Walla Walla, such as in Syrah and Mourvèdre from Zerba Cellars. These are pricey and worth the freight. Rhone varietals, indeed, abound. To get a better sense of the place,

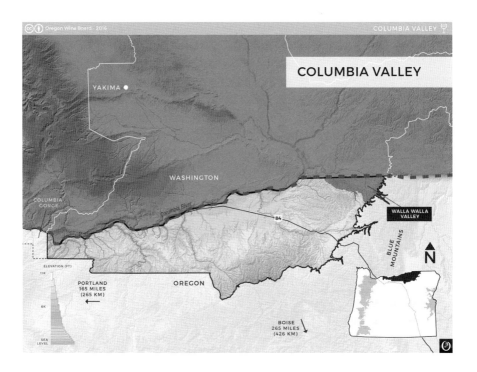

visit the Washington State Wine website (www.washingtonwine.org) and Wine Searcher's Columbia Valley page (www.wine-searcher.com/regions-columbia+valley), as each site is informative and well laid out. Insofar as the original AVA covers more than half the area of the state, from Oregon in the south to Canada in the north, the Columbia Valley wine tour is not a vacation but your day job.

DUNDEE HILLS

Remove the occasional narcissism from Napa Valley and you can experience at Dundee Hills what California's best-known AVA was like on its way to becoming a world-class playground for millionaires. Like Napa with its Cabernets and Chardonnays, Dundee Hills possesses a really singular quality in its Pinot Noir varietals and its Chardonnays. This does not diminish any other AVA; rather, the wines coming out of Dundee Hills celebrate the triumph of instinct over common sense. Dick Erath, who later founded Erath Winery, and David Lett, who later founded the Eyrie Vineyards, were

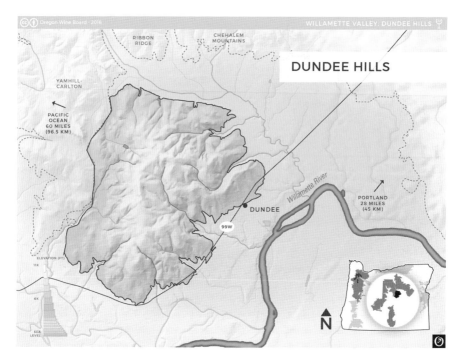

refugees from UC-Davis who did not heed the advice of colleagues when they decided that the Dundee Hills could thrive if only the farms moved out some cherry trees and planted Pinot Noir vines instead. By 1969, Erath had convinced Jim Maresh to do just that on his acreage. The can-do conspirators soon enough shared the vision and pooled their experience.

Dundee Hills feels like the locus of the industry, and this is intriguing in part because it was not designated an umbrella AVA until 2004. But recall that wine grapes were first planted here in the 1960s and that not only were Dick Ponzi (of Ponzi Vineyards) and Lett married to their enthusiasms, but Eyrie also won a Pinot Noir competition at Paris in 1979 before there was a single AVA in Oregon or Washington State. The original vineyard is here. The famous Burgundian house of Joseph Drouhin sent its legatee, Veronique, to Oregon in 1986 to scope potential for a domestic operation stateside. David Adelsheim recounted how the young woman crashed in the Adelsheim living room during her reconnaissance prior to the opening of Domaine Drouhin in 1988.

It is more than a transliteration of Burgundy in Oregon. We're in the Dayton-Dundee axis. Within the mile of the area's main thoroughfare, visitors will find names like Archery Summit, Argyle, Arterberry Maresh, Domaine Drouhin, Domaine Serene, Hawkins, Sokol Blosser, Stoller, Vista

The original Red Barn at Maresh Vineyards, where Erath introduced indicator vines in 1965. *Courtesy of Jonathan Potkin.*

Hills and Winderlea, among numerous others, whose tasting rooms dapple Route 99. At last count, 1,300 planted acres supported twenty-five vineyards and wineries.

Further, because of its proximity to Portland (twenty-eight miles), the Dundee Hills AVA seems always in the thick of balancing the needs of the vines and the expectations of visitors. Tina Bergen of Tina's, one of the best local restaurants, now past twenty years young, can tell a thing or two about changes here. This restaurant takes farm-to-table dining quite literally, and the local wines reinforce the point. To make the point about change stick even more, Tina's itself has at last changed hands, and a bricks-to-the-beach bypass is now taking shape on SR99 just past its most throttling bottlenecks.

It is best to avoid holiday weekends in most places, and it is mandatory here. But if you end up gnarled in a line of traffic, just relax. You are stuck in a good place. If you want good information I cannot see, visit www.fueledbyfinewines.com/dundee_hills and torture your peepers.

ELKTON

The latest, but this AVA really has a singular aspect. In this area tucked into Umpqua, itself tucked into Southern Oregon AVA, the surprise is a westward-facing prospect of several hundred acres in a part of the state usually associated with warm and dry conditions favorable to big red varietals and rapidly maturing Chardonnay. Ken Thomason of the former Elkton and Black Oak vineyards said, "Yes, but…" and planted Pinot Noir. And it has worked. Elkton is Oregon's smallest AVA, and the town for which the area is named boasts a population of 190 people. There's not much to do at night, goes the old joke about the former Yugoslavia, because "Tito has the car," and one ten-watt bulb lights the place (thanks, Mel Brooks).

EOLA-AMITY HILLS

Moderate elevations above six hundred feet, a soil composed of basalt base and volcanic below and cooling and steady winds from the Pacific (Aeolus, Eola's namesake, is the Greek god of winds) provide the singular qualities that distinguish this AVA within Willamette's larger AVA. Since Bethel Heights Vineyard planted here in 1977, this area has been highly regarded as a source for other Willamette vintners. Eventually, intrepid and optimistic men and women decided that if a place can grow grapes so well, wine ought to happen too.

My first encounter with its fruit in a bottle was a 2010 Pinot Gris that lived up to the virtues of that varietal—fresh fruit overall, beautiful balance and a delicate finish neither cloying nor overbearing.

The AVA runs from Amity south to Salem, and its position within the Coast Range ensures cool conditions that favor maintaining good acid in the grapes. For a modest AVA with 2,400 acres planted, Eola-Amity Hills lists well over one hundred vineyards and wineries with monikers like Iota, Redhawk and Angel Vine. The AVA extends over two counties—Yamhill and Polk—so within this relatively compact space, one can track the sources of grapes that go into making very well-balanced Pinot Noirs in particular. The website is mercifully un–not cool (www.eolaamityhills.com), and its myriad links provide a foretaste of the handiwork on these 2,400 planted acres. The secret sauce here is a notch, called the Van Douzer Corridor, that funnels marine air through a margin in the coastal range, the natural frontier of the western valley. Myron Redford is Amity's *pater familias*, and he

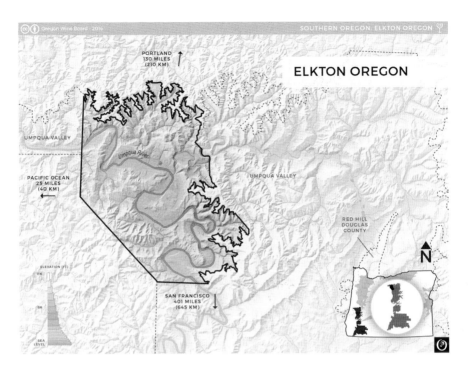

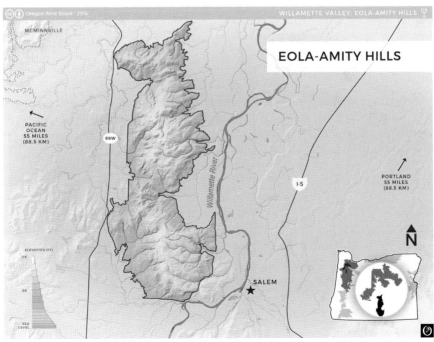

was shopping his winery property when I moved to Oregon. He has a great northwestern wine collection and stories to nibble on with them. Among the pioneers noted in chapter 2, Redford's the only one who isn't an engineer. Like several Rieslings we had one rainy night, he has been age-worthy.

McMINNVILLE

This is an American small town of the kind we used to see depicted in the pages of the *Saturday Evening Post*, drawn by Norman Rockwell. Clapboard homes with wide porches. Quiet streets shaded by old oaks and other trees. A turn-of-the-last-century hotel, the Oregon, with a rooftop bar and patio that bubbles over with characters. Linfield College contains the Oregon Wine History Project. The town has nice churches that, it seems, people frequent. So one feels part of a distant, less complicated time. But how to explain all those cool restaurants and places to honor Bacchus? So much for nostalgia.

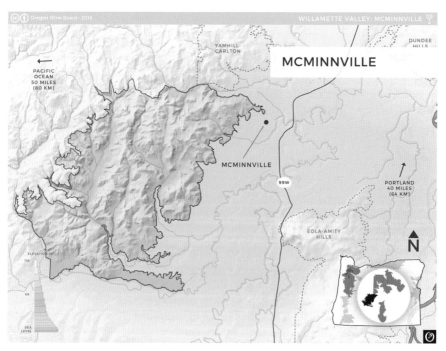

Winemakers David Lett, Dick Erath and Dick Ponzi embrace owner Nick Peirano (*second from left*) and share a laugh while at Nick's Italian Café in McMinnville, Oregon. *Ponzi Vineyards Collection, Jerald R. Nicholson Library, Linfield College, McMinnville, Oregon. Donated by Dick and Nancy Ponzi, 2012.*

David Lett and Doc at the International Pinot Noir Celebration (IPNC) in McMinnville, Oregon. Lett planted his first cuttings at Corvalis in 1965. *Courtesy of Doc Wilson.*

The AVA has six hundred acres planted, producing the three "P"s—Blanc, Gris and Noir—plus Riesling that sustain fourteen wineries. The website (www.mcminnvilleava.org) offers good, readable information. The vineyards, west of the town, thrive in the foothills of the Coast Range. Millions of years of geological upheaval have made the terroir cocktail in this AVA at once fascinating and, in terms of its wines, very positive. This lucid passage from the McMinnville AVA website deserves repeating here:

> *The significant geological history here has helped to shape a highly complex and varied terroir. The story of our soils begins roughly thirty-eight to fifty-five million years ago when the Cascade Mountain lava flows and tectonic plate movements created the Coast Range Mountains. Plate movements exposed ancient and weathered soils in the foothill regions where the AVA is located. The lava flows created "basal lava fingers," noticeable amongst marine soils in the AVA vineyards. The soils are primarily uplifted marine sedimentary loams and silts with a base of uplifting basalt. Harder rock and compressed sediments of basalt pebbles and stone are found under an average 20–40 inch soil depth, giving the McMinnville AVA a unique soil complexity on which to grow our grapes.*

The wines express these distinctive facets of the environment in their character. Black cherry, currant and spice emerge in the Pinot Noir with recall of some of their French cousins on the Côte-d'Or. Keep in mind that the International Pinot Noir Celebration, a huge annual late July draw, happens in the Grove at Linfield College smack dab in this AVA.

While this affinity can explain the name of the Coeur de Terre Vineyard, it takes a little more credulity to marvel at Noble Pig, which in 2010 planted Pommard and Dijon clones 777 and 115 on a four-acre site named the King's Table. Just how will these grapes from the AVA's newest vines dazzle us? We will have to wait, see and savor.

RED HILL DOUGLAS COUNTY

This is a mystery AVA. The Jory soil of Dundee gave that northern Willamette wine area the epithet Red Hills. One sees that is plural. When Dundee Hills became a separate AVA in 2004, it took a while for the epithet to fall off. The matter complicates even more because Lake County, a California AVA whose most famous wine flew under the Guenoc Valley AVA flag, is also

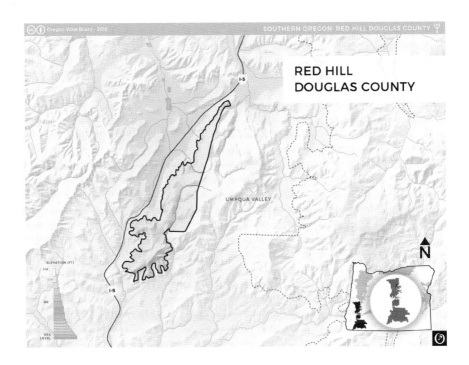

known as the Red Hills—plural once more, but also across the state line. So the southern Oregon designation for this umbrella viticultural area became assigned in 2005 as Red Hill (singular) and Douglas County (not Lake and not Dundee for that matter, either). So what is the point? Stay tuned. The AVA appears to be a clerical error until you discover that little of the iron-rich Jory soil really is here, and the area's elevation (1,300 feet) makes for cool and moist conditions in the middle of another AVA that is warm and dry. Sienna Ridge Estate is a three-hundred-acre vineyard and one of the very few that is all by its lonesome designated a single-vineyard AVA. Are you getting this? So, as in Elkton, we have Pinot Noir and Chardonnay of a different order from the majority of the output in the Southern Oregon AVA. What will they think up next time? Well, if you're able to locate Yoncalla on a map of the area, you're near the AVA.

RIBBON RIDGE

This AVA is wholly contained in the Chehalem Mountains AVA, which is in turn contained in the Willamette AVA, and at a quarter mile wide at most, it earns its "Ribbon." The ribbon extends 3.5 miles with five hundred acres

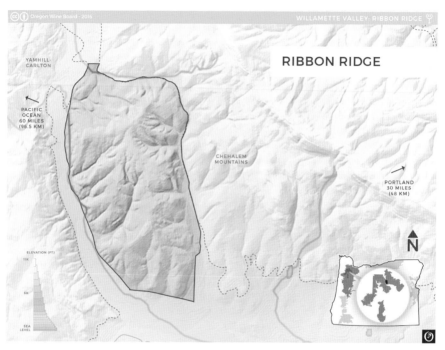

The author and James Frey—artist, proprietor and winemaker—at Trisaetum in the Ribbon Ridge AVA (Newberg) discuss Charddonnay, Pinot Noir and Riesling during a 2017 visit. *Doc Wilson Collection, Jereld R. Nicholson Library, Linfield College, McMinnville, Oregon.*

planted with Muscat Canelli, Pinot Gris and Pinot Noir. Beaux Frères is likely to be among the best-known wine brands in the AVA, which earns its status because its borderline position in the northwesternmost part of the Chehalem Mountains creates a geological boundary and its climate induces a long growing season, allowing its growers to obtain fruit of mature and intense quality.

THE ROCKS

This AVA came online in February 2015, mainly distinguished for its unique basalt formations on the Oregon side of the Columbia River. As the Wikipedia entry on this topic states, the AVA poses labeling problems for Washington winemakers. I am quite curious to try the mostly red varieties of wine to come out of this small sub-AVA, now that the government has approved the designation.

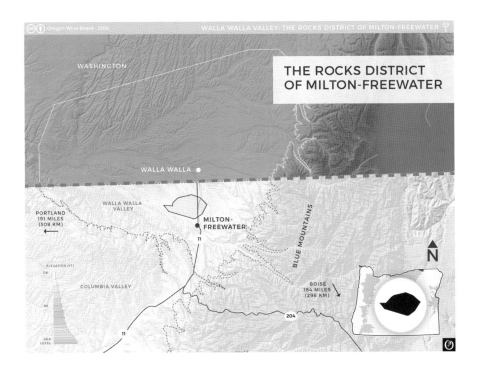

ROGUE VALLEY

Southeastern Oregon producers bear labels like Troon, which makes a blend called Druid's Fluid. It has, as Goethe once said, a certain genius in its boldness. Or maybe it has boldness in its genius. The wine-growing areas lie along the tributaries, including the Applegate River, Bear Creek and the Illinois River. More than a dozen varietals emerge from this 420-square-mile valley, including Cabernet Franc, Cabernet Sauvignon, Malbec, Syrah and Tempranillo, as well as white varietals that, along with Chardonnay, also show Gewürztraminer, Sauvignon Blanc and Viognier. The warm and dry climate is continental rather than maritime, so the growing season and output are very different from those we find in the north, as in Willamette AVA and its sub-AVAs. The rivers each contribute to a distinct microclimate that is also affected by its elevation, up to 1,500 feet above sea level, making Rogue Valley Oregon's highest-altitude AVA. Do not confuse the various descriptions of the AVA and its umbrella AVAs, although the acreage planted, the varietals produced and the wines coming from here do overlap. Although the original Valley View Winery began during the 1850s in the Applegate sub-AVA and later faded away, the next going concern in the state, Cliff Creek Cellars, opened in the Rogue Valley in 1873. It continues to produce estate-grown Cabernet Sauvignon and Merlot.

SNAKE RIVER

In the mid-eighteenth century, Britain decided to send its criminals to the colonies in North America to thin its crowded jails. Ben Franklin wrote a pamphlet suggesting the colonists send snakes to England as payback. He concluded that the Brits would be getting the better end of the exchange; after all, one could usually tell when a snake would strike. The AVA doesn't have much in common with Franklin's suggestion, but it does identify the river that separates the state of Idaho from that of Oregon. This AVA requires that 85 percent of the grapes in bottles labeled with the Snake River appellation be sourced in the designated area, a departure from Oregon's higher proportion elsewhere (95 percent). The AVA exists between 2,500 and 3,000 feet elevation; this makes the continental climate temperature spread extreme. The grapes grown are the heat-seeking red varietals such as Cabernet Franc and Sauvignon, Malbec and Mourvèdre. Chardonnay and Riesling are the predominant white varietals. The AVA is better known for its numerous

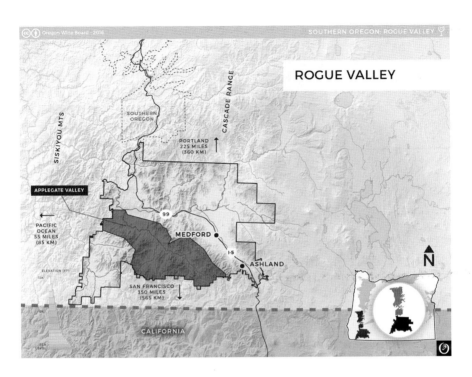

vineyards; they outnumber the wineries by about three to one. The Oregon part of the AVA includes Baker and Malheur Counties. An overview of the AVA, decidedly low-Oregon profile, appears at Wines Northwest (http://www.winesnw.com/sna.html).

SOUTHERN OREGON

As with Willamette, the Southern Oregon AVA was a geographical consideration when it was assigned in 1984. The Rogue Valley and Umpqua umbrella AVAs followed some years after and, in turn, as we noted earlier, Applegate. Elkton and Red Hill Douglas County have drilled down further. More than a dozen varietals come from the AVA and the smaller ones contained within it. As you leave Eugene, the land begins to flatten and the climate becomes more of what one expects in California: hot days, cool nights and only some rain. As of last count, more than three thousand acres have been planted for vines, and about one-sixth of the state's wineries operate in the entire area. Relatively speaking, Southern Oregon was the not-Willamette AVA when both were assigned in 1984. Nonetheless, its cities and surroundings have no lack of charm or wine lore. A readable starting place is, again, Wines Northwest (www.winesnw.com); the content there helps to orient one to this large swath of Oregon and the wineries both in its designated AVA and outside it. The Southern Oregon Winery Association posts as concise a summary of the entire area as you might want, and it bears inclusion here:

> The rugged mountain valleys and diverse climates allow for a wide variety of intensely flavored wine grapes to be grown. The cooler areas of Southern Oregon produce wonderful Pinot Noir, Pinot Gris, Riesling, Sauvignon Blanc, Chardonnay, and Gewürztraminer while the warmer, more arid regions ripen big reds such as Cabernet Sauvignon, Cabernet Franc, Tempranillo, Merlot, Malbec, Dolcetto, Zinfandel, Grenache and Syrah. Many other unique varieties such as Albariño, Pinot Blanc, Grüner Veltliner, Marsanne, Rousanne, Baco Noir, Marechal Foch, Mourvèdre, Sémillon, Petite Syrah and Viognier are also grown; making Southern Oregon one of the most diverse wine-growing regions in the world.

We can augment our perspective by noting that now more than 150 growers and wineries occupy this part of the state, having planted more

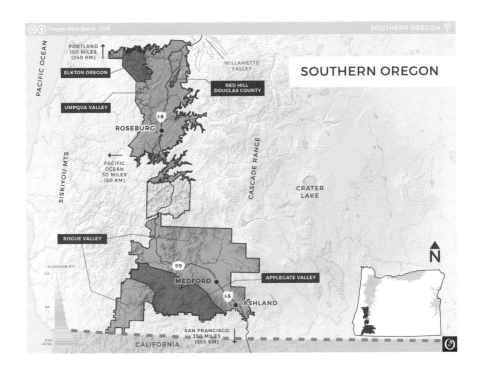

than seventy varietals. The *New York Times*, *Wine Enthusiast* and others have discovered these places in 2016 with the kind of wow-ness once reserved for Oregon wine generally.

UMPQUA

Richard Sommer is another UC-Davis veteran who disregarded the naysayers and planted the first Pinot Noir grapes in the state in 1961 at Roseburg (HillCrest Vineyard). The quilted terrain of the Umpqua region is nothing if not diverse, as small mountain ranges open into one valley after another. There are several indisputable and interesting points that distinguish this AVA. It is, first off, wholly contained in one county, Douglas. In this place, Wikipedia reports, Grüner Veltliner, the Austrian varietal, was planted first in the United States. Finally, it seems to encourage viticultural innovations, like the Scott Henry trellis system, used to train vines and manage their canopies.

The AVA is 150 miles square and is bounded by the Coast Range in the west and the Cascades to the east. Rogue Valley lies to its southeast. Umpqua's tapestry of soil exceeds at most recent count 150 types and

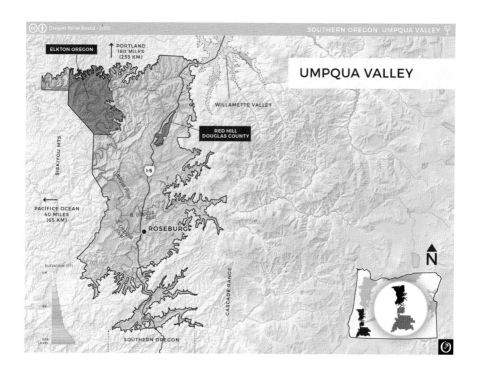

variations. Oregon Wine (www.oregonwine.org/discover-oregon-wine/ place/umpqua-valley) posts a very nice description of its climates, as myriad above as is the earth underfoot:

> *One of Oregon's more diverse climates, the Umpqua Valley can successfully grow both cool and warm varieties. It's comprised of three distinct climatic sub-zones: 1) The northern area around the town of Elkton enjoys a cool, marine-influenced climate. It receives around fifty inches of annual rainfall, making irrigation unnecessary. Pinot Noir and other cool-climate varieties thrive here. 2) The central area to the northwest of Roseburg has a transitional, or intermediate, climate where both cool and warm varieties do quite well. 3) The area south of Roseburg is warmer and more arid, similar to Rogue and Applegate Valleys to the south, making irrigation necessary. Warm-climate varieties, including Tempranillo, Syrah, and Merlot, thrive here.*

In short, this territory offers distinctions from the predominant notions about Oregon wine country and thus deserves appreciation of its natural beauty as well as its wines.

WALLA WALLA

An AVA straddling northeastern Oregon and Washington State, and contained entirely within the vast Columbia Valley AVA, this area is sun-drenched about two hundred days per year and receives about 12.5 inches of rainfall per year. As such, its vineyards produce bright and spicy Cabernet Sauvignon and big plumb-my-depths Syrah. Until 1950, no vineyards were planted in this district. Vineyards and wineries began to proliferate in the period of the American Foodie Revolution of the 1970s. Oregon's participation began in earnest over the past several decades so that today, about half the AVA's planted acres are on the Oregon side of the Columbia River. Most of the wineries operate on the Washington side. An *Oregon Wine Press* passage neatly describes the land underfoot: "Varying combinations of well-drained loam, silt, loess and cobbles were brought by a series of massive floods (known as the Missoula floods) some fifteen thousand years ago." We think real estate is a function of value; we forget how much dramatic action goes into making the land "real."

In the last winter trade tasting of 2015, I encountered some excellent Red Mountain–area wines from this AVA. There are many splendid examples of purple, bold and complex wines coming from this area in the AVA. I don't have the gift of prophecy, but the AVA process for Red Mountain, now in the works, will likely sooner than later expand this list. If you are stuck in a line of cars and trucks on Route 99 in Dundee, slide into the Zerba tasting room. Here you will have the pleasant detour of wines from Walla Walla and Red Mountain, if not with their ambient vibrations then at least providing a descant to all of the Pinot Noir engulfing you at Dundee.

Our expedition to Walla Walla reveals several truths. First, the Columbia River does not divide one Walla from another. It divides Oregon from Washington by a traffic signal. The mighty Columbia has turned left to its Canadian source. Walla Walla, a staid farm market town, has been transformed into a café and tasting room walkabout. I hope the tiresome biddies behind the lace who are not spinning in their graves will take note how wine culture can transform a place on its way to irrelevance into something lively with new infusions of visitors who can enjoy hospitality beyond watching asparagus or notable onions grow.

WILLAMETTE

Willamette is the engine that pulls the Oregon wine train. With more than half of the state's wine production contained in this region and its umbrella AVAs, the doings here affect the state's entire $3.8 billion wine enterprise. As Napa Valley came to define California wine, so does Willamette define Oregon wine. However, Napa earned its reputation not solely because of its style of winemaking; it also overcame the sheer bulk of table and wine grapes coming from California's Central Valley. In other words, Napa altered perception, and it has come at a price. Something of the spirit has been lost in the glitz.

Willamette Valley AVA faces a similar challenge—literally to keep its inspiration and spirit from becoming too commercial or too much on display. I have hope for the place at this moment because its scale is relatively small and because it's in the hands of contrarians who are also capable in the vineyard and at the winery—with many coming out of the restaurant/hospitality business as well as traditional agriculture. Furthermore, Oregon's tapestry of microclimates—a bonanza in Willamette's varied terroir—promotes green and organic winemaking. This is not just a marketer's

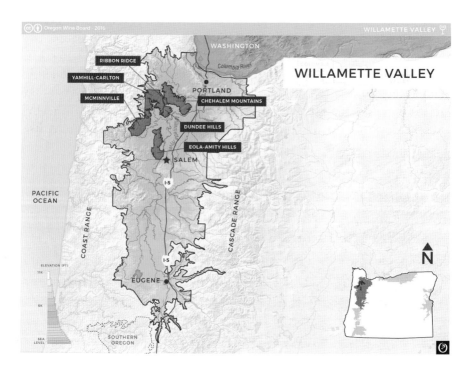

conceit. Sustainable resource management is oft at the forefront. I do not think this is window dressing; it represents a commitment that not only will keep wine quality high but also presages more innovation on a human scale. We could say all wine, being grape juice, is organic, as are the vines it comes from. But in Oregon there is a conscious attention to keeping the origins of what ends up in the bottle and stem as close to the land as possible. That is a very good thing, tourists included.

To wit, Adelsheim winemaker David Paige, who cut his chops in California, makes the point that in California, the term *organic* is not part of any commitment beyond putting the term on labels so consumers feel good. And I thought "feeling good" had to do with the pleasure of the wine itself.

Will success morph this epicenter of Oregon's wine business into just another midway for the printed undershirt crowd? We must wait awhile to find out.

YAMHILL-CARLTON

I would like to think of this AVA as the epitome of the Oregon wine scene. Its small expanse in the northwest Willamette Valley is distinguished by a horseshoe configuration of low mountains and a veritable almanac of geologic history and soil variety. Its generally long, cool seasons are representative of what appealed to growers about the region in the first place. The slow growth produces fruit of exceptional character and depth, making the region's Pinot Noir in particular a very strong candidate for the most representative wine of the entire Willamette AVA, in which Yamhill-Carlton vineyards are entirely contained. Industry pioneers like

Lenne's estate entrance sign in Yamhill. *Courtesy of Carl Giavanti.*

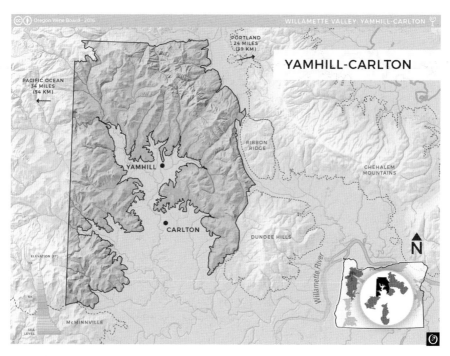

Bottom: Elk Cove Vineyards in the Yamhill-Carlton AVA. *Courtesy of Jonathan Potkin.*

Charles Coury, Dick Erath, David Lett, Bill Blosser, Susan Sokol Blosser and David Adelsheim saw the potential in this area more than fifty years ago, and that potential continues to be realized. The Campbells, Joe and Pat, have turned Elk Cove into one of the AVA's most respected pioneer wineries, with Kramer, Roots and WillaKenzie providing some of the most memorable destinations in the state.

A CONCLUSION: OREGON WINES AND CALIFORNIA NATIVES

Charles Humble, who until recently was the chief spokesperson for the Oregon Wine Board, shared a splendid 1999 Raptor Ridge single-vineyard Pinot Noir with me as we talked about the differences between California and Oregon wine country. He asserted that though Oregon winemaking has a long history, its spirit is young and still evolving. "California has its industry base more established," he said. "We like being upstarts."

The standard line about California is that nobody actually started out in the Golden State save a few indigenous peoples. We can thank some friars for the first migration, men who made their way up from San Luis Rey, establishing missions, tending to what they saw as the locals' spiritual needs and planting grapes, well before gold, land speculation and railroads drove the droves out here starting more than 160 years ago.

Californians liked their spirits and wine. German and Italian immigrants brought their historical preferences for wine over the mountains and across the vast continental expanses so that now, in the world's third-largest wine-producing nation, California is the Godzilla of the wine industry, with almost as many AVA designations as Kim Kardashian has wardrobe changes.

As noted earlier, Oregon has eighteen AVAs, and one is but a few months old. Indeed, as Napa Valley and Sonoma's riverside vines and lovely vales were taking on the traditional markets of Europe, Oregon did not even have an AVA until 1984.

If readers outside the state know something of Oregon wine, it's likely someone brought them a bottle of Chardonnay or Pinot Noir for a cookout. The wines use two of the most prestigious and popular varietals grown anywhere, including California. The typical style of wine made by Californians is big, like the state. This can come as a shock to those who know great wines from Burgundy. The California trademark Chardonnay has lots of color, butter, oak and vanilla. It can be beautiful or overbearing. Pinot Noir, a more finicky grape, has a California style, too, with wonderful notes of black cherry and currants, as well as some generous oak, usually. Pinot Noir from Asuncion Ridge on the central coast is a fine example, as are Pinot Noir from Acacia or Road 31 Wine Co. in Carneros, where Napa and Sonoma converge at the top of San Pablo Bay.

Now look at Oregon wines made from the same grapes. Chardonnay is sturdy enough to grow in the warm and dry Southern Oregon AVA, which includes all of Umpqua as well as four other sub-AVAs. But it is in Willamette that the Chardonnay takes on a style more reserved than brash, often with more lemon grass or citrus than honeyed gold. A Cerulean label Chardonnay aged some years in stainless tanks—zero oak—grows up to be clean and lean. It comes from another AVA, the Columbia Gorge, which attracts wind surfers as well as wine surfers.

Oregon Pinot Noir is a cash crop. It was first planted in the state a mere fifty years ago against the advice of practically everyone at UC-Davis, who said that Oregon was too weird and wet to make decent wine other than German-style Rieslings. But the Pinot Noir—such as Arterberry Maresh, Elk Cove, Ghost Hill, Grochau, Patton Valley or WillaKenzie, to name some—are quite unlike the fine wine made of the same varietal found in the wide expanse of California. They strike me as very bright on the nose, with cherry and at times a little chocolate, with a nice presence of oak that doesn't overpower everything else in the glass. They have structure, whereas California counterparts rely at times on special effects, big berry and oak dominant in their first impressions.

Sometimes the Oregon growing season is short, so the wine grapes get a little less sugar and come out a bit pinched or comparably more acidic. Acceptable, but very different from warmer, longer growing seasons like 1999, 2006, 2009 and 2012, which are more fruit-balanced and vigorous. The winemakers can pretty much handle the pitch Mother Nature tosses, whether a heater or a spitter. A good vintner makes good wine in any season; it seems that variables in vintage make us appreciate—yes, celebrate—these protean changes.

I think the California winemakers of renown have a fine sense of their potential for any vintage. This is also true in Oregon, with its goulash of soil types and microclimates, but the narrative is still being written. Surely part of the fun is being around, glass in hand, waiting to see how the story unfolds.

I have come over time to prefer much of what the Northwest offers in its wines to the immense output of our southern neighbor. The difference is not merely stated on AVA applications; it is also in the attitude to the land and the work it calls forth. Land has a sanctity about it in Oregon; too often down the freeway it has only an ego and a price tag. Oregonians' sense of place is not proto-Romantic; it speaks frankly of affinity to natural surroundings. Nonetheless, we can thank President Polk for his sabers and skill at poker. We have a West Coast where it belongs…and much wine to learn about.

ON YOUR DIME

Choose one varietal of your liking from each of three different AVAs or sub-area AVAs. For example, choose a Pinot Noir from the Columbia Gorge, another from Eola-Amity Hills and a third from Yamhill-Carlton. Note the color, aroma, flavors and finish. Allowing for style, how are these similar expressions of a Pinot Noir varietal?

After about fifteen minutes of air time, return to the three wines and taste them in reverse order. What qualities or distinctions can you observe that may derive from the place the wines come from? Do you perceive beyond the varietal itself a suggestion of the AVA? Are you able to perceive qualities of climate, elevation and soil that end up in your stems? Does cheese or a cracker significantly alter your perception and taste?

There is no single "correct" answer, but you might experience in this exercise what makes one AVA distinct from another. In a way, perhaps, you can experience a little oenotourism without leaving your favorite chair.

ON YOUR DIME AGAIN

Acquire (i.e., purchase) a California Chardonnay from a reputable vintner, preferably with an AVA designation, and also a comparably priced Chardonnay from an Oregon AVA. Do not chill them like soft drinks or mass-market beer. Pour about three ounces of each into two white wine stems. Compare color in the glass. Swirl each to see how many aromas you can stir up; note the bouquet. Now take a small sip of each in succession and note your first impression of flavors and taste. Cleanse your palate with some sparkling water. Wait about ten minutes. Repeat the whole business. Just how do they differ from one another? Perhaps even more important, how do familiar characteristics of the varietal appear in both?

Again, we are not looking for a right answer but rather an understanding of how the different terroir makes the wine "California" or "Oregon" Chardonnay.

I was just sent to school by a 2013 Helioterra Pinot Noir and 2014 Morgan Vineyards Pinot Noir from the Monterey, California area. These are wonderful wines and completely different in affect and character. If you can obtain a 750ml of each, drink them in tandem. You surely enjoy them; however, it's their divergences that appeal to me. Tell me what you think (kenF@decodingthegrape.com). I like this contrast well enough to risk the anachronism of a printed book for the interest of the wines *per se* and in relation to each other.

Another exercise: obtain a Pinot Noir from California's Russian River AVA and pair it with an Elk Cove Pinot Noir from Yamhill-Carlton AVA. Both will please, and I think the differences reveal complementary contrasts. Tell me if you're impressed by these mouth-filling wonders. Were they pictures, I think one as a Titian and the other as a Raphael.

Apologia: By contrasts of Oregon to California wine practices and wines, I am not dissing wines from one place to sustain the other. I have great affection for wines of both places, and my cellar reflects the balance. What I do worry about are parvenu interventions in wineries where status seeking and wealth obscure the story told in my wine glass.

CHAPTER 9

E-TICKET OR E-CHANNEL?

THE SHORTEST CHAPTER IN THIS BOOK

S ince describing what taste memory entails, it seems appropriate to put it in easy reach. Taste memory may develop through wine tourism, but it is really an aggregate of combined experiences and impressions. The customs and rituals of wine consumption constitute aspects of broader civilization, itself a sparkling façade of accepted behaviors, community and order.

When the complement in our lives focuses on its E-Channel qualities as celebrity diversion and instantaneous gratifications, its customary joys are subsumed in the frivolity of the moment. It is diverting and constitutes a slice of an evanescent good time.

This release, as it were, provides the electricity of restoration often in a context of relaxation. It differs, as entertainment, from experience one keeps, such as the memory of taste. This is a qualitative issue, for a good time does not preclude enhancing one's taste memory.

Perhaps the best way to make the distinction allows entertainment to provide contrived sensations, whereas evolving taste memory brings the matter closer to the private discovery of order as the result of varied wine experience.

This is why scoring by number assigned to wine tips the balance of wine appreciation into the maw of collective diversion as entertainment. This holds true for all mass participatory exercises based on enumerated top scores, such as professional sports, general elections, amateur showcases and other detritus invented to sell airtime and the "togetherness" of crowds.

Think of Manchester football or Nuremberg rallies or arena concerts. Rare in these does pleasure go beyond "I was there when…."

One may contrast experience, however, as something more originating in our right brain, from which our creative responses appear to dwell, as well as the very spark of creativity. In tandem with the more analytical, even linear capacities of our left brain, we begin to sort impressions of tasting wine in both a more personal and, say I, a more resonant way. It is the resonance that helps build context, and the context contributes to a confident taste memory. I like to get to the promise of the wine as a way to broaden experience, as if to say each encounter with new varietals and wines build a *mise-en-scène* for the unfolding drama, my green comedy, in which I am both actor and audience. It may be called "My Private Oregon."

Here is the gloss on these paragraphs: I like this wine. I will have to remember choosing it again.

FOUR INTERMEZZI

The following four chapters were published in somewhat different form in the *Oregon Wine Press* in 2014 and 2015. They contemplate the five "S"s of wine-tasting rites: see, swirl, smell, sip and swallow (or, less politely, spit).

These activities are familiar to wine enthusiasts; however, the positive responses to the original versions prompted me to recycle them here because the actions described actually enhance wine pleasure and because they bridge the overview that preceded with the following treks into the soul-aching adventures of Oregon wine discovery.

Jason Lett poses near a pile of prunings in 1974. *Courtesy of the Eyrie Vineyards and Jason Lett.*

CHAPTER 10

BRASS KNUCKLES

HOW TO LOOK AT A GLASS OF WINE

The mystery of art is that more is there than you put down.
—*F in "A Pimp's Revenge" by Bernard Malamud*

In the summer of 1960, the Contemporary Arts Museum Houston presented "The Ugly Show." It was an exhibit of art by another name— detritus from the bayou that at the time was snaking through metropolitan Houston, when big hats meant something. The program catalogue was written by Donald Barthelme, who was, at this time, establishing himself as a writer of infuriatingly bizarre short stories. Many of them, as he refined his style, were also pants-wetting funny. This exhibit was right up his alley.

"The Ugly Show" was making a point. A galloping horse may look nice near the gun cabinet in the den, but what of a rusted mattress spring hauled out of the Dickensian mire and stood on one corner of itself in Texas wildflower light? Although this *objet d'art* is a figment of my musings, one such exhibit item was really there more than fifty-five years ago: a set of brass knuckles.

It was mounted on a dissonant background, at least for an implement of connected rings used to break the jaws of street punks or transporters of contraband. Taken out of its accepted functional context, the brass knuckles suggested anthropomorphic elegance, like a series of wedding bands or a device to help aspiring concert pianists play block chords with even pressure. Suspending the everyday meaning and purpose and representation of objects, the show and its catalogue tour guide seemed to say, "Look at these knuckles a different way, pardner."

Now you know why it's a bad idea to drink wine from a gimme cup sporting a team logo. The cup not just changes the context; it steals it. What staring into a nice stem of wine will do is the first step on the ladder to Wine Parnassus—or, less flamboyantly, to wine enjoyment.

White wines—Chardonnay, Pinot Gris, Sauvignon Blanc, Riesling—can show the shimmer of gold, pale yellow, platinum blond or meadow straw. Each reflects an aspect of the sun, without whose Empyrean gaze no grapes would grow and ripen or, with the vintners' magic, show up in the stem at all.

If blonds do have more fun, it's because their manes call attention to themselves. So with wine, too, should we look closely. Color anticipates and the sparkle fires not only our visual senses but all the others—we can anticipate the aroma of citrus or tropical fruit; we sense the cool of the sip in our mouths; we can taste the tangy acidity or the oaky roundness or vanilla's hit and-run effect; and we can store an impression of transient springtime in the lingering finish. We start with a toast or the clinking of glasses. Thus, our remaining sense of hearing is also engaged.

And all of this happens before we sip the wine because the visuals call forth memory. The colors tell a tale, like a prologue, all to tease, "You ain't seen nothing yet." But indeed we have, if we patiently regard the appearance of the wine as a visual experience.

A rosé wine appears from pale pink of the white Zin—the 7-Up of beverages with an age restriction—to more colorations, even pallid rubies and roses caught in the light of Manet or Pissarro's imaginings. The hues of rosé contain subtleties other wines do not care to infer. We rightly associate the blush of these cheeks with the summer patio but allow neither the calendar nor the produce in season to deter our considerations.

The blush rush also calls to mind sparkling wine. A sparkling wine, pink or red or golden yellow, will talk to you in fizzy dialect, adding a soundtrack to the visual. Champagne, whether golden or rose-colored, has its own musical score. Indeed, one imagines diners on the *Titanic* toasting one another's good fortune through the lights cast by their rose-colored stemware, failing to notice that the ice isn't in the bucket but dead on course. Fizz adds fun and prickly resonance to that sparkle, and the flute encourages the bubbles to soar mouth-ward. Damn those half-frozen torpedoes! We're enjoying this dance.

Red wines show their colors another way. They may appear like the rosy nipples on the Venus of the great Botticelli painting; they can look like red satin with sensuous folds holding something back; and they can look imperially ruby-purple and defy looking through the contents. All wines capture light, but the wine refracts the light illuminating what the glass contains. Better seeing wine empowers us to see better all things.

Properly aged and stored wines sometimes lose their brightness in the stem. "All that glitters" may be gold in a Chardonnay, but over time, the striking aspect can diminish into a pallid yellow. Reds—in particular of library quality—can appear to have a hint of brown or earth tone at the surface of the wine in the glass. What such wines give up in bright fruit of youth trades off with complexity and subtle structures in aged wine; it's like becoming wise over time when once you were just clever. Linguistically, "brown" sounds a pejorative note; however, unless a wine is corked or cooked—the left-in-your-trunk bit—the alteration of color ought not deter you.

Two instances from the neighborhood suffice: several years ago, I enjoyed a remarkable reserve Chardonnay from the Eyrie Vineyards produced in President Reagan's last year in office. It was beautifully made, and what its color lacked in brilliance was more than compensated for by its complexity

Harry Peterson-Nedry and Cathy Stoller are pictured at a winery event. Peterson-Nedry is the founder and winemaker of Chehalem Wines in Newberg, Oregon. Stoller and her husband, Bill, were owners of Stoller Family Estate in Dayton, Oregon, and, as of 2018, owners of Chehalem Winery as well—Harry and his daughter, Wynn, will continue their winemaking chores. *From left to right*: Larry Walters, Steve Lutz, an unidentified woman, Harry Peterson-Nedry, George Marie Victoire, Cathy Stoller and Dick Stinson. *Doc Wilson Collection, Jereld R. Nicholson Library, Linfield College, McMinnville, Oregon. Courtesy of Doc Wilson, 2015.*

and scrupulous balance. A later pre-millennial Pinot Noir from Raptor Ridge proved that our most famous finicky varietal can lose a little hue and gain more than a semblance of classic character.

If you pop a cork, pour a draught, chug it down—well, that's like using brass knuckles to break a jaw—or at least, as we say in polite society, focus another's attention on the intent of our communication. Even a humble jug wine will want to express itself visually. So give it a chance, not a concussion.

Winemaking is an art, but like making pictures and hustling collectors and galleries, it is also a business. As we regard a work of art visually, it seems apt to look at wine pictorially, as something on display for our private pleasure. Perhaps this explains my impulse to present the subject here in terms of famous artists and paintings. Who misses the connection between a place that gives us Titian and Amarone? Or one that gives us Poussin and Puligny-Montrachet? It is of a piece and it enriches us. It establishes value like Malamud infers, beyond what the maker and the viewer expect.

Re-frame your wine drinking the way successful athletes anticipate taking home the big trophy and the big payday. They visualize the win. You visualize the wine.

ON YOUR DIME

Put on your knuckles. Oops! Wrong book.

Use your good, clean stemware for this. Place three glasses on a white surface in adequate lighting. Pour three white varietals into the stems. Since we're in Oregon, pour a dry Riesling or similar Austro-German wine in the first glass. Pour Pinot Gris in the second. Pour Chardonnay in the third.

Using good stems improves the visual trip you now take. Hold the glasses by their respective bases and hold each to the light. If you're holding the bowl, you're looking at the back of your hand and also putting greasy fingerprints on it—not to mention the transfer of body heat from your mitt. Table etiquette really does have a point; it's not too late to impress your mother-in-law with a few things that spell pedigree.

Now look at them. Look for the differences of clarity, color and overall appearance. Write down the first word impression for each or stretch the word into a brief phrase. What's similar? What differences do you see? Color will vary, often palpably. You might find the variations between the second and third wines to be more inferred than dramatically stated. It will depend on the wine. To extend this palette, add Sauvignon Blanc and/or Viognier to the lineup.

Even the half blind can, with a little concentration, pick up the variations in appearance. The idea is to distinguish, so your reasonable expectations will be met when you purchase wine from a list in a restaurant or off the shelf in a market or bottle shop.

This exercise will hold true for rosé wines produced for summer by many Oregon and Northwest vintners. The colors range from the modest blush on the cheek of an anchorite to the Kewpie doll pout of the girl you took to the county fair and didn't win a doll for her collection. Get your own toy, you tart! Rosé wines probably offer more contrasts in color than an art school analysis of Cézanne paintings. Add wines from southern Europe to this mix and the spectrum expands.

Red wines are equally challenging to view. To assert the point, just start with three Pinot Noir wines—the first from, say, a single vineyard in the Willamette Valley sub-AVAs. Compare this with a "Willamette Valley" designated AVA (one, in other words, that is 95 percent fruit from within the valley but from various places). Now for the third Pinot Noir, try one from Yamhill-Carlton AVA or the Columbia Gorge. The wines, of course, are all red, like many apples, cherries or even table grapes. But they do show differently. Imagine, then, the following.

Compare an Oregon Pinot Noir with a Syrah from within the Southern Oregon AVA. Then introduce a red blend from Walla Walla located in Washington State. The appearances run from regal to rustic, from sexy to subtle, with marvelous reflections in light angles as you hold each up to the light.

A last pass at color. Cooper Mountain in the Red Mountain AVA, about sixty miles north-northwest from Walla Walla, makes a primarily good Cabernet Franc. The color alone bespeaks the impulse for in-your-face brightness and character in wines justly prized. Don't forget to pet Buddy the winery dog. He is a milk chocolate Lab, and this pairs well with the Bordeaux grapes, of which Cabernet Franc is one of five. The wines produced in this spare AVA have a flair for looking great in a wine glass.

CHAPTER 11

MY GRANDFATHER'S ARTICHOKE

WHY WE SWIRL THE WINE

R emind me to tell you about the time I looked into the heart of an artichoke," Bette Davis snarls as Margo Channing in *All About Eve*. It's one of cinema's great bitchy moments.

During my starter marriage, at our starter house with its earth tones, throw pillows, poster art and ginger jar lamps set on Parsons tables, my grandfather came to Sunday dinner. He encountered an artichoke for the first time, just a bit into his ninth decade.

"What is this thing?" he asked. Here was a person who was born on a farm in New Jersey about a decade before the Wright brothers flew at Kitty Hawk. And he remained topside well into the decade after Neil Armstrong put that famous small step on the surface of the moon. Technically, eating an artichoke that day proved as challenging as calibrating a re-entry vehicle's descent. What Charlie—that was his name—did next seems, in retrospect, intuitive. He turned the artichoke around and around. "What am I supposed to do with this thing?"

My former wife the journalist came to his rescue, pulling a tender outer leaf from his starter course and dipping it into a mix of butter, garlic and olive oil. He simply took the whole leaf, bit into it and swallowed it. "Good garlic," said he. And then he continued to turn the artichoke—nay, swirl this odd appetizer in its functional dish—around some more.

I recall this event because we regard food and drink often by turning it around, like an idea or proposition, not in our heads but on the plate or in the stem. Like the dread drip of garlic butter and oil onto one's tie or trousers, swirling wine poses a parallel risk: the swirl that goes airborne before it lands where it does not belong.

This bit of domestic history aside, swirling the wine is more prone to slapstick than skewering. Like the gargles of Alan Rickman or Paul Giamatti, the swirl step in wine-tasting rites makes the swirler look pretentious if not ridiculous.

I offer one caveat: do not swirl the wine in the stem with the vigor a mixologist applies to shaking a designer cocktail in the hip place of the moment. The wine has a place, and it is not on your lap or tank top or on the furniture. So why bother? After all, Charlie's most excellent adventure with an artichoke occurred only one time.

Be not intimidated by the swirl. Rather, consider it a practical and vital step in the apprehension of wine. It has scientific and aesthetic purposes; thus, in a way, it extends the vintner's art in terms of chemistry, climatology and physics.

On the website of the *Telegraph*, a post called "Why Swirling Wine in a Glass Makes It Taste Better" points to the physics of "orbital shaking"—a form of motion perhaps exemplified by the hula hoop. When the wine is swirled, the encounter between wine and air creates a vertical force that allows tannins to soften and aromas to increase, especially at the rim and the surfaces just below it. In a study conducted at the Swiss Federal Institute of Technology in Lausanne, researchers were able to apply this orbital principle to pharmaceutical and biochemical invention, proving, once again, wine's many benefits to humans. Then, too, consider how these natural laws affect the art implied by wine.

The swirl is vital because wine needs air. To enhance its qualities, wine needs room to breathe after its seeming resurrection from the suspended animation of its time in the barrel and the bottle. As the folks at VinePair express it, when a wine breathes oxygen, it opens. I would agree but add that once in the stem, the wine begins to tell its story, reveal its secrets and merge history and place with the moment. The famous opening of Beethoven's Fifth (750ml?) Symphony would not sound without oxygen; the air vibrates when the C-minor chord sets the whole thing in motion with a triplet of a diminished third down to the held tonic, the C-note. (And without oxygen, none of us would be around to hear it.) The music of the wine also begins when it takes the air. Like a symphony, the wine unfolds texturally and over a period of time. The winemaker, in effect, composes wine as Beethoven composed a string quartet or a piano sonata or any one of his nine symphonies. The basic elements synthesize, and the oxygen carries the idea along as its sensations, in turn, stimulate awe and wonder, joy and pleasure.

So, to further this comparison, I am reminded of how Dick Erath described the appeal of winemaking to an engineer. The resources today available to growing grapes challenge one's technical know-how, whereas the making of wine *per se* appeals to one's creative impulses—a left to right brain relay—but we might add that both aspects of the product, from vineyard to wine newly bottled, marries the outer world to the individual mind and/or soul.

Surely, as we noted in the previous chapter, we first see wine in a glass. But it's the swirl that sets the dancer to dance.

The nice thing about the swirl is that, as my grandfather demonstrated, it is intuitive—and also instinctive, as if we are assaying our prey. Give your pup a big meaty bone and look at his eyes when you come near. That's not Fido—it's Margo Channing marking the turf. The swirl marks the wine because it unleashes the potential energy held in the bottle and bruited about by wine merchants and wine writers before the energy becomes kinetic. The famous four-note pattern of the symphony is nothing if not the release of potential energy into explosive kinesis. We know what wine's supposed to look like.

Having just flogged the *why* horse, let's ride it. Despite the instinctive turns of stemware, there exist certain little principles that keep the swirl from becoming a Basil Fawlty sight gag. Start with the stem. Bubbly wines make their own fizzy music, and the champagne flute takes its slim profile from its purpose, matchless pairing of form and function. Uncorked, all those CO_2 bubbles soar up to escape into the air. Few things elicit more pleasure, except for the caviar.

Other wineglasses are more bulbous, and if the flute channels the air, the larger stems throw wide open, so to speak, the wine windows. Consider the Pinot Noir stem: the flare at the top promotes the oxygen but also bars flying gobs of wine. It's good to practice with one of these glasses; the VinePair writers make the common-sense suggestion to practice with water in the glass so mistakes don't lead to dry-cleaning. Approximately two ounces of liquid is enough to work with.

In my own practice, I move the glass—holding it from the base or the stem just above it—in small circles on a flat, taut surface (a party-favor tablecloth does not, as a rule, have the body to neatly accommodate the pressure). I tend to swirl this way throughout the tasting or meal simply to keep the air going. I realize that I do this often without even thinking about the action, sort of like my grandfather's natural response to the conundrum of an artichoke. You may prefer to swirl the glass on an angle, holding the stem aloft; this can reassert the visuals the wine offers.

Some sommeliers make a big deal of vigorous motion well above the surface. One writer calls this a faux lasso and terms the effect "obnoxious." As Queen Gertrude tells Polonius, "More matter, with less art."

Swirls liberate aroma in the wine to allow its flavor profiles to emerge as alcohol evaporates when it hits the air. The swirl is for rosé and white wine as much as for the more densely textured red wines, which have the most dramatic color for swirling. No matter the varietal, the swirl contributes to the purpose and value of the wine-tasting rite. One needs to keep this in mind as one keeps the swirling contents in the glass.

If you remain skittish about the swirl, just recall Charlie's close encounter with an artichoke. You are never too old to discover something that combines the utility of the sciences with the pleasure of the arts. As I noted earlier, Ernest Hemingway wrote that memory is hunger. I demur. Memory is thirst. Just ask Charlie, wherever he is, doing some serious orbital shaking.

CHAPTER 12

THE NOSE KNOWS

The nose is a fleshly gas chromatograph.
—*Mary Roach,* Gulp: Adventures on the Alimentary Canal

Is it perfume from a dress / that makes me so digress?
—*T.S. Eliot, "The Love Song of J. Alfred Prufrock"*

I cook with wine; sometimes I even add it to the food.
—*W.C. Fields*

"Is that a lanthorn, or just your nose?"

This book began as a query when I wanted to try my hand at taking some mystification out of wine terms. The most challenging terms involve our sense of smell. For example, an Oregon Chardonnay will smell differently from a comparable California wine made of the same varietal. After one or two encounters, we readily can tell the difference. The former may be full of fresh citrus and minerals. The latter gives off strong floral scents and often enough oak to build a writing desk. Then, too, we may mistake the nose by hundreds of miles. Why?

If you can, recall the passage where T.S. Eliot, everyone's favorite prissy modern poet, described how, while walking, a person can smell steak cooking as its aroma wafts from an open window, while thinking simultaneously of lovemaking or reading Spinoza. ("Noza"—get it?) Eliot addressed an idea about "dissociation of sensibility," meaning in his modern world, human experience had been atomized to the degree that individuals became alienated from one another and life in all of its plenitude became fragmented or reduced to the superficial.

For us, though, smelling that steak will likely remind us of our desire for such a slab, posted on our plate with a big baked potato, washed down by a gutsy Zinfandel or a supple Merlot. In other words, our olfactory bulb, located just below our frontal lobe, triggers emotions (I'd love a steak right now) and memory (yes, let's meet in the bar at the Ringside or another notable chophouse).

The sense of smell is fascinating to those of us who barely survived high school biology. For instance, humans may possess a capacity to detect trillions of distinct odorants. We do not have, however, the hundred-fold capacity of dogs to make active use of this ability. Or consider some bears that can smell free food from as far away as eighteen miles. Salmon, a favorite ursine meal, use smell to know which river is Spawn City—just watch out for the bears. Last, women smell better than men—yes, I mean in both ways. Smell is one way a mother distinguishes her child from a changeling.

Odorant molecules actually act like keys to specific neural locks, and these galloping ganglia in turn activate our taste buds. The person who can detect a wine's place of origin is not merely engaging in a parlor trick. Olfaction fascinates because its myriad degrees impact our emotions and lead us directly to specific memories. Sniffing the stem entails more than showbiz. I think it is the central stimulus in appreciating a wine's merit at the point of tasting and more likely than other aspects of the sequence to challenge or confound us.

Then we have persons at our table sniffing a cork only to proclaim, "Good nose!" as if the cork were the personification of W.C. Fields. One learns very little from a cork unless it signals that it has failed its duty to preserve the wine. Does a "nice nose" refer to the aroma (smell) or the bouquet (fragrance)? I believe impulse suggests the former, as it exists as an effect of the wine in our glass greeting the air. The latter refers to the sensations we experience as the wine alchemy transmutes in the glass. One may say the aroma derives from the natural characteristics of the varietal. A Sauvignon Blanc will exude grapefruits and freshly cut grass or hay. A Pinot Noir will often reveal cherries or strawberries with a hint of the local hillside. A Riesling exudes blossoms and even something akin to ineffable honey or candied fruit—not necessarily sweet, but inviting.

Left: The original Oregon Wine Wizard (Doc Wilson) casting a spell over the Essence Table. Like shards of the True Cross, there are many false claimants to the honorific. It's as bad as the "Ray's Famous Pizza" rivalries of mid-town Manhattan. *Doc Wilson Collection, Jereld R. Nicholson Library, Linfield College, McMinnville, Oregon.*

Below: The Essence Table in the foyer of the Rex Hill Winery in Newberg presents a catalogue of thirty-six distinct aromas and taste sensations that wines elicit. This provides a marvelous illustration of what makes taste memory. *Doc Wilson Collection, Jereld R. Nicholson Library, Linfield College, McMinnville, Oregon. The photo dates from November 2017.*

The bouquet more likely emerges over time as a testimony to the skill of the winemaker. The effects are deliberate, if not exact, and they enhance the natural smells of the varietal as they also excite us. If a wine's bouquet reminds you of Spinoza, I suggest you visit a public library. If it triggers associations of place and plenteous bounty, then you're likely in the swing of things the wine expresses.

Each time we follow W.C. Fields into the kitchen and use wine in cooking, we cause the alcohol to evaporate—the exciting hiss—and we reduce the wine to its varietal essence as a way to complement or highlight the other ingredients. So Petrale sole in white wine butter contains the soul of the varietals but not the literal feel and taste of the same stuff as if we were drinking it. This brings to mind an off-road but significant detail: cook with wine you can drink, that you enjoy drinking and whose flavor profile appeals to you in this kitchen iteration.

Earlier, I noted that a gimme cup does nothing for looking at wine. Not merely does it obscure clarity and color—it also assassinates smells. Its material offers convenience, durability and easy disposal—virtues at a tailgate party but not conducive to allowing wines to breathe and therefore influence our experience of the wine. The cork, once removed, and the swirl, once or twice accomplished without dry-cleaning, animate the aromas and the fragrances of the wine. The shape of the stem elicits autonomic triggers and also sensations of which we are cognizant.

The sequence of wine drinking surely affects our perception, participation and summary in the enjoyment of wine. We go to wine tastings rather than wine sightings or sniffing parties. In my taffy-pulling metaphor mode, I suggest we look at the steps my musings describe—see, swirl, smell, sip and swallow/spit—as if Aristotle in his *Poetics* wrote of oenology rather than Oedipus and his unfortunate family. By this I mean a sequence exists, and if we break its components into separate parts of the whole, we will greatly enhance our apprehension and appreciation.

Oedipus in the backstory frees Thebes from the tyranny of the Sphinx. He becomes king and marries the widowed queen, and we meet him as he tries to save the city from great famine. We may consider the setting of the scene the same way we look at the character of wine once we see it in our stem.

The swirl stirs things up as alcohol, released, meets the air. In the play, this exciting incident, called *peripeteia*, is the problem of the plot, at least from the POV of the main character. Of course we know better than he. As Oedipus inexorably goes ahead to unravel the cause of the gods' anger, we also approach the apex of the dramatic complication. This moment is akin to the point at which we experience wine by its smell and fragrance. I consider this step the apex of our likely response to the wine in our glass. It is the open window on the wine; it's the threshold to the doorway through which we stride to at last taste the wine.

We know the Oedipus backstory and his secret—he kills Papa and marries Mama—just as we know that a Pinot Gris or a Pinot Noir will possess certain familiar aspects based on our tasting experience. So this is potentially the most complex and intuitive part of apprehending a wine.

When Oedipus discovers the truth about his crime, he endures suffering, the *hamartia* for his hubris, his go-it-alone pride. The moment of discovery, called *anagnorisis*, is where the grapes, so to speak, hit the fan. And in these revelations, we who have considered the wine (or, by taffy pull, the play's unfolding) reach a condition of release, emotional and physical. We have tasted the wine, and in its effect and finish, we arrive at our likely point of satisfaction. This catharsis becomes part of our wine memory, and what remains is the finish and the effect the wine has with the meal supporting it.

This analogy does not infer or express that the sequence is tragic, per se, unless you discover you paid way too much for a wine or it doesn't live up to its press. Rather, it is to show that wine enjoyment is a process as is viticulture and that, yes, the gods will amuse themselves at our peril. Experience of the nose, as it were, is part of a greater whole we access both consciously and *sub rosa* to define the pleasures of wine.

Oedipus gave Freud a name for an entire barrique of neuroses. The father of psychoanalysis was oft badgered on the topic of the Oedipus complex, and in giving advice to those who saw mother fixations everywhere, Freud admonished, "Sometimes a cigar is just a cigar." Just so the dinner guest who sniffs the cork and goes on and on about the provenance of the grapes and other imagined details. Please gently advise: "You know that sometimes a cork is just a cork."

ON YOUR DIME

On small plates, place five kitchen herbs or seasonings you normally use. Turn off the lights and go out of the room as someone else arranges these plates willy-nilly. Come back into the room. In what order do these hand-selected items call your attention? Do they call your attention? Make a marinade with the ingredients for future use.

The point is to locate olfactory memory, not as a technical element of a larger process or as an end in itself. We are simply experiencing certain prepared smells in our environment. Which of these stand out? Which confuse us by masking or accentuating another smell? We are experiencing, so to say, our senses in slow motion by focusing on these impressions.

Next, pour and swirl in two stems two identical varietals from two producers. Allow the wines to open. Consider the initial impressions each makes in terms of aroma (which comes from the grapes) and bouquet (which derives from the winemaker's craft). How do they compare? How do they differ? How do they change in the air and, ultimately, how do they change over some time? How do aromatic qualities change, if at all, with appropriate food?

We seek to disambiguate the smells presenting their stimuli by experiencing them in a slightly controlled context. The answers are your own and need only be consistent with your impressions at the moments you identify them. We are slowing things down to learn how smell and bouquet contribute to how we perceive and then experience wine in order to cultivate taste memory.

I deliberately start with a global impression—the particular elements will come soon enough to appreciate.

CHAPTER 13

THE SIP

DR. KEN'S CATCH-AND-RELEASE PROGRAM

The best fugue will always be that which the public takes for a Strauss waltz.
—Robert Schumann, nineteenth-century composer and music critic

C.S. Lewis is best known as the author of the *Narnia* tales and as a principal character in the film *Shadowlands*. Anthony Hopkins played Lewis, a Cambridge don who fell for an American widow late in life. Lewis was a very smart literary observer and historian. In one of his books, he asserted that few people know how to describe things. Most are content to respond emotionally; the best they can do on paper is to say "I like this" and "I don't like that." An evaluation, then, is little more than prattle. On the other hand, description takes the speaker's egotism and personality out of the equation, so more specific and expressive language can better communicate the sense of a thing. We taste wine to acquire such a sense of it.

A writer who writes about food or wine—both matters of experience and taste—spends more time trying to describe than to react with preferences. What a writer prefers usually becomes explicit as he is describing something else.

We need a starting place. I comb the annals of other writers on my subjects and season the stew with analogies and metaphors from music, as before, or history, pop culture and sports. In short, I am in search of a language to describe meals taken and wines enjoyed. As long as I listen to books, play music and get some garbled newscasts, I am well set in my descriptor inventory.

Will forgetful snow improve taste memory? *Girardet Vineyards and Winery Collection, Jereld R. Nicholson Library, Linfield College, McMinnville, Oregon. Courtesy of Philippe Girardet, 2013.*

The series of steps that contributes to the wine experience moves from colors to aromas to the place where, idiomatically, the grape meets the road. Tasting wine is the object of wine tasting. A wine can sometimes fool or mislead us.

Here's my *mea culpa*: in late 2014, I went out to taste some wine but first scarfed down a brisket sandwich in Newberg. That's not normally my mode. I like to taste wine on a relatively empty stomach so as not to clutter my febrile mind or my palate. But passengers cannot always get their way. So up we drove to Panther Creek. After several different wines, we encountered a premium Pinot Gris. However, my olfactory senses were in the break room, and what my brain said had zero to do with what shimmered in my stem. "I think this a pleasant Chardonnay, very restrained and subtly fruitful."

Wrong! I believe the misconception arose right out of the barbecue pit. While dry crackers and low-moisture cheeses may not dramatically complement the wines tried at tastings, the reason they appear in tasting rooms is that they don't leave a sensory trail both labyrinthine and misleading. In wine pairing dinners at their best, the courses really show better with their viniferous companions, and many wines that first taste somehow incomplete or rough suddenly comport themselves as if they just left finishing school. Likewise, wine tastings often begin with a starter wine or two. These are palate teasers and set the tone for other flights to follow. No matter the rites observed, in this catechism we always come back to one point: there's no accounting for the taste of others. There is no other way to explain the success of *Love Story* or reality television. But still we ought to try.

THE PARTY IN YOUR MOUTH

The tongue and salivary glands form the organs of taste; with our teeth, used more for food than wine, we can take a bite out of texture. The tongue comes equipped with buds—usually three to ten thousand per person—and these sensors register sweet, sour, bitter, salt and umami, or savory. Known as papillae, they are found not just atop the tongue but in the cheeks and way back in glottal regions of the mouth. Although they are specialized sensors, they can all sense and transmit each of the five tastes. There's more: the taste buds replenish about every two weeks; one might say nature has provided us a built-in palate cleaner.

When we sip wines to taste them, we may go through a gyration or two so that we expose the papillae to the wine both close to the air in front and further away toward the back. If you sustain a condition or disease that impairs your salivation, you will soon discover your apprehension of taste has gone into the witness-protection program. The next time you light up a Camel, consider this.

We ought to recall that the five-S etiquette manual suggests not wearing jump-me perfume or macho aftershave. It behooves all of us, whether moving through a trade cattle call wine expo or sitting at a tasting-themed meal, to put sufficient distance between ourselves and the other participants. A few moments of silence also helps to focus attention on the wines rather than the latest gossip. At some tastings, we issue a gag order of ten minutes' duration so we can individually draw our inferences from the stories told by the grapes. It's not silly—if you plonk down the equivalent of a mortgage payment, it's prudent to spend a few moments with the wine. You may go home with it.

Persons new to this rite will perhaps think everyone is crazy. They sip and then appear to gargle like actors in a Listerine commercial. What's this about? Aeration, to begin. We sight the wine to determine its body and clarity. We swirl the glass to help liberate the alcohol into the air. We smell the wine to gauge its character and potential. And we taste the wine to confirm or confound these prior impressions. The aerodynamics have been compared to drinking with a straw, but I don't drink wine with a straw. The effort intends to get the wine to the papillae in front and elsewhere in our mouths. The taste is not a frat house gulp; it draws on the perhaps 1.5 ounces of wine in our stem and calls for concentration and focus. Less is more. Wine is a food, but it's not fast food.

Next we swallow and linger; let the wine express its varietal characteristics and winemakers' skills. Allow the impression to remain, as if you just kissed your sweetie good night. Of course, refrain from kissing anyone with a mouthful of wine.

Paul Gregutt, writing for the *Wine Enthusiast*, has a nice peroration on the tasting portion of the wine rite: "A complete wine is balanced, harmonious, complex and evolved, with a lingering, satisfying finish. Such wines deserve extra attention because they have more to offer, in terms of both pleasure and training, than any others you will taste." The point scales used to dissect a wine—and then score it against an ideal—work as well for value wines as for first growths. But we're not all actuaries; the steps in the tasting rite are meant to enliven and expand wine experience and knowledge.

What about the sixth "S," the spit? First of all, in a sequenced tasting where a vast number of different wines in generous pours face you, it may be advantageous on the first pass to get rid of the remnants by pouring them into an aptly named "dump bucket." Failing that, outdoor tastings have bushes. I prefer "spew" to "spit"—more Rococo Cupid than Bowery—and "swallow" to both.

It should become abundantly clear that a considerable sampling of wines will come with an accumulated release of alcohol. Anyone who drinks wine will admit that a salutary virtue is the buzz the alcohol elicits as it works its way into our bloodstreams. There are numerous good reasons to be mindful of the transformative power of ample wine on our inhibitions. One of these is not offending others with loutish mien. Another is that car with the flashing lights pulling us aside later on. Still "spit" has its residue of poor manners. "Spew" doesn't cut it. So swallow when you're able.

The entire tasting is for inquiry, not intoxication. But remember: good balance applies to more than the wine in your stem. Still, although we gather impressions at our peril a little, the insights and discoveries are usually worth it.

Many descriptors insinuate themselves in the taste. Take this one: "simple and complex." This strikes me as a hazy phrase intended to send me on the hunt for better words. Is the wine lacking a personality but also blessed with an interesting feel, structure or texture? Perhaps it's not so simple. Other descriptors occur often—"citrusy," "chocolate," "earthy" and "toasty" come to mind. The "barnyard" of some Burgundies is perhaps the most intriguing descriptor of all. But these are our papillae talking to our brain as we talk at one another. I think the sip reveals the harmony and structure—the feel and then the finish of the wine we put in our mouth. It's the sense of the sense, not oeno-Bingo or Scrabble for sots.

We taste flavors or adumbrations of flavors—coffee, eucalyptus, mint—as our taste buds do their thing. But depth, fullness and harmony are, we might say, the metaphysics of tasting wine. They convey character, and the relationship between flavor and effect makes "the sip" into a moment of private truth.

THE COSMOS AND THE SIP

The epigraph at the top of this chapter refers to a music form, the fugue, "a contrapuntal composition in which a short melody or phrase [the subject] is introduced by one part and successively taken up by others and developed by interweaving the parts," according to the *Oxford English Dictionary*. Earning one's stripes in a winery is akin to learning how to compose a fugue. Each is technical and each is also an art form.

Schumann, who later composed a festive overture on the German Rhine wine song, suggested that at its best, the fugue, with its rigor and predetermined structural rules, takes on the ease and lilt of a gay waltz. The listener hears the happy music revealed; the underlying strength is artfully concealed.

Is this not like wine? Is not the point of the exercise of the tasting rite a pleasurable discipline and a path to enjoyment? We can take this analogy further. Music scores are symbols put to paper. They're realized in performance. The experience of the musical narrative occurs within a time sequence. Thus, as the sand in the musical hourglass runs down, so conversely does the impact of the music increase as the score inevitably moves to its dissolution, its coda and its ultimate silence as the music fades away.

Likewise, the story in the bottle paradoxically becomes more comprehensible as the contents gradually disappear. The rites of the tasting lead to something greater than the particular steps; we have presaged the sip in order to excite association and memory in the context of the moment.

Thus, when Benjamin Franklin wrote that wine is "a constant proof that God loves us, and loves to see us happy," he put the pleasure of the moment into a beneficent and universal dimension. Anyone who buys wine for hospitality sales will work quickly through the "S" steps to come up with an order. But whether a novice or a sommelier or a wine merchant, we are reminded by the steps to give the wines and our palates the fairest chance to acquaint and appreciate one another.

To sell the vintage, the winemaker and the vineyard manager carry in their souls the knowledge that sooner or later, the wine child born will meet the larger light of the world and do just fine. *Sans* swallowing, we run the risk of missing something miraculous or transcendent.

Remember Leonardo's immortal *The Last Supper*? There's no dump bucket on the table.

ON YOUR DIME

The sip and swallow are the final steps in the sequence of five "S"s. The goal of these steps is not to impress others with your wine savvy but to gauge an impression of the wine overall. Even those comfortable with the Alpha Critic bromides sooner or later must make a call about a given wine, and trust me, it ain't a number. It is made of words, and these words approximate the feel, flavor and finish of what we experience.

If you know how to set the timer on your mobile device, the next time you go to a wine tasting, set the interval for eight minutes. Why eight? It endures more than five minutes and less than ten. It is arbitrary—like the Alpha Critic numbers—but here I am simply using the interval to spell one word: P.A.T.I.E.N.C.E.

Our 24/7 world so dreads silence—what in broadcasting is called "dead air"—that we feel compelled to fill up the empty air with babble. Thus we condition ourselves and others to be first responders. Wine tasting isn't like ringing an alarm bell. It is a rite, and it bestows the privilege of contemplation and reflection, two modes closely associated with the innate characteristics of the wine itself. If we wanted instant feedback and uniform responses, this book might be called *Decoding the Coke*.

So use the seven minutes to ogle the attractive single across the room, having first visualized the wine, swirled it confidently and then enjoyed its intrinsic smells, its artful bouquets and taken a draught to obtain an idea of what the wine promises. Then wait.

Here comes the written test. Write down the first impression obtained from the above. After the first seven-minute interval, repeat the exercise. After the next interval, say twenty-one minutes in, eat some food that pairs with the wine. For each interval, write down what your impressions have suggested.

Finish the bottle. Now, was this a harmonious wine? Did the art of the fugue in your glass demonstrate skill and inspiration wed to nature?

I leave this exercise with a quote I heard on *60 Minutes*, supposedly from Galileo: "The sun, with all the planets revolving around it, and depending on it, can still ripen a bunch of grapes, or even a single grape, as though it had nothing else to do in this universe." In a way, the great astronomer was telling us to be patient, smell the roses and crack the whip only when the grapes are harvested so they can be crushed and begin the alchemy implicit in the winemakers' skills.

A SHORT CODA

One finds help to comprehend wine from many sources. As this book was going to the publisher, Madeline Puckette released her weekly online newsletter for October 5–6, 2016. It presents nine terms that she claims will assist anyone wishing to make an informed choice about purchasing a wine. She is spot on, for my money, though I added one term to the list. I demur on only one term that echoes the thunder of the herd. (See www.winefolly. com for the entire post.)

- Fruit forward
- Earthy (also "savory")
- Body (light, medium or heavy)
- Tannic (a wine with mild or prevalent tannins, with astringency you can feel)
- Sweet, or not dry
- Finish: what happens after you swallow a dram
- Typicality: or, the *genius loci*, the sense of place in the grapes expressed in the wine

- Complexity: the layers revealed in the wine as it interacts with air in your glass
- Crowd Pleaser: I demur—too many undershirts in a room too small; a term for supermarket shelves (less a descriptor than a sales pitch)
- Food-Friendly: when not spoken by a person posting images of plated food on Facebook; it suggests pairing but is less academic or technical (e.g., milk and cookies)

The terms do function as a gloss on our four intermezzi and suit my evocations with a shorthand a wine merchant or steward in a restaurant will know. In turn, you will be closer to obtaining a wine you will more likely enjoy.

Thank you, Madeline.

One thing more. You will often see the term "silky" or "silken" used to describe the impression made by a Pinot Noir. Is this impression emanating from one wine area such as Burgundy or in Oregon, the Yamhill-Carlton AVA or from California's Central Coast? Is it accurate? I know it when I encounter silkiness in wine, but I wonder whether we are all experiencing the same sensation but need a better word. Go figure.

PERSPECTIVES

The close of the prologue at the outset of this book cited Northrop Frye, and we can return to his take here. The tasting steps revisited in the preceding pages walk through five sensational impressions. These represent empirical and experiential actions we can take to better sample a wine or a group of them.

The conclusions we draw from our observations in these steps depend on our acuity as it engages the glass of wine. Of the food products we use, wine is rare in that it starts to change after we pull the cork and over time we pick up these changes.

Wines differ from beer, as it will soon fizzle away. Spirits, distilled to a pristine condition, will live on in a liquor cabinet until emptied next month or until your granddaughter graduates from medical school. But wine changes when the cork comes away, and no small measure of its quality occurs in the transformations as the outer world meets what's in the bottle.

The five "S"s remind us to take time to enjoy what took time to get to our table. The sound of the cork removed, the nearby waft of some new thing in the air fills us with an anticipation based on discovery and the promise of pleasure. When Frye wrote of exuberance, he wrote about poetry. He could have been writing about a glass of wine.

CHAPTER 14

PERDITION HIGHWAY

HOW CARRIE NATION AND MADISON GRANT TAUGHT OREGONIANS HOW NOT TO DRINK

PERSPECTIVES

By mere coincidence, this chapter is the center of my book. Telling the story of majestic failures, it provides my take on social experimentation of foul motivations. In telling an Oregon wine story, readers should gratefully hoist a glass, lest we have no stories to tell at tables adorned only with glasses of weak tea and green Jell-O molds filled with marshmallows and canned fruit cup. It looks outside the frame of my Oregon wine snapshot to illustrate that wine culture's existential threats include what others believe make people better by invading their persons, property and good will based on false premises.

It is kaleidoscopic history on fast-forward. Although the "Noble Experiment" failed, its residue still pollutes our wine-drinking habits and our very ability to learn about the ways in which it improves life's most appealing moments.

RUST

The Perdition Highway is a road ultimately arriving nowhere and strewn along its shoulders by the wreckage of bad ideas turned into hulking detritus by social engineering. How this hoax got foisted on our forebears is less significant here as its "why" and the consequences of such narrow prejudices.

Good intentions drive this car; the other occupants neither help pay tolls nor psy for the gas—and there's a lot of *that*. They are Ambition, eager to advance an agenda to advance a career. Next in ergonomic infant restraints long outgrown sit Righteous Indignation and Zeal, determined to save the "people" in abstract for Heaven, though such a place tends to resemble a camp meeting or a very exclusive country club run by commissars.

Their parents, Envy and Resentment, who work as community activists devoting much time to shouting into television cameras, are as usual in the hotel in Acapulco calling the cabana boy over in tones intended to show their solidarity with the little brown fellow in the white tunic.

Sometimes, an Enforcer, riding a tricycle, shadows the car, ready to punish those not cowed by codes, regulations, statutes or lower court orders.

HULKS ALONG THE WAY

We count wrecks of different magnitude, but they're all wrecks. A good place to read about them is Paul A. Johnson's affectionate *History of the American People*. They're all here. From Columbus's five voyages to landings at Jamestown and Plymouth Rock to the opening of the frontier to Buffalo Bill's cowboy expos, the New Deal and the Marshall Plan, one can find perspectives made to fit bottom-up writers of history, such as Howard Zinn, to top-down accounts like those penned by Ron Chernow or Samuel Eliot Morrison, where readers may have to guess about the sympathies the writer has for his subject.

Nor were social engineering big mistakes gone by the time we got color TV. Less than successful were various wars on poverty, or drugs or education; however, some proved far worse in our time, like affirmative action and its litany of reverse exclusion, our domestic edition of the Nuremberg Laws. We know how that turned out.

That our infrastructure built during the '20s and '30s bears more than passing resemblance to Stalin's apartments, Mussolini's fen fixings and

Hitler's autobahn is no coincidence. State-ism and steam-rolling were in the air and on the march. By then our biggest FUBAR projects were sour memories.

THE FIRST REALLY BAD IDEA

The monumental hulking wrecks include Reconstruction in the South, which followed the Civil War with vindictive inefficiency and malfeasance, leaving the former slave states in the dust of new industrial expansion elsewhere and the freed slaves like poor whites left holding bags of injustice like litter after a big picnic.

The result? A new kind of race hatred and social tension. This was a very big wreck; had President Lincoln not been felled by an assassin from the dream of the "Lost Cause," the time may have proved more propitious. But that is smoke.

To illustrate, one need but consider some black students on college campuses at this writing, more than a half century after desegregation of housing was effected, demanding separate dorms from whites and, of course, overachieving Asians on campuses. This is the kind of baggage in Good Intention's car.

The other great wreck is Prohibition, federal law from 1919 to 1933 on which we now gaze.

THE STAGE ARMY OF THE GOOD: CHURCH LADIES ATTACK PLANET EARTH

The wreck of Prohibition owed much to women, enfranchised by the Nineteenth Amendment, just after the booze ban of the Eighteenth.

Several strains coalesced in both big mistakes (Reconstruction and Prohibition) borne aloft by shouted high ideals and crude political calculation. Antislavery advocates included politicians and preachers, newspaper editors and institutional interests such as banking and manufacturing and, above all, women.

The concessions to slaveholding states was a can kicked down the road. It blew up at Fort Sumter. Leading to this explosion was the fact of women's productive capacity. The settler population was a baby juggernaut. In Malthusian terms, the American destiny owed more to the ovary than to ironclad ships, rifled cannons or even the telegraph. The pioneer stock—Anglo-Saxons, Dutch, Germans and Scots—were a randy lot. Ask Reverend Dimmesdale. The geographic miracle of the North American continent, buttressed by two oceans, was wide and rich enough in natural bounty to accommodate a large increase in its population. And God's blessing was behind it.

The women pioneers have been roundly romanticized. But reality demonstrates their adeptness in things other than reproduction. They managed a household brood. They fed the lot of them, cleaning all well. They encouraged and oversaw book learning for their scrappy kids. They could stand up to most interlopers and trespassers—consider Jessie Fremont. All the while, the putative head of household was somewhere liquored up, manifesting some destiny. Often a woman was repaid with boozy horseplay or worse. It was not *The Little House on the Prairie* but more like *Hellraiser.*

Women bore the brunt of rowdiness. However, as guardians of the hearth, they offered the spiritual nourishment of the family. We need not deal here with two Great Awakenings of religious zealotry in the middle years of the eighteenth and nineteenth centuries, but the moral force of arguments against slavery and human trafficking came as much from behind the apron as from behind the pulpit.

To illustrate: Louisa May Alcott went to the White House and there met President Lincoln. He looked down at this diminutive bonnet, author of *Uncle Tom's Cabin*, saying, "So you're the little lady who started this big war."

The demographic and economic realities notwithstanding, the Southern slave states saw their peculiar institution in peril. They backed down only when Tennessean Andrew Jackson threatened to kick their cotton butts to Cuba if they attempted to secede from the Union. They called this bluff nearly thirty years later to a cost of about 660,000 American lives. So, for some even now, the Deep South isn't deep enough.

The evangelical movement also was a moral uplift movement. Thus, the antislavery lobby was also a nascent prohibition one. Both flew under the flag of women's suffrage. From the Seneca Falls meetings in 1849 to the empowerment of women as a voting class, the reform virus spread in the national DNA, as more Americans became rich and had means to express their convivial instincts on a frequent if not always lavish scale. Women stabilized the home and vociferously defended its unique character with more courage than cant.

Freedom of conscience cut two ways. On the one hand, it wished to build on the teachings first heard at the Sermon on the Mount. For this, we can admire Jane Addams's Hull House and many others for their efforts to assimilate new immigrants into American society, almost exclusively from Europe though with notable exceptions. These were urban resources, self-funded, and continued a tradition of self-help and charity through the neighborhood parish, rural or urban. Good works were tallied in some heavenly tome, like a record of payments to the feed store.

But another theme in this highway to Salvation was very different. It manifests strong Calvinist dogma appropriated by the original Puritan exiles coming to North America. God brought them here to rule without ecclesiastical furniture.

As in its initial inspiration, the reforms made faith wholly dependent on the vernacular Bible and placed each soul in direct contact with God. This proved profound in establishing the dynamics of American faith across all sects. It was Mosaic in its adherence to the Commandments but positioned the new settlers as the successors to Zion, not its acolytes. It was an inventory of musts and don'ts. Therefore, it gave away both the mysticism and mystery of Judeo-Christian earthiness and colorful rituals. The new Israelites eschewed the world and its allure, seeing pleasure as an e-ticket to Hell.

Not even blinking, it saw material gain as proof of God's favor. Plenty confirmed reform, and reform sustained personal contacts with the Lord. The reform virus coursed down every pew in every Protestant sect from the stony shores of Maine to the Gulf and way out there to the end of the Oregon Trail.

What each of these armies of the good preferred was altruism and exclusivist aid. To this they salted the stew with a bitter edge that maintained that pleasure of any sense is the snare of Satan. Americans, alas, are oft spiritually bereft and bipolar in their pleasures. Conviviality—one of my main themes in writing about wine—has no place in the America wished for by the church ladies from cow pie country (to salute H.L. Mencken) or dour Brahmins or high church (i.e., Anglican) substitutes.

To dine in luxury was a sin. You ate food in order to have the energy to plow the back forty and your wife. Children in the farm villages meant a foothold on other worth. Accumulations of grain or produce indicated God's pleasure with his newfound flock. The moneyed powerful would help spread the faith and attract the disaffected or heathens. Over time, descendants had to admit that being rich was sort of a "Get Out of Hell Free" card.

These spiritual gymnastics need no safety nets—God will catch you.

MEET CARRIE NATION AND MADISON GRANT

Even dead, these very intriguing opposites connect. One is entombed in flyover country, near Manhattan, Kansas. The other rests at Sleepy Hollow thirty miles north of the real Manhattan. He bunks with the likes of Washington Irving and Andrew Carnegie. The two principals could hardly be different. And they attacked different interrelated aspects of domestic habits based on allied prophecy and eugenics.

Carrie Nation is self-invented as much as Madonna or Andy Warhol. A woman from the middle states, she bounced around with two husbands, one who died of drink and the other a Methodist lay preacher. Nation worked variously until she was called by Jesus (collect?) to destroy saloons ahead of armies of hatchet-wielding *hausfrauen*. Her career ran through the first decade of the past century and ended in a loony bin. But Nation shrewdly advised local media of her intentions. Further, she lectured over the land and abroad. She said she was like a dog faithfully running under Jesus's feet. Since she stood six feet tall, she had to believe in divine magic.

Conversely, Madison Grant was a New York City attorney descended from Bay colony stock who came to America in 1623. During his life, he was a respected conservationist. WASP elites were big on preserves and state parks. It was good form for the betters to let the teeming masses know they were in a special land, even if they would never see it.

In 1916, as national feeling ran just below a slow boil, Grant published *The Passing of the Great Race*. Not a best seller, more than twenty thousand copies were out there when Grant passed away in 1937. One A. Hitler owned a copy, says the urban legend department.

The book promulgated a simple solution to a perceived big problem. Pioneer stock was diminishing, not only because reproductive rates had fallen dramatically but also because consanguinity was marred by intermarriage. In time, the white race would go the way of the Indians, whose birth rates had petered away. Replacing the old stock were prodigal procreators from southern and eastern Europe (Balts, Basque, Greeks, Italians, Jews, Levantines, Portuguese and Poles) who could augment the booming populations of Irish immigrants who escaped famine and oppression—real or not—from British overlords.

About 20 million people arrived to stoke the engine of the industrial boom in America between 1880 and 1920. The arrivals accompanied black migration from the backward agrarian South. All competed for jobs and residences to stake claims on the advertised dream. The melting pot metaphor of Israel Zangwill was actually melting down.

The most obvious imported vices were radical ideas such as farm communes and labor unions, expressed emotionally in vast quantities of beer and spirits or homemade wine, all old-country imports. Carrie Nation and the Woman's Christian Temperance Union (WCTU) associated such habits with abuses women had endured for far too long. The tavern had supplanted the congregation meeting hall.

For Grant, without surcease of these migrations, the good old pioneer stock would be swamped. Therefore, the nativist imperative supported the movement to ban alcohol, and in anticipation of women's voting strength, established pols caved in before the footlights, no matter the snorts taken elsewhere. Taking a drink began to look like race suicide at the fringes of the Noble Experiment. Grant proposed sterilization of the unfit (i.e., those swarthy types reeking of garlic and cramming English in night school) but soon settled for slamming shut the Golden Door of American passage—or at least reducing the flood to trickle. He got his way. Nativism not merely Evangelism was in the air, giving the nation a spasm of moral uplift.

Both themes coincided with the ratification of the Nineteenth Amendment, which enfranchised women to participate in national elections. So, it is easy to see how different ideals produced a nasty suppression of pleasure.

How did it work out? Well, if we ready ourselves to learn some history rather than to skew it to false agendas—or deny it, rewrite it or ignore it—we will learn a bit about the world around our barstools, tasting rooms and wine and martini lists.

WOODROW WILSON: AMERICA'S LEAST WORTHY "GREAT" PRESIDENT

H.L. Mencken called President Wilson (1857–1924)—aloof and tall, blessed with an air of condescension—a "Christian cad." Was he without grounds?

Wilson, son of a minister, came from Virginia. He possessed southern charm. Beneath, however, he burned with ambition and sanctimony. His *pince-nez* sneer derived from a successful book on Congress, he made his way to full professor rank and then dean, president of Princeton and governor of New Jersey; in a split-party race, he won the White House.

Academics usually classify Wilson a very fine president. After a century, this is like awarding O.J. Simpson a good neighbor plaque. Wilson was a phony. He was a typical academic resting on a textbook rep. But he was arrogant, secretive and self-righteous. Even Sigmund Freud co-wrote a disdainful account of our twenty-eighth president. He made some interesting cabinet appointments, and for good or ill, the Federal Reserve and income tax occurred in his first term, by which time the war in Europe had begun. When the oft-ill twenty-sixth president Roosevelt asked to enlist in the army, Wilson gallantly demurred. He did not want his spotlight dimmed.

His second term was a disaster. He entered the war against his recent claims. He dictated the peace with improvised points he jotted down as if taking a quiz. At Paris, he towered above the other allies, but diplomatically, he was a midget who hijacked the idea of a league of nations without assessing its viability and then stubbornly resisted all advice and took his idea on a domestic campaign tour that broke his health. The reformer left office discredited, but his sneering pride kept him around long enough to see that as an international ideologue, he blew his chance.

As have other holders of his high office, Wilson imagined himself above law. His attorney general, Mitchell Palmer, conducted "Red Scare" raids that ignored the precedence of habeas corpus under two espionage and sedition laws. One 1916 candidate, Eugene V. Debs, went to jail. The Bolshevik takeover in Russia, like the German-led Central Powers, elicited intense nativist feelings in America. So seizures of persons or their property was the signature of Wilson's "reforms." As the two amendments worked across the country in accord with the terms of the U.S. Constitution, Wilson was absent, both as commander-in-chief and as foolishly idealistic peacemaker. Crippled by three strokes, he left office to general relief. But most historians still pretend that his progressivism excuses the bungling.

Wilson was not the first chief to expand federal power, nor the last. The international situation surely commanded his attention, but Wilson preened himself like a big bird on a worm hunt. He ignored the consequences of the pending alcohol ban as much as manipulating to good effect the belches of xenophobes to advance his ends as a politician. Thus, he abetted the forces of moral and demographic terror the Eighteenth Amendment and the coming quotas would impose on a nation just stepping onto the world's stage.

The hatcheting, hymn-singing *frauen* of Carrie Nation's army and the legions of nativists noticed and wanted to take back the USA. Back from *what?* Whatever. Wilson wanted the new women's vote.

OREGON AND THE BOOZE BAN

Like thirty-five other states, Oregon was "dry" years prior to ratification of the Eighteenth Amendment. The interesting thing is how the state, already going its own way, managed to keep the party going despite the ban. This points further to the bromides swallowed about the leaders after Wilson who were Republicans and who presided over the most vibrant and exciting decade in the century.

Like Gershwin's *Rhapsody in Blue*, performed in 1924, the decade saw many firsts. It read or banned books by Sinclair Lewis, Theodore Dreiser and William Faulkner; elevated the Broadway musical; and saw the birth of the Museum of Modern Art. People flocked in time to see pictures with sound. It was the great era of baseball and aerobatics.

Above all, it roared with innovation and liberation. Its gadgets birthed the modern kitchen, which freed women from drudgery their grandmothers experienced on the way west. They listened to radio, and the major networks came into being. It was the decade that book clubs took off and telephones were ubiquitous. Community orchestras were more numerous than cases of influenza.

Above all, America took to the road for fun. It quintupled the number of automobiles. This urgency to be on the move repeated the pioneer push west a century before, but its circumnavigations of blue law bans was compost for other alleged vices. These included push-backs like radio preaching, mass Sunday services or Klan rallies. It was heady.

The clerisy would see the '20s as a roar of nativist empty capitalism that saw its bubble burst. Although an element of poetic justice runs through these professors of resentment, the real point they ignore.

In 1929, the United States produced more than 34 percent of the world's GDP. Even before that, say 1910, we were already years ahead of all industrial nations by dint of hard work and class fluidity based on money power. How well did Prohibition fare?

Even in the first dry state, Kansas, one could enter a town and in about the time it took to settle into a hotel room, one could buy a drink, said one congressional witness.

Like Gershwin's famous music, so typically American with its melding of klezmer clarinets and African American blues, it was a bit sassy, poignant, raucous and insouciant. It was us, Carrie Nation be damned.

In Oregon, as elsewhere, per capita income rose with the jazzy music. Public works helped to tame rivers and their traffic, moving more lumber and produce from its farms, forests and orchards. Fruit like apples, berries and cherries could make good homemade brandy. Still rural in its character, Oregon was accustomed to dry towns. But it simply meant that getting around the blue laws was not new.

BAD GIN AND GOOD TIMES

Listen to actual recordings cut in the '20s and one is immediately struck by its paradoxes (campy and frantic) and its spirit (energetic but wary). As the big winner in the Great War, our national soul was electric and skittish, as if as a people, like Carl Jung wrote, we began to dream.

Wilson left office believing that isolationists were his problem, not his insufferable demeanor. His three Republican successors—Harding, Coolidge and Hoover—wore the goat's beard for the crackup when it arrived, a convenient way to set the stage for FDR while ignoring the expansion of the economy and its spur to mobility, automotive and social.

These three men saw it meet to let the government actually buffer the hum of the marketplace more than routinely interfere. They pretty much allowed Prohibition to function with few teeth. Treasury agents, not the Justice Department, tried to enforce laws that most people disdained and ignored.

President Harding had buddies in for action, meaning poker and whiskey. Coolidge, dour and puckish, prided himself for his laconic mien: "Most of the people who come to see me want something they shouldn't have. If I sit and say nothing, after five minutes they run away." Here was a president allergic to social engineering and throwing millions at a moral uplift chimera.

Only Herbert Hoover, a successful engineer who came up from a dirt-poor Iowa farm to oversee feeding Europe's war-starved populations, was an interventionist chief magistrate. Yet he, too, quietly ignored the booze ban. Having let go of a wine cellar, he was known in his days as commerce secretary to stroll home by way of the Danish embassy. There, he was literally stepping abroad so he could have a nip prior to dinner.

So what Prohibition did best was inspire people to work their lives around it. And President Harding pardoned the socialist Debs so he could "have Christmas dinner with his wife." Some Christians are cads and some are not.

PARTY ON IN WEST EGG

Should one want to know how the majority of Americans viewed the Noble Experiment, look no further than the lawn party scene in the middle of F. Scott Fitzgerald's *The Great Gatsby*, appearing in 1925, right in the middle of the booze ban. Starlets, ingénues, judges, aldermen, movie moguls, *schnorrers* and tycoons cut the rug with abandon and champagne, cocktails and cock-teases.

As Carrie Nation's saloon smashing was already old news, statistics gathered in 1910 revealed that Americans imbibed about 7 gallons of spirits and other alcoholic refreshments per capita per annum. By mid-century, the quaff per capita stood at 2.7 gallons per year. Did the Noble Experiment work? Tracking consumption of booze is like tracking the Taliban; it is impolite to ask people how much they drink. And such numbers do not account for a minimum 60 percent jump in population by 1960.

We do know that Boston's eight hundred saloons going dark in 1920 were replaced by four thousand unlicensed taprooms. Public drunkenness in dry states became as visible as grain silos. And not all that grain made bread. But the foolishness of the entire experiment had no place in American society or elsewhere, with the possible exception of Easter Island. It proved bad legislation, and it cost plenty nearly a century later.

As a general rule, a person who refuses a drink or glass of wine is really wanting you to be unable to obtain a drink for yourself. Sobriety is no longer a choice but a blue Medusa that will turn the drinking classes to stone.

DAMAGE CONTROL AND YOU

Oregon in the '20s did not exactly resemble the big industrial states of the Atlantic seaboard, but it was no less affected by the pointless rigors of Prohibition.

The ostensible goal of the Prohibition movement was to curb the drinking of immigrant males. It became instead a moral crusade against pleasure, abetted by politicians afraid to oppose the intrinsic stupidity of the whole business. They anticipated the impact of women's political strength, and these men did pander to the prevailing impulse. The ostensible goal also was compromised by nativism and xenophobia. The Noble Experiment could not last; Americans were too accustomed to their liberties and entrepreneurship. Still, the experiment did take effect.

One paradox in our time seems to show that Oregonians, who took the pledge, then became vigorous brewers, distillers and vintners since, with a populace given to drink. The fruit boom described by Katherine Cole in her overview of the state's wine history ("Oregon Wine Story," posted on the website of the Oregon Wine Board), as well as in the opening chapters of Paul Pintarich's *The Boys Up North*, suggests that home-farmed fruit long provided spiritual refreshment, prior to and throughout the period of the commercial ban.

Throughout this book, I have noted the fragility of commercial ecology. The social uplifters never think of it because they impose only their respective agendas. Putting others out of business by seizing their inventory or destroying their places of business or coercing growers to pull up vines looks like totalitarian bullying to me.

The busybodies and scolds wanted the teeming masses to be woven into their illusory kind of America, shedding their old habits. The marketplace accomplished a kind of assimilation not foreseen. The demand for liquid pleasures was a need newly minted Americans fulfilled. The traffic and manufacture in brew, spirits and wine was overseen by the very people whose presence in the new Zion was obnoxious at best. Bootleg commerce provided big money to gangs of ethnics controlling defined territories. These tycoons were Irish, Italian, Jewish, Polish and African American, and these groups soon supplied goods for other vices. Most customers were the effluence of good colonial stock whose offspring gravitated to the vibrant cities across the land. Prohibition made crime pay. It paid off judges and police for protection. It helped organize organized crime. It advanced logistics with precision that spawned other services needing just-in-time product. Harriet Tubman, meet John Torio. Above all, the millions made in illegal booze in two generations had been recycled enough to move to the suburbs, fund legitimate businesses and send the grandchildren of the tough guys to private schools.

Even presidents skirted the law. Americans like their liberty on the rocks with a splash of soda. Scoffing the law was in fashion. And where personal choices occur, enforced morality will never take in a society founded on the pursuit of happiness. Why social engineering failed raises some interesting points.

Readers may wish to look up the lyrics for "Lady Liberty Blues" from the 1927 *Revue des Ambassadeurs* by Cole Porter. The singer, passing the Statue of Liberty on a ship inbound from Europe, laments the chains and shackles of the church ladies temperance' scam.

PERSPECTIVES

In a 1996 article called "Alcohol and the Bible," Daniel Whitfield tallies 228 discrete references to drink, principally to wine. Of the total, 59 percent are positive references, 16 percent are negative and 25 percent are neutral, as interpreted by the compiler. He asserted that the writers of scripture had no animus against wine, for, among other things like corn, honey, milk and oil, wine was an expression of divine favor.

What the homily and research suggest is that vine tending and winemaking were already well-established activities in the time of the prophets. Moreover, the central metaphor of the sacrifice in the Gospels turns on bread and wine. God's bounty (Old Testament) and God's mercy (New) put vineyards and wine center stage.

So where is the Don't Touch that Drink commandment? In the febrile brains of the reformers. It is not in scripture, and this should not surprise anyone who follows the story about the mission of Jesus. He makes wine the central metaphor of his sacrifice. There is, as previously noted, no dump bucket at the Last Supper. So who laughed last?

We have invented a pathology, part criminal and part warm and fuzzy—a cottage industry bringing traffic enforcement and psychologists of the hand-wringing variety together in order to fleece drivers who fail breath tests. We have to endure the negative behaviors of binge drinking, selling false IDs and spiking the punch at the prom. When drink is a dare, it is not convivial. It is dumb. Interdictions against drink promote furtive drinking of brew, spirits and wine, so many parents fail to cultivate a palate for enjoyment of wine as food paired to other food.

I think the saddest effect of the whole business is the assault on conviviality. Here the abstemious and the alcoholic can compete for the dubious distinction of removing the convivial from the American table. Chronic drunks no less than behavioral terrorists took the convivial impulse away from the customary gathering. Instead of a sharing ritual, a reinforcement of social connection and hospitality, the table became a crossover between a place in the pews and a refueling stop. It's not surprising that the convivial was not invited to sup. Even now, despite the ubiquity of food-wine pairings and martini menus, the conviviality seems, if not forced, then at least an after-market enhancement, like mud flaps and fender skirts. Wine festivals too often more resemble arena rock concerts than a celebration of abundance and comity.

At the last, it made consensual standards of morality and philanthropy into commodities that community activists, mountebanks and professional politicos could exploit for gain and position. Prohibition intended to purify; instead, it spat into the porridge. The fact that a national law was roundly disobeyed marked a turning point—the consensual morality ceased to be voluntary but a contrivance of compliance and coercion. This, in turn, affected the spirit of philanthropy: "If you do as we say, we will help you."

Orson Welles, someone prone to conviviality on a large scale, said near the end of his life that Prohibition ruined America by destroying the trust symbolized in a handshake. More to the point, the local results across the nation have produced a crazy-quilt of regulations that make business transactions and wine events subject to all kinds of petty variations built these days by fear someone will fall into the flowerpot and then sue you. Liability makes cowards of us all. And fees and revenue made governments small and great prefer managing the system than trying to stop it.

A winemaker in a control state such as Oregon can occasionally just sigh. Tom Monroe, co-owner with wife Kate Norris of the Southeast Wine Collective in Portland, said, "We're still jumping over regulatory hurdles that make little sense and vary from one place we sell wine to the next. It's nuts."

Empress of food writing M.F.K. Fisher asked, "Which came first, the Blue Nose or the Red Nose?" One winemaker who once worked for pioneer David Lett recalled his complaint that "it's easier to ship ammo out of state than a bottle of wine." Carrie is still out there, with God's private number on her speed dial.

If you require commercial illustrations of the residue of the failed experiment in Oregon, I call readers' notice to the December 5 celebrations to mark the death of the Eighteenth Amendment. Taste on 23rd in Northwest Portland features bubbly to customers aware of its promotion.

More explicit is the sale from pioneering Gaston Elk Cove. It is Oregon Wine Country thumbing its nose at Carrie Nation:

Decoding the Grape

Prohibition Ended December 5, 1933

Dear Elk Cove Fan,
The 18th Amendment was repealed 84 years ago today. What a great excuse to celebrate on a Tuesday and delve into a bit of Elk Cove history…

Pat's great grandparents were Swiss farmers and winemakers in Helvetia, Oregon in the early 1900s. Did they make wine during Prohibition? If you were a subsistence farmer with 4 kids, 12 grandkids and 5 acres of Chasselas grapevines, what would you do?

~

One popular option for Prohibition era winemakers: bricks of wine, dehydrated blocks of grape-juice to reconstitute at home. Blech! Meanwhile, Joe's uncle Clyde Cordner toured the midwest giving rousing speeches on the evils of alcohol as a prominent temperance advocate.

{Instructions: After dissolving the brick in a gallon of water, do not place the liquid in a jug away in the cupboard for twenty days, because then it would turn into wine.}

~

Clyde's vision of an alcohol-free utopia wasn't realized, but decades later his nephew fell for the descendent of (alleged) bootleggers. In the early 1970s Pat and Joe Campbell joined other "Oregon Wine Pioneers" to revitalize Oregon's long lost wine industry.

So let's raise a glass and be thankful we're not drinking brick wine, bathtub gin or swill. Cheers!

—the Campbell family

CHAPTER 15

NEW YEAR'S DAY 1934

CHANGING THE WORLD FOR OREGON WINE AT HONEYWOOD

Anybody who has walked into a winery tasting room and walked out with a bottle or two of wine owes a tip of the cap to Honeywood Winery in Salem, Oregon. It took a demure, gutsy lady who owned this venerable business for part of her forty years on premises to persuade the state's legislators to alter regulations so you can today visit tasting rooms all over Oregon.

Add to these details the fact that, for a time, Honeywood Winery was the only continuously operating producer in the state. It puts a little resonance into stories from the Oregon wine country. And a woman ran the place before it was politically correct. Look another way.

When Richard Sommer planted those first fabled Pinot Noir cuttings in the Umpqua Valley, Honeywood, formerly known as Columbia Distilleries, was almost thirty years in business, having moved away from the still and manual labor to automated bottling. Four decades later and in the hands of the very people who acquired the Honeywood brand the year Gerald R. Ford became president and other vines were growing in the Willamette Valley, this singular heir to the post-Prohibition fruit wine boom soldiers on.

Wine enjoyment and wine lore resemble baseball—each a version of pastoral. Both pastimes are defined by place; one can say Rogue River or Côte-d'Or and the initiated know exactly what's meant, like mentioning the Green Monster or the "House that Ruth Built."

Left: Vintage Honeywood Blackberry Wine label. *Courtesy of Honeywood Winery.*

Below: Honeywood Tasting Bar. *Courtesy of Honeywood Winery.*

To place we add memory and statistics, for both wine and baseball revolve about these poles. Both glory in good years; both endure sub-par seasons. Remember 1984 in Willamette? Thus the history of each one is loaded with subjective recall inspiring passionate assertions.

Over the past year of researching and writing this book on Oregon wine, I was repeatedly drawn to Honeywood Winery. It marks an intersection of past and present. It seems right that Messrs. Ron Honeyman and John Wood wanted to be close to lawmakers and regulators while running a distillery. Call it influence pouring.

If readers care about stats, swirl on this. Honeywood (aka Columbia Distilleries in 1934) received bonded winery license no. 26 from the Oregon Liquor Control Commission, which it holds to this day—the lowest number in the state. What happened to numbers one through twenty-five? It's like asking who played first base for the Yankees before Lou Gehrig. (It's Wally Pipp, and you can look it up.) The present facility stands very close to the original wood-frame warehouse, and it is more plant than pastoral. Within, Marlene and Lesley Gallick preside over a kitschy assortment of wine accessories and paraphernalia, not to mention more than fifty SKUs of ciders, fruit and viniferous wine. It's fun without being cheeky. "Beaver Believer"? Well, almost.

Eighty years young, the business has survived its share of challenges and almost closed in 1963, before its office manager, Mary Reinke, bought the place at the behest, as she recalls, of the local investors who likely enjoyed fruit wines up close and personal. They could thank Reinke, who, before she passed five months after our interview at age ninety-five, was likely the Oregon wine industry's most venerable and vivacious citizen.

She was fifteen when Prohibition ended, a bright young thing who graduated from high school and began a distinctly liberated professional life that closed out forty years to the day from the 1934 launch of what would later be called Honeywood. A daughter of Italian immigrants and born in The Dalles, Oregon, Reinke soon moved with her family to Salem. She recalled that her bedroom stood directly above the cellar where her father made his own wine, as was the custom among old country arrivals to the New World. "I heard a tap-tapping on my floor," she remembered, "as corks flew out of fermenting bottles."

After graduation, she took business and secretarial courses, landed a job at a credit bureau and, along the way, also began a party- and wedding-planning business, although this recollection came down without a date. We do know, however, that Reinke began working at Honeywood in 1943.

One can imagine this energetic woman seventy years ago, the Lois Lane of the place, happily scampering over ten thousand gallons of wine held in huge redwood casks long since replaced by stainless steel. She oversaw myriad business functions. "I was a good study and jumped whenever John Wood growled at me," she recalled.

Honeywood installed its first bottling machinery in the mid-1950s, and the cases rolled out to the loading platform at the rate of 1,200 bottles per day. Evolving fashion and tastes gradually caught up to the winery, and nearly thirty years after it emerged from the shadows of Prohibition, the

Great Depression, the Second World War and beyond, Honeywood Winery faced bankruptcy. This crisis was Reinke's opportunity.

The way Reinke described it, she was asked by the shareholders to rescue the business. One suspects, however, that Reinke, who was familiar with the financials and the equity players, had a good notion about what Honeywood required before she was asked. And so, in the time of tail fins and Sandy Koufax, she owned Honeywood Winery.

No stranger to publicity, this demure lady with bouffant hair was often seen, huge Bundt cake in hand, in the local newspapers or other media. And she had just begun. The regulatory reforms Reinke instigated were sound business practice. She foresaw, to a certain degree, that wine tourism could move product and that consumers liked the convenience of sampling wine where it was made—today's tasting room—and thus, where they could acquire it.

Reinke was good press, too. She retained her profile as a woman who entertained. She had her own advice column, an unabashed marketing tool. And she traveled the national market promoting what were now her wines. Her presence in the largely male-dominated industry was one part novelty and two parts savvy. She integrated her party planning, her recipes and wines into what we now call a "lifestyle"—when American quaffing preferences were for beer and spirits.

Reinke emerged as one of those unanticipated outcomes of the Prohibition aftermath. Clearly Honeyman and Wood were doing under-the-radar business that the Twenty-First Amendment now allowed the light of day. We can infer, though, that the introduction of production technology took longer in winemaking than in making canned peas because the industry was for public consumption, off-line. Reinke became known as the "Dutch Cleanser Girl" for her scrupulous attention to plant hygiene before commercial standards were codified and enforced. Again, it would seem that the 1920–33 hiatus at first set back and then allowed for a period of deliberate speed in winemaking practices.

A Minneapolis group acquired the Honeywood Winery in 1974, and the Gallick family still operates it. The original building was sold to Willamette University and the University of Tokyo in 1991; the present facility and lively tasting room stand diagonally across the rail line from the original building. Today, the winery produces thirty thousand cases per annum, and both Gallicks assert that the wine is considerably drier than in the past, although it's impossible to miss the fruit. The winery also produces viniferous wines from established growers and its own estate, twenty-one acres in Eola-Amity Hills.

And yet as Lesley Gallick pointed out, Honeywood is an anomaly. "We have to lobby hard to get the wine writers' attentions." Think elderberry wine without thinking *Arsenic and Old Lace*. After a pause, she added, "We're typecast: wines for spinsters. But we are far more than that; we have a large and varied portfolio. And a good following." Their 2012 Pinot Noir argues against the pigeonhole.

Even forty years after relinquishing Honeywood, Reinke had until the end a cordial relationship with the Gallick family, who arranged my meeting with the former owner. At the end of that conversation, Reinke looked pensive. Then she said, "My only complaint at my age is the bursitis in my hands. I can't pull the lever on the slot machines."

Will fruit wines enjoy resurgence? Perhaps the growing local distillers' offerings will pique the palate for wines originating from a cornucopia of plump berries and golden ripe hanging fruit. It might even reduce the angst in some tasting rooms, where the fruit wine heritage of the Oregon wine industry has been overlooked, if not forgotten.

Honeywood is not alone in carrying forward the fruit wine boom that began in Oregon immediately after Prohibition was repealed. The various berries and other fruit bases that one expects in cordials and liqueurs seem to produce very interesting effects in main dishes and desserts when fruit wine takes its part. Those who sneer at wines made from peaches should remember, recalling baseball lore, that the "Georgia Peach" had the best lifetime batting average in the history of the game.

And if you cannot spike the second baseman like Ty Cobb did, you can at least spike the wine.

A POSTSCRIPT

The original version of this chapter appeared in *Oregon Wine Press* in 2014 and elicited some obloquy from the present owners of HillCrest Winery in Roseburg. They claimed that we erred by saying Honeywood was the oldest operating winery in Oregon.

Some people should avoid staking out positions that are indefensible or just plain wrong. Who got where first doesn't matter if there is no longer a there where once it was.

Richard Sommer, who passed away in 2008, planted the first Pinot Noir vines in Oregon, to his credit, in 1961. By then, Honeywood was long in business and had been, in one or another form, since 1934. As noted earlier, the Oregon Liquor Control Commission issued Honeywood license no. 26. It issued Sommer license no. 43. On my planet, twenty-six comes before forty-three by a difference of seventeen places. So, Honeywood was here first.

The contretemps calls attention to two things. First, in twenty-seven years' time, only sixteen other licenses relating to distilling and winemaking in Oregon were granted by the commission. This suggests how damaging the Prohibition amendment proved in the evolution of wine drinking and wine marketing. The second point derives from the first. The successors at HillCrest do not really consider wine made from fruit other than grapes to truly be wine. It represents a kind of barnyard snobbery. Both grapes and peaches can produce wine. That we tend to dismiss or ignore wine made from other fruit again returns to the damage caused by the failed experiment of the Eighteenth Amendment.

I have seen part of the e-mail exchange between the owners of the wineries in question, sent by Honeywood to me for comment. I tactfully refrained. It seems to me that both wineries made a contribution to the industry we celebrate in this book and need no other defense. I just hope people remember how to add and subtract whole numbers.

Finally, the reader can place himself or herself in the time when the iconoclast Sommer insisted that Pinot Noir and Chardonnay vines would do nicely in southern Oregon. To put perspective on the relative youth of the wine industry in the United States, we might remember that at the time, I was flunking algebra and the White House press corps reported that President Kennedy told the Ruskies to can their Cuban missiles. Maris and Mantle were chasing Babe Ruth. Cars had tailfins. And how much would you pay for a first growth? Twenty bucks?

Yuri Gagarin flew into outer space. Adolf Eichmann habituated a glass booth in Jerusalem on his way to the gallows. Gasoline cost nineteen cents at the Gulf station on Route 25. You could ride the subways of New York indefinitely—or at least until the equipment failed—for fifteen cents. None of these incidental details occurred very long ago. Oregon wine was a story about to be written.

Be grateful that Oregon has since produced wines worthy of admiration by wine lovers everywhere.

A SECOND POSTSCRIPT

If you have not sampled fruit wine other than marijuana mouthwash bought at convenience markets, you owe to yourself a sampling of rhubarb wine produced by Honeywood. It has that little bit of sweetness you encounter in a moderately dry Riesling, but minus the floral notes. Rather, it begins by making an earthy, mildly tart impression and then goes a little honeyed silk on the way down. Fruit wine is comparatively less expensive than still wine made from grapes, so you can experiment with varied fruits without killing your budget.

My other recommendation is the Eola-Amity estate Pinot Noir. The 2012 vintage proves again the attractiveness of this fruit. There is a fullness in the mouth and a fine finish, with the overall impression of the varietal— layered texture, good cherry and earthy notes, as well as just enough of a light touch to make it a wine at home with the good china or on the deck. I think it will keep for a number of years if you can locate a bottle or two. In the event this sparrow has flown, try a later vintage and decode a little bit of the Pinot Noir DNA. Sommer, by the way, primarily came to farm Cabernet Sauvignon and Riesling at Hillcrest. Syndicated wine columnist Dan Berger still thinks that Oregon's prize varietal is Riesling. It appears to be enjoying a Riesling *resurgimento*.

Wine survives changes of fashion and taste even being fugitive. Honeywood brought winery retail sales out to the front porch.

CHAPTER 16

THE NAKED CITY

REFLECTIONS ON URBAN WINE

"I THINK WE'RE GONNA NEED SOME LAW"

A story filed in the *Oregonian* dateline October 22, 2015, and called "Grapes of Wrath: Urban Winery Owner Recovers Stolen Barrels through Dogged Sleuthing," corrected this writer's mistaken belief that crimes of industrial scope don't occur in Portland city limits.

This misconception actually was corrected firsthand at the winery featured in the news story, the Southeast Wine Collective. "Collective" here is a kind of misnomer; it has fortunately not too much of Karl Marx or Mao in it. However, the shared assets playing host to ten wineries in one space suggests the kind of collaborative spirit I praise throughout this book on Oregon wine.

John Bayley, the Oxford critic who collected the short stories of Raymond Chandler about fifteen years ago, observes that Chandler's narrative gifts and sense of place provide the impression of a cozy normality beyond the mayhem of the main characters and their deeds. The streets of L.A. may be mean, but most people go about living outside the cruelty and vice. In a sense, we may view urban winemaking as the reverse image, where the collaborative and convivial spirit plays out against a cityscape not immune to crimes of property but relatively benign, day and night. Portland prides itself on being a bit weird rather than hard-edged.

But this collective of ten operating wineries sharing equipment, space and vision is different—it's a spot on the city property tax rolls that does some good, especially for anyone passionate about wine. Urban wineries express a pastoral impulse in concrete and steel rather than rolling vineyards surrounded by birdsong.

So, when some miscreants steal stuff here, there accrues to property loss the simmering indignation that comes from having one's privacy and property invaded. When the latest theft—one of six at the collective (!)—was discovered, I was into my third of five wines poured by the owners of the property. Needless to add, my interview stumbled to a halt.

The good news was that the latest stash was recovered from a fence in Gresham, a dubious suburban outpost about twelve miles away. The fence, who uses Craigslist to sell "used" winery equipment, remains at large. Portlandia logic sends both fences and the just to Craigslist. If some of the thousands of Portland bicycles purloined annually appear in posts on the website, both the scurrilous and the affronted can browse the site for goods of dubious provenance. Call it virtual coney-catching. But it indicates how inured we have become to the customs of urban life, both good and ill.

Collective manager-owners Thomas Monroe and Kate Norris knew exactly where to start their hunt for wine barrels: by going online. The recovery meant avoiding a hit of more than $3,000, something no business owner will countenance. For most wine collectors and acolytes, this side of the industry is all but invisible. The recent news story therefore provides a nice corrective as it also attests to the resilience of wine people, whether they pound the pavements or tractor the furrows.

Here I propose to survey a few urban wineries. Some make wines on premises. Others use the urban spaces for retail sales. Still others combine different operations into a single building that has been refashioned for such grape appreciations. The urban setting is postindustrial and postmodern. Lest we believe this a novelty, Kate Norris of the purloined wine barrels reminds us that in her year of apprenticeship in Burgundy "the wineries are lined up on the main road going through the main town, Beaune, and the vineyards surround the town and the course of the road." After perhaps fourteen centuries, residents have become accustomed to the notion of "urban wine."

It would serve to recall that across the English Channel, the great poet Chaucer, whose Harry Bailey organized the wager that is the premise of *The Canterbury Tales*, was the son of a vintner. Thus in fourteenth-century London, urban wineries existed but without websites; wine traveled with despoilers and discoverers of the New World; and before this time, the spice roads from Asia enabled the movement of wine along the routes of the

Middle Sea. That helps explain the ubiquity of vines in Europe south of the Nordic boundary, with its blood oaths, herring and proto-vodkas.

The making of the modern world is as old as supplying the Roman armies with good drink. Call it Gresham's Law minus the fences noted. You can't plunder and rule the known world on an empty flagon.

My interest incorporates the idea of place transposed. The land is out there, but not outside the garage. The polyurethane transports arrive with their native urgency to a former foundry site or warehouse near the tracks. The birds overhead are aloft and usually en route.

Starlings do a star turn annually in northwest Portland, but migrating birds aim mostly for vineyard pickings. The city is less a roosting paradise. There are too many disturbances. Are urban wineries producing better or lesser wines than country folk? You would be wise to avoid such a litmus test. Rather, drink up the city's mix of mild intimidation and enjoy what's poured. The postal code is just a way to use a GPS. The view may not inspire a great landscape painting, but you've arrived at the wine by streetcar. Or by mountain bike or skateboard. However one pedals toward an urban winery facility, the wines made in these confines do not, for the most part, disappoint.

Urban wineries offer a number of advantages. Ryan Sharp, owner of Enso Winery on Southeast Stark, with its factory ambiance close to curbside, noted some good reasons to run a winery in the city: "We are close neighbors to many of our customers, so freight and handling are pretty simple." He looks away, toward the rear of the building where the wine is made, thinking he has heard a foreign noise, a possible snafu. None has occurred. "Another thing—if equipment needs a replacement part, one can usually find the supplier at hand. Time to age wine in barrels has a slow clock, but when the grapes come in from the field or the press arrives at the roll-up front door, you want to move fast. So proximity to the guys who make the gaskets and rings keeps our winery in gear."

At Seven Bridges on Northeast Harding, a winery operating in a former auto and motor works, owner and winemaker Bob Switzer pointed out another benefit: "We are close to our trade customers. We get fast feedback from the marketplace." Seven bridges can be seen from this winery—hence the name. Portland, like New York City or Sydney or London, is defined by the soul of water, usually a river network or harbor. Nothing defines a place and its living tempo more than a river. Ask Mark Twain.

Another thing, too, emerges: wine people in wine country who have grown up amid vines, may have acquired formal credentials by a combination of round-robin pickup jobs and well-defined classes at local colleges or, for many, from the UC system to the south. But the people inside the city postal codes often came to making wine from other parts of the hospitality business, particularly bars and restaurants. The perspective is complementary to more agricultural venues, but as Jon Grochau (who has worked his vines in Eola-Amity as well as in the Rose City) noted, the restaurant experience firms up fundamentals of consumer relations and, just as important, the relationship between the wine and the food. As Madeline Puckette of the blog *Wine Folly* said, rather than pick the wine based on the food (e.g., Pinot Gris with picnic-temperature cheeses and meats), select the wines before preparing the meal to serve with it. This is simple and terrific advice.

Most people have long been habituated to washing down their food with some kind of drink, whether a shake with a Big Mac, a can of Budweiser with a chili dog, a glass of milk with a ham sandwich or served on artisan bread or, most famously, Dr. Brown's cream soda with a corned beef pastrami on rye—all at times delicious but consumed more as utilitarian fuel rather than the ingratiating ritual that a table well laid represents. It's those damnable Puritan defects in our DNA that for too long and for too many have gotten in the way of forethought and sensation going into a meal.

What red wine starts a meal with grilled salmon as its protagonist on the plate? David Rosengarten and Joshua Wesson wrote a whole book on the subject in 1994 called *Red Wine with Fish*. Be counterintuitive. Urban wineries represent more than thinking outside the box. They put new wine in old boxes once used for something else. Where Sharp gets it most right is in what he told this writer: "Of all the logistical things that put Enso on SE Stark in the city is the fabric of being in my neighborhood. I can get my kids from school. I can hang with other businesspeople including winemakers who have a similar regard for the urban vibe. I think that allows me to experience the best of both worlds." To this I would add, "Look well to your wine barrels," as Brabantio tells his fellow Venetians in Shakespeare's play (where the possessions aren't barrels but daughters of marriageable age).

On the first day of May 2016, the PDX Urban Winery Association gathered for a tasting at Switzer's plant. It formerly looked, on our first pass several years ago, like London during the Blitz—a working winery in there somewhere. Now it is still patently industrial, but it is spacious, with barrels reaching high into the clerestory warehouse. The fourteen wineries assembled had much to offer; there was accomplishment and focus and, yes, more than a little Rose City pride. And the wines continue to improve, in both quality and variety. The crowd included wine visitors from Nebraska.

"Why not start our wine vacation in the city?" one said. "We have options at hand. It's really a fine way to start a vacation."

The room attracted more than waving-grain retirees. Plenty of Portlandia hipsters cruised through the space, and the event, despite almost immediate arena-crowd energy, was a happy one. The organizers and members have plenty of cheer to cheer.

The first urban wine is made from local fruit, but its pedigree is very old and very distant. It's an Amarone-style wine produced at Southeast Seventh Avenue at a converted industrial space called Urban Crush.

As we drive the several miles from Seven Bridges, we can count the Willamette River crossings embedded in one brand, but speaking to one of the Rose City's most endearing and enduring features. Thresholds to pass like the doorways to our taste memories. Keep in mind that this city and its surroundings stand not apart from farms and vines. They're the top of our wine country; indeed, you're in it.

JULIET'S VINEYARD

"A rose by any other name would smell as sweet" is Shakespeare's ingenious deconstruction as uttered by Juliet. In other words, if the *fiori d'amore* were not spelled "r-o-s-e" and, instead, represented a less salutary smell spelled out in four letters, what would we do? Personally, I would find another Romeo.

Juliet's words and their capacity to identify meaning relate directly to the wine in question here, Amarone. The storied wine has been made for centuries in the Valpolicella wine district of Verona, Italy, the location of the Bard's most famous romantic tragedy. Nowadays, Verona hosts the largest show of its kind in the world, Vinexpo—the Super Bowl halftime event for winemakers and wine lovers.

As the story of the star-crossed lovers has traveled so well around the globe, so, too, has the famous wine from the hills and dales surrounding Verona.

Amarone, which means "great bitter one," refers not to an emotional state but to the fact it is not Recioto. Great moments in winemaking can occur by mistake. Recioto, left too long in some barrels, lost some of its native sweetness, becoming Amarone.

Five wines derive from the Valpolicella designation: Superiore, Classico, Ripasso, Amarone and the aforementioned Recioto. Three varietals go into fashioning these wines: Corvina, Molinari and Rondinella, with certain allowances made for other varietals. What makes Amarone the pride of this litter, however, is the technique used to produce it. Ultimately, we must ask not merely how the techniques used translate elsewhere but also whether the effort pays.

For instance, the acidic Valpolicella Superiore will strike new palates as astringent and thin. Pair with fruit or charcuterie plates and the message softens. Likewise, the "baby Amarone" inherits its well-defined acid-to-fruit balance by having been exposed to the pomace of Amarone—the remains produced from the fermentation stage. In our New World market, driven by Cab Sauv and related red blends, the Amarone matrix may seem daunting when it is, in fact, approachable—you can reliably build a five-course dinner around this family of wines.

People who become infatuated with this wine are an interesting group, defined by their love both of the machinations needed to produce it and its sheer voluptuary abandon. It's a wine that rewards anticipation.

As easily as the Amarone style evokes appreciation—nay, passion—we ought to remember how much preparation goes into it, including the method of sun drying applied to the harvested grapes, called *appassimento*. While the ultimate quality is fashioned in the vineyard, we would be wise to appreciate the unique tasks performed to produce these marvelous wines.

"It's risky business," said Gino Cuneo, who has produced Amarone-inspired wines in the Pacific Northwest since about the year 2000. "Each step of the way can impede your making it turn out the way you want it to." By this he also means the farming at his Walla Walla sources. Unlike his forebears in the old country, he uses local varietals of Italian pedigree—the Tuscan-born Sangiovese, the Piemonte-born Barbera and Nebbiolo. To date no one has tried to root the Veronese varietals in the Pacific Northwest.

Before drying the grapes, one must tend to the clusters, leaving plenty of room for air to pass along the individual bunches. The purpose is to ensure the health of the skins, which bring the tannins, color and intensity of flavor to the wine. Usually harvested in early fall, the grapes, as at Cuneo's Walla Walla facility, go onto mats—straw or canvas—to work on their tans up to four months.

Desiccation, said winemaker Ed Fus of Portland's Urban Crush, reduces the entire crop by volume, thus concentrating the incipient flavors to emerge in winemaking. As the fruit dries, problems can occur. Exposed grapes may be subject to bacteria and botrytis, ruining the suitability of the fruit. And this gamble, in turn, illustrates the nature of the *appassimento* process—for there is method in this madness.

The Romans of imperial times sought a substitute for honey, at that time the primary sweetening agent for wine and other foods. The roads led up the boot to places where grapes were sun-dried, producing a solar sugar before Western civilization invented the plantation. The process itself seems to have immigrated to Italy by crossing the Adriatic, where it arrived from Crete at the far end of *outre-mer*. This "discovery" by phalanx and sword may have occurred as recently as the late third century AD.

Importer Ciro Cirillo of Mission Wine Company exclusively imports about sixty Italian wines, including Amarone and Ripasso. He pointed out that even on the straw, one considers what will happen next.

"It depends on the final proportions of the primary grapes. In one way, the Amarone has flavor profiles like port. In another emphasis, the raisinated grapes show best. Then, in a third way, the effect may come from the relative lack of acid in harmony with the relatively high alcohol content, producing a mouth-filling bonanza." He stressed that there is not one correct approach. "All emphasis will produce wonderful wine almost too intense to drink every day. For that, we have Valpolicella Superiore."

Once dried, grapes go to crush and fermentation, long after other wines. "This is the point that poses a second chance for spoilage," Fus said, adding that the juice must be moved into new French oak to rest for as long as fifteen to twenty months. In Italy, new French oak is one of three kinds of barrels used, the others being Slovenian and Slavonian. Even after this step, the wine, once bottled, must wait two to three years for release.

Joe Meduri, whose Cinzia label is produced in Oregon by Fus, noted that the numerous stages of production increase the cost of making the wine. "This is a labor-intensive wine, and we make it because we love it." Like this writer, Joe and his wife, Cindy, fell for Amarone decades ago, but they only recently decided to try to produce some wine in the style of their favorite.

Meduri sources Zinfandel, Petite Syrah and Primitivo for his production. This choice offers a wonderful symmetry. Zinfandel, long spurned by Cab-obsessed type-A money-brokers, is once again getting a little respect. And its kissing cousin, Primitivo, from Apulia on the Adriatic coast, has recently been traced to a Croatian vine that survived history and its trials since the time the Romans searched for a proto-sugar.

The major distinction of Cinzia's production comes from the Meduris' family business located in Salem, now operated by their sons. They are the dried fruit emperors of the state; they use their sophisticated drying system to replace the *appassimento* sequence. So their production curve is flattened and speedier.

So, does the effort pay? I think these wines acquit themselves very well. I recommend letting them take the air in order to allow their copious aromas and textures to stimulate the senses, the way Juliet must have done to Romeo. The high alcohol sails on a galleon over a sea made of sinew, spices and suggestion. No wonder they eloped.

The wines we tasted from Cinzia used to be made at Carlton Cellars in Carlton, one of the best one-blinker towns in Oregon. Now they're produced at Urban Crush, as noted before, on the east side of the Willamette River in a refitted factory space on Southeast Seventh Avenue. Here, too, Fus and his wife, Laureen O'Brien, make their own wines: Angel Vine Zinfandel and Primitivos.

I learned at this writing that the cellar is producing for Cinzia, a Ripasso made from Pinot Noir fruit for a restoration of the Odd Fellows Lodge in Salem, a mixed-use inspiration of urban re-imagining. This may help readers grasp the magical fullness of this wine, even when imitated conceptually with different grapes half a world away.

Amarone makes people do remarkable things. Perhaps how the Amarone-style wine found kindred spirits for big, powerful and spicy wines with some subtlety bound into its overall aggression also is very romantic. And few things are more elusively romantic than Shakespeare's lyrical tragedy.

What's in a name was the question leading to Juliet's disquisition on the name and stink of the rose. Apparently the answer, no matter your zip code, is everything. Put another way—Amarone-style winemaking releases pheromones. Romeo has competition.

Sourcing varietals from different Northwest climates and vineyards poses challenges that winemakers accept readily. Thus, we can anticipate descendants of notable Italian, French and Spanish vinelands coming to a winery near you. This is particularly true in the urban wine districts, as their greater populations support many restaurants looking to pair their cuisine with indigenous wines that express a wider vernacular than first impressions limit to the most popular wines for which Oregon is best noted.

I leave this little tale of translation from old-world wines with a comment by Dan Berger, a well-respected columnist. Years ago, he said to me over dinner, "It's a shame so many Riesling vines in Oregon are being pulled to make way for the money varietals, Chardonnay and Pinot Noir." Oregon's best wines came from Riesling for decades, he said. And the old should still elicit respect. What prompted Berger in the early 1990s to make this point, however, has been modified by the turn of history's wheel: the warmer and drier AVAs in southern Oregon are now producing grapes associated with other places, such as Bordeaux varietals, Tempranillo and Italian grapes like Primitivo, Sangiovese and Zinfandel, a California translation of the Primitivo gene pool. Likewise, the Columbia Gorge, the Columbia Valley and Walla Walla provide much of this fruit destined for urban winemaking, not to mention a stunning array of wines produced where the varietals are grown.

Anyone with a thirst for wine must bust out of the Willamette Valley and discover the rest of America beyond the Cascade Range rain shadow, just down I-84 East. Blends emerge from this fecundity. Rhone varietals such as Grenache, Syrah and Mourvèdre appear at times as single-varietal wine to generally good effect. In blends, known as GSM, however, they seem to complement each other. These wines, easy to drink, do not belie their manifold charms or the artisanal skill that goes into their invention. Decidedly, they display layers of interest as much as a *feuritille* filled with Mediterranean shellfish in brandy cream. The variety of varietals seems to inspire winemakers to go about like kids with a new chemistry set, producing rockets of flavor.

Byron Dooley of Seven of Hearts in Carlton is my favorite mad scientist in this regard; he orchestrates grapes sourced from disparate AVAs to make very appealing wines. In addition to the GSM red, he produces whites including Rousson and Voignier. The urban wine scene seems catholic in approaching blends with varying degrees of appeal. Blends are volatile, and although it is easy to manipulate juice fermented from different varietals, it takes more than luck to produce a wine that is more than a patio pounder. Blends, however, make good ports of entry for tempest-tossed refugees from soft drinks and faux fruit juices.

But we should turn to the venerable varietal that perhaps owns the oldest pedigree in Oregon: Riesling, first planted in the territory when James K. Polk was president.

The varietal likes residual sugar, the kind one savors in the bite of an apple or the afterglow of apricots and peaches in high summer. Along with Grüner Veltliner and Müller-Thurgau, Riesling is the go-to varietal of the lederhosen set—testimony that the first great transatlantic population migration to America from the mid-seventeenth century to the mid-nineteenth century comprised German-speaking peoples, nearly twice as many as later transfers of Irish or Italian peoples. But taste memory accesses the better narratives of the past, so while these pleasing whites may fall from fashion, they will never disappear. Nor should they. Each is versatile, and in the manner winemakers make them in Oregon, they are moderate to bone-dry.

Winemaker and proprietor Byron Dooley (Seven of Hearts) at his Carlton tasting room. *Courtesy of Jonathan Potkin.*

In a March 2016 blog entry in *Wine Folly*, Madeline Puckette, inspired by an episode of *Wine Library TV* in which Gary Vaynerchuk actually paired a Spätlese Riesling with breakfast cereal, paired five wines with cereals and lived to tell about it.

One ubiquitous white varietal, Pinot Gris, with an Italian relative, provides not only a vineyard and winery location in the Portland city limits but also a pirate ship.

"Keep Portland Weird" is a local mantra. We could better do with "Keep Portland Eclectic." The urban wine scene lives up to it. Of more than seventy varietals commercially farmed in Oregon, it's more than likely you will find some blue-jeaned enthusiast making a single variety wine around the corner, between the bakery and the machine shop.

SEVEN SAILS WINERY PINOT GRIS: UP TO THE BIG HOUSE, MATE

In the 1940 thriller *Farewell, My Lovely*, detective Philip Marlowe drives up to the Grayle mansion and describes what he sees in laconic understatement uncommon to postings on Zillow.com—vintage Raymond Chandler to be sure: "The house itself was not so much. It was smaller than Buckingham Palace, rather gray for California, and had fewer windows than the Chrysler Building."

So, imagine my surprise when I encountered the house lording over the vineyard at Seven Sails' pirates den, based in Portland's western hills. I'm accustomed to quirky and historic framed homes of the early twentieth century, but it is a rare dwelling that combines prestige writ large with a great sense of humor, as if Rabelais were a house—and one comes upon it from below, making its imperious presence more dramatic.

If this experience does not suffice, imagine this: the vineyard proprietors style themselves as pirates—the skull and crossbones kind—who also pilot a 1971 ketch-rigged privateer and are serious purveyors of musical entertainments. Kate Larsen, one of the principal "avast ye mateys" swashbucklers, traveled the world as a singer on cruise ships; she is also a first-rate gourmand. Her partner in this venture, a kind of island creature washed onto the mainland, Shuhe Hawkins, is an actor, arts educator, puppeteer and now vineyard manager. They met during a Portland theater gig at which both performed.

Together they founded the Portland Pirate Festival in 2006, attracting an average of fifteen thousand patrons annually—due to venue matters beyond their control, the event has taken a hiatus; they hope to resume the event in 2017. Larsen and Hawkins also perform in the BilgeRats & Pyrettes, a multi-genre band with, you guessed it, a pirate theme.

The wine business adds a new component to their personae; after all, privateers liberated gallons of spirits and wine at the time they cruised the world's commercial routes.

To a certain degree, Larsen and Hawkins are accidental vintners. As growers on the estate, they dealt with gophers and burrowing bureaucrats—both are pests surmounted. Nature provides the sneaky mammals, Portland the compliance codes. This vineyard once stood as an amenity of comfortable wealth. It seemed to Larsen and Hawkins, if not at once, that the landscape ought to pay its way, or at least make an attempt. This determination is more than a matter of will.

Commercial wineries are flypaper to compliance engineers, the horde who conjure and enforce all manner of codes. To this, one must account for smaller yields and limited case production and manage the path from bottling to marketplace. Pinot Gris is a respectable varietal for which many Oregon winemakers do justice. But it is not the state's headliner varietal.

You cannot hide three hillside acres of what were then fifteen-year-old vines planted by the former owners of the house, who made wine with more of a sense of amusement than ambition. When Larsen and Hawkins decided to make an official effort, they started with all the appropriate agencies. Good thing they did, as the prior owners ran rogue—bottling their harvests mostly for friends and not for commercial sale.

"It was good to put the formalities behind us," Larsen said, "because these hills are filled with people who like being left alone. Had we ignored protocol, who knows whether we could have launched this enterprise meaningfully." One imagines federal tax agents in Sikorsky helicopters droning over the staid West Hills enclave.

Whether it's growing Pinot Gris or performing as pirates, Larsen and Hawkins waste no time. "We jump into everything we do with two feet and expect to figure things out as we go," she explained.

The *Royaliste*, their privateer, was built in Nova Scotia. Our pirates found it marooned in Kentucky, not noted for its intercoastal geography. Built as a floating historical attraction in 1971 for the Canadian War Museum, it first migrated to the East Coast and ended up trekking the Oregon Trail by flatbed truck. Larsen and Hawkins intended to use it as a show and tourist venue in the Northwest. Four years ago, they participated in one of those ersatz Columbia River marine festivals arranged by promoters to sell memorabilia and who knows what else. All was shipshape until the local paddle wheeler—you can see it on the river downtown in Portland—backed into the commerce raider, pushing it into the concrete bulkhead along the riverfront and unseaming its sturdy wooden hull in many places. Suddenly, Treasure Island had become *Titanic*, and Hawkins found himself knee-deep in bilge water, bailing it out with a bucket.

Well, it was feet first. And all this mayhem the local news cameras captured for worldwide *schadenfreude*.

The wine story is less leaky, although the small output precludes commercial distribution at this time. Vintage 2013 sold out of its tiny 46-case output; 2014 still has about half of its 240-case yield; and 2015 pushed past 300 cases. The economics do not favor marketing blitzkriegs, thus Larsen and Hawkins, vineyard owners and pirates, find themselves calling on local markets and restaurants on a case-by-case fire drill method. Readers can visit Seven Sails' Facebook page or margotproductions.com to find the wine, the limping ketch and the pirate shtick.

Although damages paid for the *Royaliste* mishap amounted to six figures, the boat still needs a comparable sum to fulfill its intended purpose. That leaves one other open question: How is the wine?

Most urban wineries source grapes from out there, wherever that happens to be. Seven Sails reverses course, sending Portland grapes into the countryside to produce its wine.

Larsen and Hawkins engaged John Derthick, the winemaker of the former property owner. They walked the vineyard with him, asking that the wine be made according to their input. This imposes a premium on production costs and, in turn, affects the reach into the market.

Larsen said, "Since we didn't have a clue how to do anything with vines or wine, we naturally needed his help. We have learned a lot both from him and from the small crew who help us from time to time. They used to laugh at us, but I think a bit of respect is beginning to come into play at last."

Respect is due. I tasted the 2013, in 2015, and liked its acidity and finish. At the same time, I was underwhelmed by the 2014. But now, with another year in the bottle, this second pirate vintage drinks beautifully. And Brie or Irish cheddar do it even more justice. The 2015 possesses a long, crisp finish, and after a surprising flash of green midway on the palate, the second pass a week later rounded the impression fully. You taste this hillside, nearly one thousand feet up, in the Portland postal code.

Who would have thought pirates drank anything but rum? Wager that the sailing will grow smoother in time as well.

CERULEAN SKIES OF HOOD RIVER AND ITS PORTLAND ART GALLERY

Well, if a winery can be run by pirates (whose e-mail signature contains Mark Twain's prayer for God to let boys become pirates), then a Columbia

We found good Cerulean wines in Hood River with perfect serendipity. *Courtesy of Jonathan Potkin.*

Gorge winery can simultaneously operate an art gallery space with a full bar and a restaurant and operate its second tasting salon.

Thus, Cerulean Skies straddles the Hood River neighborhood in the Gorge and northwest Portland. Hood River boasts several dozen wineries and tasting rooms. Located about fifty-five miles east of the Rose City, it offers, like Walla Walla upstream another two hundred miles, wines of thoroughly different flavor profiles from even similar varietals that make Willamette Valley so distinctive.

The two geological features that determine so much of the identity of Hood River, subsumed in the Columbia Gorge and Valley AVAs, are the Columbia River itself and the leeward side of the Cascade Mountains. To make matters more singular, the Gorge functions as a classical Venturi experiment. In the summer, the heated air of the continental land mass mixes it up with the maritime air stream, creating the most agreeable conditions for people whose idea of fun entails windsurfing beneath the cliffs that lord over the northern shores of the river. This is Washington State. The southern shore is Oregon. Imagine crossing the Hudson River where two states contend for shoreline and you will get the idea. Rivers form psychological as well as political boundaries; the grapes often flourish at high altitudes in soil that is very different in composition from that found in the Willamette lands. This is tough, rugged dirt pushed into shape by volcanoes and floods. Its character is cinematic in its breadth and impact. But no Pixar here; this is the hand of nature unbridled.

So expect the wine to express its characteristics differently—more acid, more concentrated fruit, wines that are lean but full of sinew and textured layers. The salmon don't swim upstream to take baths; they come here to spawn and fight and then come to dinner less as guest than as menu item. I think this stretch of America made Lewis and Clark gasp with awe as they made the last part of their trek to the Pacific.

I stepped into the tasting room on Oak Street, one of the main thoroughfares in Hood River, one spring afternoon and began tasting my first Columbia Gorge wines.

One notices the astringent character of the whites, even when the varietals recalled might not suggest this kind of crispness in the mouth and cleansing in the finish. I acquired some 2009 Chardonnay, fermented in steel. It took little time to notice that this wine did not aspire to honey over oak that made California wines of the same varietal so popular—and so misleading. On a Long Beach, California patio, Billy Bob—a wine broker and collector—took a draught and remarked, "My goodness. This is frog wine," meaning it reminded him of a classic white burgundy, made from the same varietal. It was a compliment of high order.

This was exceptional wine. Subsequent years have produced on occasion other Chardonnays, sometimes aged briefly in oak. The effect remains very good. What we taste in these different vintages is the terroir, the ambiance of this windy and elevated land. The difference startles; the wine possesses a kind of equipoise between citrus, minerality and lean texture. I like it.

For instance, the May 2016 cellar club tasting featured the 2009 as well as the Cerulean 2008 Pinot Noir. The Chardonnay expressed the comely balance of acidity to fruit, coherent structure and elegant finish—in short, an Oregonian wine speaking French with an American viticultural accent. The Pinot Noir, incidentally, expressed dense layers of black cherry, minerality and long finish. Again, an indigenous wine with its Gallic heritage easy to appreciate.

Making the tasting event even more pleasant was the 2013 Chardonnay—French in spirit, Columbia Gorge in physique. Readers unfamiliar with wines produced in this AVA will be impressed by the magnificent differences these wines show in relation to the better-known wines of the Willamette Valley. I have stretched the city limits, as it were, to make this point.

The principals acquired their vine land from a neighbor after already owning a home above the Gorge on the Washington side of the river. I take "under" as way above, some surveyor's idea of a joke. Jeff and Tammy Miller, however, are also Portlandians. So they have a parallel universe in the city at the corner of Northwest Marshall and the 405 elevated highway. This old bonded warehouse has gone considerably upscale, a vision of white on black, sharp angles and expanses of the linear punctuated by new exhibits of art and sculpture. The environment expresses the elegance of chic without becoming ponderous; I like the feel of the place. The full bar is also the urban tasting room for Cerulean Skies. Add to this a capable chef and extensive northwestern menu and the destination fulfills its multipurpose inspiration, less urban winery than urbane wine space. "Space" is a sobriquet in this part of town, the Pearl District, because numerous old buildings have been refashioned as upscale venues where "space" connotes experience—of art, food, music, wine—and the company these amusements keep in the city. It seems to have been inspired by SoHo in New York, as loath as we are to imitate the Right Coast. Rather, it captures the vibe, dare one say, "the terroir of a metro street."

The origin of the grapes belies the municipal zip code. Nonetheless, the dichotomies of city lights and removed pastoral glimmers make Cerulean Skies into a city destination—resonant, if one contemplates enough of their portfolio, of some serious country earth.

An instructive experience concerns the Cerulean Pinot Noir of 2010. The growing season in Willamette Valley was noted, as mentioned in an earlier chapter, for the onslaught of birds. This year did not set records for heat or bulk. The Columbia Gorge is accustomed to very dry, warm growing conditions by way of comparison. These affect the grapes' characteristics. The 2010 Pinot Noir was austere and a bit closed. Then, after four years in my cabinet, voilà! A remarkable red wine with lavender scents rolled over my palate. I called owner Jeff Miller to ask whether he had a similar impression. He was laconic: "Don't you think it matured very nicely?" Understatement becomes these wines a mere streetcar stop away (Northwest Fourteenth at Northrop).

ENSO

Since its opening in 2011, the Enso Winery on Southeast Stark has been increasingly adventurous. Owner Ryan Sharp likes to point out that despite contracts with growers, he is not tied to a fixed area of vines. He can source, when available, from numerous growers and thus make wines he thinks his customers will enjoy.

Sometimes commercial virtue results from a mistake. A few years ago, Sharp bottled a rosé that subsequently went into malolactic fermentation.

The wine started to fizz, an unintended outcome. Laurie Lewis, a partner in the urban winery Hip Chicks Do Wine, added to the collaborative reputation of Oregon's wine people: "Don't dump it! Make Sangria! When we have lousy wine, fruit and spirits come to the rescue." And so Portland Sangria arrived from Enso like Minerva out of the head of Zeus. Well, maybe not—but it's a good tale. Packaged in cans, this SKU has made its way in the jungle warfare of supermarket shelf space in Portland to the tune of a projected ten thousand cases at this writing.

Other bottlings are not children of misfortune, however. Take the Rhone varietal Counoise, a light, bright and acidic wine that balances the heady, sugary intensity of Grenache and Syrah, the two dominant varietals in Châteauneuf-du-Pape, the signature wine of the Avignon popes. Study your papal history, quaffers. In the fourteenth century, the Roman church was removed from Peter's seat because the Romans proved intractable misfits and brigands and held a regimen of ungodly habits. The papal seat in the Rhone Valley proved to breathe fresh air into a religious institution that had suffered for at least three centuries from spiritual constipation. The second Avignon prelate, John XXII, takes honors for introducing Châteauneuf wines in 1324, according to historian John Julius Norwich. (The church also moved the treasury. No wonder its wines became legend.)

Bartender at Enso, a Portland urban winery. *Courtesy of Enso proprietor Ryan Sharp.*

Sitting area at Enso. *Courtesy of Enso proprietor Ryan Sharp.*

What always impresses me about varietals comes down to the way they translate from one growing area to another longitudes distant. The primary Rhone varietals—eighteen by statute can go into Châteauneuf-du-Pape—can reappear in Paso Robles or the Columbia Valley without a pope, without an inquisition, but with equal fervor for the grapes.

Urban winemakers thus are quite catholic in exploring varietal preferences and, when conditions warrant, make good wine consistently. A street scene in Southeast Portland will do just fine. Enso's Sharp seems to this writer the epitome of an urban winemaker. He follows his instincts, certainly, but he follows the Henry Luce dictum that all business is a future calculation. The outputs may be small: a portfolio offering a dozen or so wines, which represent less than four thousand cases available to customers willing to drop by without the occasion of a tour. The feedback does not take long to register. In this respect, the more commercial Sangria in a 12.5-ounce can is entirely different, and Sharp intends to spin the operation into a freestanding wine company.

"Based in the city, I am not dependent solely on wine club members or tourists," he pointed out. Also, the space has become a venue for events, largely social meetings, that further root the winery to the surrounding neighborhood.

An urban winery may not, with its clerestory sliding garage door, open on vistas of gentle hillocks or rows of vines set against a background of puffy clouds. But in its own manner, like an eccentric neighbor, it warms the fabric of its surroundings. An urban wine excursion ought to become an agenda item for anyone visiting the Rose City—bicycle thieves, meter maids and all the rest.

A BOUQUET OF URBAN WINERIES

A list provides readers with starting places for the urban wine iteration of the Oregon Trail. Take a bus; leave the pack animals on the farm. As noted earlier, the wineries of the city continue to get better.

What we must keep in mind is that not only are we visiting nontraditional winery spaces, we are also participating in the creation of wine-production traditions. The establishment of a wine reference library has to begin somewhere. The city winery people have, ultimately, themselves to rely on in order to introduce principles of style, methods of production and systems of distribution and consumer education. It is not exactly the first day of school, but it's close. Even if we aren't awestruck like the poet, silent on a peak in Darien, we can experience traditional practices in winemaking surrounded by the varied sensations and asymmetry that seem to mark urban life now (and—for my money—always have).

The transactions between city and country go both directions, as the passage on Seven Sails earlier demonstrates. Helioterra Wines started operating out of the Southeast Wine Cooperative managed by Tom Monroe and Kate Norris. The winery is now far closer to its grapes if no longer to the number four bus. The wines are made by Anne Hubatch at Bjornson Vineyard in Eola-Amity. Why? Well, one reason is scale. In a wine collective, the access to the facilities is almost by appointment. When the fruit is ready, the winery must appear. Grapes do not wait. Hubatch spelled out the reasoning for me in an e-mail dated May 9, 2016:

- *My production had grown large enough that I was occupying too much space in the SEWC.*
- *The cost of making wine in the city at SEWC was very high. I wanted to increase my margin by capitalizing on lower overhead.*

- *I moved to a space that had a larger capacity, so I was able to take on two clients as their custom crush winemaker. This allows me greater creativity and new fruit sources to explore.*

Thanks for asking!

It brings us to this observation: wines are sourced from many places. One 2013 Pinot Noir from Brooks Wine in Eola-Amity Hills arrives in the bottle from ten different vineyards. The winemakers' skill is in the assemblage, blending these diverse outputs into a wine expressing the character of the varietal and, paradoxically, the place of origin.

Consumers in California, as noted in the front of this book, can identify a Napa Valley Cabernet Sauvignon when its juice is 75 percent from the valley vineyards. In Oregon, the threshold to call a wine Willamette Valley Chardonnay, Cabernet or other varietal is 85 percent. This is not to say the standards in California are slipshod; the difference is reflected in output. In 2015, as the California Wine Institute reported, growers harvested 3.8 million tons of wine grapes. Varietal output may vary from one grape type to another, but the general rule is that a 60-gallon barrel of wine in its aging will offer up twenty-five cases. A ton of grapes produces on average 150 gallons of wine (give or take 25). The yield amounts to 750 bottles of wine per ton without factoring other variables like varietal and climate and terroir. The landholding grower and winemaker can anticipate yield and thus is master—for better or worse—of his or her fate at harvest.

By contrast, the urban winemaker is subject to a supply chain at the point of the dog's tail. One breaks the chains of servitude on one hand only to fashion a different set of commercial manacles. Life, however, could be worse. We speak of making and drinking wine, not wading among rice paddies.

Basing one's varietal component at one remove (i.e., not farming the grape crop itself) would seem to provide more

Doc Wilson and Joe Campbell, founder of Elk Cove Winery. *Courtesy Doc Wilson.*

flexibility and surely more choices for an urban winemaker. But this picture misleads. Most winemakers source grapes from myriad vineyards, even if they're owners. One might say collaborative instincts begin with the dirt.

At least in theory, an urban winemaker has a little insulation from the vicissitudes of farming. But urban winemakers source almost all of their fruit away from where wine production occurs. No matter how often one goes to contract sources to coddle vines, the reality is just like urban contours. You have to invent everything.

Perspectives: Pinot Gris 101

Pinot Gris has an identifiable pedigree dating to the late fourteenth century, having emigrated from Burgundy, where its sibling Pinot Noir became the varietal of choice. It wasn't until 2005, when two UC-Davis researchers mapped the DNA, that Pinot Gris was revealed to be a mutation of Pinot Noir, to which its molecular profile is a near match.

As with so many discoveries, the urban legends go on. Dick Erath pointed out that the "gray" of the gris owes as much to monastic fashion as to the color of the skins. Those Franciscans who early cultivated this varietal wore gray robes. And Pinot Gris with its mendicants took to the road toward Switzerland and into Germany's Palatine. It also became in time a go-to grape in Alsace. Here the varietal's hang time is long, and the ripening clusters develop body and a mouth-filling sweetness that is distinct but not syrupy or cloying. It soon migrated to northeastern Italy, as in Friuli, acquiring a wonderful character of acidity married to the pleasing color of light straw. Its name derives from the root *pinot* as in "pine cone" and *grigio* as in "gray," or *gris* as in *éminence grise*. It remains widely popular.

The New World from Australia to Mendoza is filled with vines of Pinot Gris, as it is a wine that can enter the market early, with far less time after fermentation compared to oak-and-butter Chardonnay to make it onto wine lists and retail shelves. More than half a dozen states in the United States have Pinot Grigio or Pinot Gris on the vine, including California, Idaho, Michigan, New Jersey, Oregon, Virginia and Washington. California calls its more acidic output "Grigio," as Italy does, whereas the mid-bodied Oregon varietal remains "Gris." The grape's European travels moved into the Balkans as well, ending up in the Ukraine on the shores of the Black Sea. Chinese Pinot Gris? The twelfth-century roads to old Cathay eventually landed in modern China where, it seems, everything but oxygen has gone to be re-engineered more cheaply.

As noted, we owe David Lett, Oregon pioneer, the credit for planting cuttings of Pinot Gris in 1965. Many years later, in 1991, King Estate Winery championed the varietal, capitalizing on the wine's rapid track to market. Readers can quickly grasp what new and exciting times we live in with respect to developments in the regional wine industry. Pinot Gris is still a kid here. If you pick up Eyrie's Pinot Gris, for instance, you pick up Jason Lett's obeisance to his father's early planting.

———❖———

CHAPTER 17

"WINE COUNTRY" IS A COMPOUND NOUN

Historian Garry Wills ended a 2005 book about Henry Adams—diplomat, gadfly, historian and WASP extraordinaire—with the comment that the family farmer of the colonial nation (and to this day) provided the moral center in American life as if sacred. The point interests us because in the year 1800, 6 million farmers populated the United States, 20 percent of all. Today, there are still 6 million farmers in a nation ten times more populous, and Wills included agribusiness under this halo.

Readers need to keep this respect for the land in mind. The land is good, and its fruits reward care, labor and good stewardship. What is in the bottle retains this authority of nature and its spirit. If this sounds romantic in the nineteenth-century sense of the term, so be it.

I think at some level we like the country air, the dirt, the vines and the absence of mindless buzz other than a few honeybees. It is pastoral more in imaginings than in reality, but the scene offers a break. Although I cast some shadows about in comparing winelands of the West, I remain a fan of what strikes me as balance between the commercial and practical demands with handling vines and their abundance. Despite Buncombe and drive-by tastings, keep in mind the fleeting footfalls of Lewis and Clark and the boundless optimism of pioneers picking up and moving with the frontier wherever it lured them next.

Willamette Valley is the largest and one of the three original AVAs assigned in the state. Localized even more, "wine country" means SR 99W in the middle of Dundee, about twenty-eight miles away from Portland. I offer this rhetorical refreshment to illustrate that "Willamette Valley" stands in for the whole Oregon wine enchilada. This sleight of hand allows me to tell some stories here that

Ted Casteel has Robert Casteel on his back while he harvests the first grapes to be produced at Bethel Heights Vineyard, located in the Eola Amity Hills in Oregon. *Courtesy of Bethel Heights Vineyard, Jereld R. Nicholson Library, Linfield College, McMinnville, Oregon. Courtesy of Pat Dudley, 2014.*

represent the wine industry as a whole, without rewriting the *Rerum Natura* of Livy, thus letting some parts stand for the whole. From these one can sally into the charms and range of more than seven hundred wineries in the state.

LOST IN PARADISE, OR, NAPA REDUX

In 1994, John Berendt published his novel *Midnight in the Garden of Good and Evil*, a screaming success. He followed in 2005 with the nonfiction work *The City of Falling Angels*. The fiction occurs in and around Savannah, Georgia, the nonfiction in Venice—not the one in California. Berendt commented that these settings, though distant in GPS terms, had something in common: "Both are isolated. Both are inward looking. Both turn on tradition. Both have a deep sense of place."

These stories both describe the frisson of good intentions contesting with unsavory ones. The sense of place was violated. I think something akin to such a conflict occurred within Napa Valley, a victim of its own remarkable rise.

From my first of thirty-plus visits, Napa was synonymous with "wine country," even if it represented a relatively small pile of dirt and grapes. Today, more than four hundred wineries and growers operate there, and for years, only Disneyland lured more visitors. Yet about twenty years ago, the passion and informality that seemed to highlight wines made with artisanal and regional pride became sullied in the muck of celebrity and impudent money.

What really happened was this: Napa Valley winemakers started going for the gold, the high score rating, and believed their own press far too much. Some wineries lost their institutional focus and sense of place. Any billionaire bozo could buy a winery, and some did. Tradition went the way of rabbit-ear antennae and the wall telephone in Mom's kitchen. But the lost focus slowly returned, and if one looks around, one sees that it really never left us. "Don't cry for me, Pasadena."

So what follows pours a little of my heart into a fine glass filled with wines that kept the faith while navigating reef-strewn channels of the lives of the rich and famous. To put it another way, this chapter looks at how Oregon wine pioneers, like teens eager to assert their independence from parents, sought to escape from what literary minds call the "anxiety of influence." *Plus ça change.*

The historical reality, as this book has variously shown, is that agriculturally endowed Oregon had a wine industry, including a notable fruit wine boom. But it took a longer while to separate the psychological reality from the heavy blanket of California's much larger and less regulated wine industry.

Perhaps propriety insists that we tour a little of Oregon's wine country with an express appreciation of Napa Valley wine lands. Oregon's contemporary wine situation and its commercial ecology owe much to California winemaking, both by its example and by reacting to it. Space and the limits of my mobility do not allow me to exhaust the wineries of Oregon, so a few will have to do. Although in the early pages of this book California wine culture is taken to the woodshed, fairness to its inspired examples dictate that we offer just praise. Wine orbits a shining sun of traditions honored.

When California wine culture faltered, it lost sight of traditions that informed its achievements. Readers should consider that my Oregon wine stories represent traditions in progress, and the health of the industry and the fruits of labor produced by many depend on maintaining traditions and, by doing so, keeping the stories alive.

Between 1973 and the early twenty-first century, my business and pleasure travels brought me to the "California wine country" about three dozen times. Then, after a hiatus of five or six years, I went again in 2009 for a wine magazine.

I was stunned. The whole place seemed transformed, as if I had over the years been visiting some other parallel universe. What I saw in 2008–9 was a very different place—a crowded amusement park for well-heeled, name-dropping and cash-impudent Californians. The rustic amenities I once fondly recalled now seemed all tonied up. The once pricey wines of thirty-five dollars now were not pricey enough at eighty dollars. The demand drove a belief in success, American-style.

As this occurred, I renewed my visits to Oregon, a quarter century after my first visit, and experienced what I felt lacking in California, which also was to lack yours truly.

Americans love success and then feel guilty about it. Worse, we take great pleasure in observing the falling away from it—especially when the ruin is owned by the next guy. Napa Valley seemed to this writer to have undergone such a dubious transformation. Too much ego and not enough distinctive wine to support the self-adulation. The value proposition was not in the bottle but in the "experience" of the bottle. Imagine going to the dentist. You don't go for the "experience"; you go because your movie-magic smile is marred by a broken crown. So it seemed that Napa Valley broke a tooth.

The watershed year was 1993 in the run-up to the bursting of the Internet bubble, when Bubba was president and "Stand by Your Man" was just a song. That year, Robert Mondavi, visionary owner of one of the nation's great wineries, decided to take his enterprise public, raising $500 million in equity. What happened, though, was not pretty: the company's closely managed family

Boys and men shovel soil and use pickaxes next to Bonded Winery no. 7, located in Douglas County, Oregon. *Jereld R. Nicholson Library, Linfield College, McMinnville, Oregon. Courtesy of Shelley and Mike Wetherell, 2013.*

A man stands next to a wine vat that is being used to bottle wine before mobile bottling lines made the job easier. *Jereld R. Nicholson Library, Linfield College, McMinnville, Oregon. Courtesy of Shelley and Mike Wetherell, 2013.*

grew very rich overnight and soon enough were mired in poor decision making that ultimately led to selling off the whole name and repute to a bigger firm, Constellation Brands, for $1.36 billion. So the rich got richer and the tough old scion passed into history, if not beloved then surely admired for his success. (We will look at this corporate exemplum in a bit more detail later.)

The lesson was simple: a closely held business can bury its internal conflicts, but a public company is naked once each quarter. This outcome was further complicated by a kind of corruption of the spirit of the place, the vineyard. The wine lost its institutional memory—that is, what made Mondavi wines so compelling in the years shortly following the 1966 opening of its Oakville landmark went missing. And the wine became ho-hum. And the market makers, Goldman Sachs, got away with this travesty. They had oodles of money and not a thimble full of the passion that once made this a great brand. They were too busy being rich and famous to notice the toothache. The wine today has found new direction, but it won't be the same as once it was.

This impression seemed to sum up Napa Valley wines as less an expression of the life in the landscape than its lifestyle. Happily, the news has gotten far better. Napa Valley, if once lost, is again found. It cannot return little homes on the valley floor to four-figure mortgages, but it can assert the peculiar genius of the place to produce wines worth celebrating. Too many seemed to have lost sight of the fact that this is agriculture, not a place for sports celebrities to park their millions. And this is good news.

Two wineries that maintain their institutional memory reward us for knowing where to look.

The late Joe Phelps built his premier winery on a St. Helena slope. Joseph Phelps Vineyards had started producing by the time I first came up the I-5 in the early '70s. The main estate of six hundred acres is largely in trust, a perpetual resource protected from developers, heirs and well-meaning politicians. (Not!) The original winery building, designed by the architect John Marsh Davis, was completely reinvented to retain its harmonious place in the landscape and provide a staging area for the wines. The winery is home to a first-class Sauvignon Blanc. But it is primarily the source of the Phelps Cabernet Sauvignons that strive to the pinnacle of the Insignia blend. At $240 retail, the latter wine isn't for leftovers. Its most recent vintage, 2012, is elegant and vigorous, worthy of age and worthy of its owners' legacies. Pricey, yes, but at an event horizon where the value and quality intersect. It is first-class from first pass to finish, a worthy iteration of a wine first produced in 1974.

Down the Silverado Trail and off State Route 121 is Tulocay Winery. The skipper is Bill Cadman; his assistant winemaker is daughter Brie. These two are further encouraged by their companion, Buddy the dog, and various hands. The website promises to send shipments to the nearest intersection for wine club members who live in their car. It is as down-to-earth a winery as Phelps is ethereal.

Cadman started his business in 1975, although he moonlighted for the Mondavi Winery until 1999. His approach to winemaking is all about making wines with the guts to express their varietals, whether his two present Chardonnays or his Cabernet Sauvignon. He originally sourced this wine from vine rows in the Stags Leap District, close to the Phelps property. Where Phelps produces more than 50,000 cases—an industrial scale in relative terms—Tulocay produces fewer than 2,000. There is enough, then, to go around if you know what you're looking for, and the consumer pays far less to enter this little slice of paradise. But money matters less where results speak most to the pleasure of it. Namely, two wine companies that didn't let success go to their teeth. They preserved their institutional memories by continuing traditions to which they once aspired.

Boosters of the "wine country" may predictably take umbrage. There have been excellent wines coming out of Napa and Sonoma for decades. However, when I mention a brand in mixed company, responses tend to yawns. Someone in the group will recommend a wine no one else has encountered or even heard about. I attribute this to market clutter—too many options but few distinctive ones. Second, too much hype. But the most telling is an absence of tradition that connects one family to one brand and one slice of the landscape. Rather, the fluidity of land grabs and consulting winemakers and oenologists tends to ensure well-made wines that like the well-made plays of the Scribe two centuries ago have long since gone into the corners of darkened theaters. We don't remember what's-his-face or his wines. The tradition is subsumed by the idols of the market—the media awards, the point ratings, the obscene prices and celeb nameplates—instead of the measured and respectful handling of land and the rituals of the table.

Although some will demur, I stand by the claim that without an institutional memory, winemaking and buying are senile. It's grand to recover this memory of what made the effort worthwhile once upon a time; it is, however, far better to share in traditions not inundated by tides of fashion and self-regard. Indeed, I submit that for all of the present notice, the winemakers of Oregon work to establish tradition so as to measure and preserve their accomplishments.

So, return to the parable of the Hebrew and the Himalayan—place and timing is all. Oregon's wine industry is teetering on the edge of that moment when it can still build on its beginnings and evolving traditions.

As you visit Oregon tasting rooms, often so cozy and welcoming, remember the return to Napa. Will the wines you drink and the stories in the glass reveal the union of nature with dedicated skill? Or will you be an alien visitor on a planet populated by cheery Stepford wines appearing to be the real thing? Context is the special ingredient in an Oregon wine. It's not just an iPhone picture. It's place.

NOT RODEO DRIVE BUT WORDEN HILL ROAD

A right turn off Oregon state road SR99 will put you on local Ninth Street in Newberg and then on to Worden Hill. A few years ago, the last mile or so to its terminus at State Road 240 was gravel. Now it's paved, and rather than listening to stone-thumping sprays of gravel on metal, you can take the curves and the view with attention where due.

Worden Hill Road is home to a number of fine wineries, and the flow of traffic will suggest to visitors that there are good reasons to follow it. Along the way to the one intersection of consequence in Dundee, you will encounter, among others, Panther Creek Cellars, Four Graces (where I fell in love once), Wine by Joe, Chapter 24, Argyle Winery (where I also fell in love once), the Ponzi Vineyards tasting room and trattoria and the area tasting room for Zerba, with its wine barrel furniture for sale if you haven't bought too much of its wine, sourced from its upriver Walla Walla farms on the Oregon side of the state line. The Zerba tasting room is cast against type, since its reds are sourced from Bordeaux varietals such as Cabernet Sauvignon or blends with bright, layered flavors. Zerba stands right in the middle of Pinot Noir heaven.

Here above is the estate home of the wine country pioneer Dick Erath, surrounded by thirty-five acres of Pinot Noir vines. Dick and Susie are grape veterans who spend more time now on pet projects. Winemakers and growers both, they survey the Willamette Valley from a prime perspective. Although they have sold this prime Pinot Noir vineyard to Silver Oak of California, they can still enjoy their view. For that matter, contiguous neighbors Tom Fitzpatrick (Élevée) and Mo Ayoub (Ayoub) can share the view if not the sales proceeds.

Along this view, visitors will find Domaine Roi et Fils, Winderlea Winery, Maresh Red Barn, Alexana Winery and the esteemed growers at Abbey Ridge. Upslope right is the Utz family's Black Walnut Inn, a Tuscan villa of

Pat Dudley pours a glass of wine for her sister-in-law, Marilyn Webb. The four co-owners of Bethel Heights Vineyard pose together for a celebratory photograph. *From left to right*: Pat Dudley, Ted Casteel, Marilyn Webb and Terry Casteel. *Bethel Heights Vineyard Collection, Jereld R. Nicholson Library, Linfield College, McMinnville, Oregon. Courtesy of Pat Dudley, 2014.*

Dick Ponzi works in the winery. Ponzi is co-founder and winemaker at Ponzi Vineyards in Sherwood, Oregon. *Doc Wilson Collection, Jereld R. Nicholson Library, Linfield College, McMinnville, Oregon. Courtesy of Doc Wilson, 2015.*

Roland Solles (*right*), winemaker at Argyle and owner of Roco Wines. *Courtesy of Doc Wilson.*

immense comfort and refinement, overseeing regiments of Pinot Noir vines in stately procession. Hollywood money has scarfed this property down at this writing, so hurry along.

This is the kind of dirt wine growers sift through their fingers like bullion, if people do such things. This is Jory soil, an iron-rich clay more red than brown, leavened by alluvial soil full of fossils and minerals deposited by ancient floods that shaped the hillsides and plains, dug the Columbia River trench and still allowed in time for the invention of wine country tourism. Elevation (450 to 700 feet above sea level) and favorable sub attitudes make this a compact example of the Dundee Hills AVA—superb color, brisk aromatics, harmonious balance and fine finishes once poured from bottle to glass to happy mouth. The land encourages a style of winemaking that rewards complex, layered varietals and is justly prized.

Although the pages following will note wines from recent vintages, the nature of the printed word—even with our post-Gutenberg ethos—means that these vintage years go into libraries at wineries, private collections and restaurant select lists. So, reader, please work from the winery, its maker and the available vintages. If your instincts for research match your patience and wallet, perhaps you can experience a wine as mentioned here, albeit at a different time and place. In a way, despite claims made in earlier chapters, sometimes one settles on a vintage that by custom and law is absolute and yet also indeed relative and a result of what's available.

The wine tells a story; trust that story and not the ones experts command that you trust. A wine label, too, is veracity impaired on the reverse side. Run away from wine descriptions that talk of "state of the art," "hand-crafted," "award-winning team," "gold medalist" and the rest of the ubiquitous weasel phrases. In a career described by its snafus as much as by its evanescent victories, this writer has come to distrust most of all a wine that "will exceed expectations." "I was adored once too," the forlorn Sir Andrew Aguecheek confesses. Enjoy the pour and skip the propaganda. As D.H. Lawrence averred, "Never trust the artist. Trust the tale." If you believe in the wine poured, you hardly require the crutch of oxygenated adjectives any more than numeric ratings.

Just south of the Ninth Street intersection on 99, you will shortly arrive at Domaine Drouhin, Domaine Serene, Archery Summit, Stoller and Sokol Blosser, among many, to name some of the prized and industry-involved wine companies. And we have not driven many more than sixty minutes from downtown Portland. The transition is as dramatic as it is convenient. A veteran of Napa, Sonoma or Lodi will discover myriad wines at the remove of a few backyards.

Few places conspire to wile away the time as does Worden Hill Road.

In addition to the aforementioned wineries, visit Maresh Red Barn, one of the pioneer testing grounds for viticulture in this AVA. Near the junction with SR 240, Alexana will dazzle you with its myriad Pinot Noir blocks—nine different ones—on the property. Each has its own peculiarity, and the differences between one block and its neighbor will demonstrate how Pinot Noir can behave within a near space of different elevations, soils and exposures. The love-child of a Houston-based surgeon, Alexana has a parallel universe in Argentina's Mendoza province, producing pricey, gorgeous Malbecs and other blends.

Tom Fitzpatrick serves as GM at Alloro Vineyards in the Chehalem AVA (Sherwood). Note the qualitative differences between the Alloro wines—more minerality and lean (svelte)—and his own Dundee Hills Élevée wines, with their brighter fruit and potentially forever finishes. "Wine is a compound," he said, "the ingredients are grapes, people, and time," adding that the special character of Oregon wine derives from a "small is beautiful" way of life—hands-on, high touch and down to scale.

On the opposite side of Worden Hill stands Winderlea Wine, the gemstone of Donna Morris and Bill Sweat. Their take on Pinot Noir sourced from a handful of estate and related vineyards summon up wines of beautiful scents and textures. The view southwest over the property will live in your head nearly as much as the memory of the wines.

THREE VIRTUES

Here are what I consider the cardinal virtues of the wine land in Oregon, as articulated by the people tending the vines and making the wine:

- collaborative cat herding
- plenitude as organized chaos
- the building of traditions

I will visit and by inference recommend some winemakers and wine brands that exhibit these impulses and traits. These exemplify the attitudes in circulation in the expanding story of Oregon wines. I offer them as starting places in the context I have created in the preceding sentences. These suggestions derive from my observations about Oregon wine accumulated by design and haphazardly for more than thirty years. Use what you can and leave the rest.

"Collaborative cat herding" describes how wine industry pioneers and those since comport themselves. Competition is leavened by a genuine regard for what the grower over the hill is up to. Many a notable in wine lore has had a cameo in another person's wine. RJ Lint of Plum Hill Vineyards recalled how a neighbor vintner, informed of something amiss in Lint's acreage, dropped his activities to help Lint solve his winemaking obstacle. Dick Erath, more than a decade past the sale of his brand to Chateau Ste. Michelle, took part in helping out Dave Rasmussen at Purple Cow in herding a few cats at the assemblage stage. As Dick and Nancy Ponzi remembered at the founders' celebration in 2015, described earlier in this book, the impulse to help others starting Oregon wine industry came about with alacrity in part to prove to skeptics that the state would produce first-rate wines. Consumer acceptance just reinforced the determination to wow the flat-worlders.

Nonetheless, readers ought to avoid the tendency to believe everything told to them. The prevailing mythology begins with the pioneers, who proved starting fifty years ago that the experts got it wrong. Yes, there were many flubs in the vineland—expensive equipment did not work as advertised or worked too well. Ken Wright described having to reverse his decision to automate stemming with a costly French machine that was *too* efficient at a critical point in his winemaking.

There were yards that did not like certain plantings. Forest blazes in southern Oregon literally smoked some vintages, with the perverse result that consumers and critics like the wines. Ask the folks at Troon Vineyard,

The Bethel Heights Vineyard owners pose in front of their sign, located toward the front of their property in the Eola Amity Hills in Oregon. *From left to right*: Terry Casteel, Ted Casteel, Marilyn Webb and Pat Dudley. *Bethel Heights Vineyard Collection, Jereld R. Nicholson Library, Linfield College, McMinnville, Oregon. Courtesy of Pat Dudley, 2014.*

which has a tasting room in downtown Carlton. Although mishaps are endemic to new ventures especially, we should remember that the Drouhin family of Burgundy planted vines and opened a castellated winery in Dundee in 1987–88 to good effect. This is Joseph Drouhin. With Gallic élan and insouciance, his storied Burgundy wine property settled in Dundee Hills, inspiring two decades of French investment in Oregon's prime Pinot Noir vine land. The wines produced by these colonizing winemakers show their pedigrees, but they have accomplished a translation that remains very good wine made in Oregon. It pays a great compliment to Oregon, like that lady on Liberty Island in New York Harbor, a large hostess gift from France to America.

Investment has its hairy underbelly. The California corporate wine supermarketer Kendall-Jackson had the effrontery to purchase Oregon wine land as if it were coming off the shelf at Costco. Here the effect is not yet known. California imprint La Crema introduced Pinot Noir from Oregon a few years ago; in addition to its acreage appetite, it has since acquired Penner-Ashe and Willakensie. No amount of flak-yak can make this cynical optimist imagine that everything will change but the views from the tasting rooms—splendid—until recycled as water parks and homeless shelters.

Then we have John Olson of TeSóAria in Roseburg and Medford explaining how he came to Oregon looking for something to do and with a friend drank himself into a mild stupor that ended with buying a vineyard and a winery. This constitutes part of the folklore circulating among the denizens of the state's wine industry. Sheila and Bill Blakeslee of Blakeslee Vineyard Estate in Sherwood noted that they bought a beautiful wine property only to discover they were in the wine business. Oops! Do not be deterred. The wines, like their surroundings, show beautifully. Similarly, the owners of Seven Sails sailed into the wine business by being less than prepared for all of the curves in the road. The view is grand, as noted, and the wine helps to explain that wishing for a winery is also a wish for scads of paperwork even prior to trying to sell what one makes. In a continuously evolving industry short on precedent, it soon dawns on the enthusiast that there is no end to the work around the romance of the vines.

So, remember that the self-deprecations cover for a great deal of hard work, reinvestment of capital and collaborative cat herding where the terroir is nearly as fickle as the drinking public. It makes for good copy, and beneath the funny anecdotes lie veins of high esteem for the land from one corner of Oregon to its extent. For the many reversals of fortune there is, at the end, the pleasure of the sip, the well-laid table and those happy cats. One example suffices.

Marilyn Webb of the Salem-based Bethel Heights took me out into the vineyard after I tasted Pinot Noir from two blocks. Designated East Block and Southeast Block, these vines are separated by about the width of a tractor axle. And yet each is remarkably distinct. Webb said, "Now imagine if these two blocks were even closer, would they taste this differently?" The variations of varietals that are nominally identical is an astounding characteristic of grapes grown here. Indeed, differences can be appreciated elsewhere in the wine world, but Oregon makes the point that terroir can be a matter of a few feet. Elsewhere in Willamette Valley, the two gentle slopes of Patton Valley Pinot Noir fruit grow on slight angles looking toward the Chehalem Mountains. They, too, make a complement of differences measured by the yard. Youngberg Hill Vineyards in the southern reaches of the McMinnville AVA grows fruit on two levels of land about six and eight hundred feet above sea level. The altitude is in the wine, and even persons new to the Baileys' property will note the variations. In other words, micro differences matter, and Oregon winemakers like to accentuate these permutations.

There are several other details to illustrate the folklore that reinforce the notion that hard work is the ground bass of vineyard practice. Bob

Aerial view of Youngberg Hill Vineyards in McMinnville. *Courtesy of Carl Giavanti.*

McRitchie of McRitchie Winery and Ciderworks followed Bill and Susan Sokol Blosser to Oregon, he recalled over a burger and brew at a McMinnville eatery. "I came up here to help out some friends. What did I know about wine? I was trained in the natural sciences. I could tell you about the sex life of a flatworm, but not about making wine." Well, he did produce some wine, and that collaborative effort contributed to the Sokol Blosser brand, earning some serious respect among the cadre of experts who also recognized the rise of the pioneers from adventurers to a coming force in the national wine scene.

Likewise, Trudy and Keith Kramer put aside the mortar and pestle of pharmacy to plant their first vines in the mid-'80s, with Kramer Vineyards opening for real in 1990. So, they are in a midpoint in the evolution of the Oregon industry and remain for me one of the favorite wineries in the state. As readers recognize, the Kramers came from an applied science. Their founder predecessors were often engineers—builders of ideas—like Erath, Ponzi and Harry Peterson-Nedry. Joe Campbell, MD, continued to practice medicine as he and wife Pat built Elk Cove. Only Myron Redford, who sold Amity Vineyards in 2014, was considered a displaced hippie rather than a refugee from applied technologies. In the more recent generation of winemakers, like John Olson and Dave Rasmussen, the change to

Doc, the author and Bob McRitchie, winemaker in the early days of Sokol Blosser Winery. *Courtesy of Doc Wilson.*

winemaking came from their respective careers in the inimical enterprise of construction and development (read "destruction and envelopment"). Jim Maresh really was growing his cherries and plums at the time when he was urged to plant vines.

There are some tales also beyond stringing garden hoses. David Lett, late of Eyrie Vineyards, could be witnessed chasing birds away by pretending his cane was a gun. Dean Fisher translated his army experience into building a de-stemmer and conveyor from scratch for his Gaston ADEA brand. The Ponzis still regard with affection their improvised wine press, prominently on display at Sherwood. Honeywood still displays funky wine bottles from the 1940s; the Oregon Wine History Project can pull out a genuine Knudsen-Erath bottle—drained of contents—from its archive. The examples abound.

The contests and improvisations go on. Lett pretending a cane would serve when the propane gun used to scare feathered predators ran out of propane; Shuhe Hawkins and Kate Larsen going after gophers on their Portland hillock; Monroe chasing stolen wine barrels using Craigslist; and Ryan Sharp transforming secondary fermentation snafu into a Sangria brand.

But lest we become too glum, the story has an upside. *Down to Earth* is the name of the environmentally correct newsletter issued online by the California Wine Institute. Not only has this industry association been of

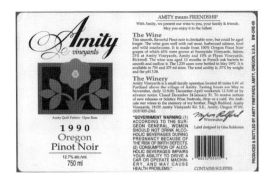

Left: This wine label from Amity Vineyards describes its 1990 Oregon Pinot Noir. Designed by Lisa Rahkonen, the label features an Amity quilt pattern (Open Rose). *Courtesy of Amity Vineyards and Myron Redford.*

Middle: Myron Redford poses near wine barrels. *Courtesy of Amity Vineyards and Myron Redford.*

Bottom: Myron and Vicki Redford and the author. *Courtesy of Doc Wilson.*

217

Jim Maresh explains how he gave up growing cherries to grow wine grapes. *Courtesy of Jonathan Potkin.*

help to me for various research in my editorial and writing duties, but it also points up significant distinctions between California and Oregon.

Environmental considerations are not new. But only last year did the Wine Institute start an awards program. In my column for *California Homes*, I recently wondered aloud what took so long to promote this aspect of wine land management. Dave Paige of Adelsheim in Dundee, who migrated from Jekel Vineyards of Monterey, California, thinks that the California wine industry uses the buddy-to-nature trope for marketing but is glad the industry is giving the uses of land another look: "I think in Oregon we just take for granted that caring for the environment sustaining the vines is as important as tending the vines." This is one difference worth noting since it now appears practices in both states are more consonant.

Here is another difference: despite boasting more than four thousand vineyards and wineries—just think, once-sleepy Lodi AVA has more than one hundred thousand acres planted!—the Golden State is not dilatory in crunching numbers. Annual harvest figures come out swiftly given the size of the market.

One might think reasonably that a state one-tenth the size in terms of population alone could count its harvests with dispatch as well. But that

David Lett tastes wine at the Eyrie Vineyards winery in McMinnville, Oregon. Tom Ballard took the photo for an article in the *News-Register. Courtesy of the Eyrie Vineyards and Jason Lett.*

would make sense. Oregon's pace is languid by comparison. You can thank the Oregon Liquor Control Commission in part for that difference. Oregon wine production contends with an additional layer of government regulation, a self-sustaining bastion of exceptions nonexistent in the Golden State and recently jettisoned in neighboring Washington State. Sleepy tonnage reporting seems one way to manage cash flow. For pecuniary reasons, too, every grape before and after fermentation is *pro-rata* justification for some entity to claim its share of value. (For this reason alone, expect the alcohol content reported on wine labels to shave a little; it is common practice and is frowned on with a winking eye.) Nonetheless, with the absence of a liquor authority, the states above and below Oregon seem to trade off some orderliness and price stability for the dynamism of the market forces at work. I note this difference without prejudice, but you will sense that Oregon winemakers will put up with the requirements until the law changes. And this eventuality is possible. Still, the proliferation of wineries in Oregon since I began writing this work—from 452 to 720 in three years—can be credited at least in part to the foundation of state-imposed controls, especially the COD requirements that support new enterprises emerging from vineyards.

In addition to the distinctions just noted, California has taken to sustainable vineyard practices with gusto, having discovered that consumers pay attention to how the winery operations integrate with what I call the commercial ecology of a place.

For thousands of years in thousands of places separated by natural and political boundaries and customs, wine was made with a feel for what would do to produce good product. We have benefited from the scientific revolutions that allow us to note and understand winemaking on the molecular level. For historical reasons dating to the earliest twentieth century, California has taken a lead in this applied research, and its progeny now exists in Oregon as well. Call it left brain wine science.

Likewise, wine knowledge to the nth remove teaches us in rational terms what was once intuitively, if less precisely, measured. No decimal point can by itself express the way broiled prawns with spicy apricot chutney pair well with a dry Riesling or Pinot Noir Blanc, even as such a technicality will point us in the right direction. Winemaker notes can inform, but taste memory ultimately remains a sit-ups or listening to motivational speakers.

Thus, I consider Californians' rediscovery of wine country as more than its value as real estate both welcome and exciting. It represents a reframing of attitudes worthy of a great agricultural economy. We ought to recall Byron Dooley's thirty-one varietals planted on his Yamhill-Carlton acreage—science applied minus the spirit of the artisan makes for dull drinking. Luminous Cellars advises that Byron is having fun. And Mme. Mad Scientist makes chocolates sold to pair with the wine, sold out of the same tasting room. And while here, drop in next door at Stone Griffon for Terry's Tempranillo.

Oregon, for reasons as salutary as they are unclear, has instinctively managed land use with far more grace and certainly far less hoopla. Its success derives, in part, from the "escape from Disneyland" impulses of people like the Sokol Blossers, tooling around in their Cheech and Chong VW camper, seeking to express a counter view to the wine business in place that made jug wine the go-to beverage of the masses in the 1950s and '60s before the fine wine culture gained traction. In this regard, Oregon has herded its own cats with an eye on the impact of their labors.

The *Down to Earth* newsletter, recently inaugurated in the Golden State, reminds us that our appreciation of wine today owes much to both states for

The founding members of the Yamhill County Wineries Association raise their glasses in a toast for a publicity photograph for the first "Thanksgiving Weekend in Wine Country." *Front row, left to right, kneeling*: Joe Campbell of Elk Cove Winery and David Adelsheim of Adelsheim Vineyard. *Back row, standing, left to right*: Bill Blosser of Sokol Blosser Winery, Don Byard of Hidden Springs, Myron Redford of Amity Vineyards, Dick Erath of Erath Vineyards, Fred Arterberry of Arterberry Winery, Fred Benoit of Chateau Benoit and David Lett of the Eyrie Vineyards. *Courtesy of Sokol Blosser Winery and Susan Sokol Blosser.*

doing the right thing. The Oregon growth limits passed in 1973 tossed a gauntlet that its southern neighbor has at last picked up.

But collectivist tendencies designed to encourage collegiality have an unintended effect. The shared crush facilities carry the me-too virus. Don't get me wrong. The Carlton Winemakers Studio is one of those places worth visiting on any oeno-tour. The issue comes down to money and its logistics. A man or woman passionate about making wine may not come from banking or software millions. The custom crush can squeeze out the personality of a wine because there exists a disconnect between the land and its expressive varietals.

Collegiality doesn't force an orthodoxy; however, the proximity of winemakers sharing the same sandbox leads to a certain overlap because the facilities are levelers of technique. So, if winemakers make wines for others or operate in the same locale, the inevitability of some likenesses may be attributed to the shared production itself.

To see how the custom crush venues work, visit one, such as the aforementioned Carlton Winemakers Studio, co-founded by Eric Hamacher, or Urban Crush in PDX or Day Camp in Dundee to experience the vibe.

Its very organizing principles seem at variance with a winemaker who tends his own vines and makes the wines out there, just over that hedgerow in the shed with the weather vane.

At Analemma Wines in Mosier or Purple Cow Vineyards in McMinnville, for example, the entry into a place that one could nurture came out of satellite mapping in one instance and home-building development—my private Antichrist—paired with a sense of purpose that to do it right one needed to personally manage the vineyards as well as the winemaking. Fortunately, many have been able to realize this outcome. It depends on luck—like inheriting your great-grandfather's filbert farm and vineyard—or a lot of money.

Still, many others work from a relative distance that can too easily enable the phone-in winemaker. As you swirl your Chardonnay by the pool, you may be surprised to learn that your wine may come from there—but the grapes came from here and there and the winemaker from several other simultaneous points of call. As Gertrude Stein mused, there may in the end be no *there* there. Readers can assess and assume this risk because the market has become saturated. As in the "international" style of architecture once in fashion, the same designs on winemaking can produce capable wines without a zip code or underlying premise. It is as if Ray Kroc made the wine. Thus, provenance has much to contribute to your wine enjoyment and should not become obscured by ratings, cost or buzz. The land remains more important than as a background to a picture taken on your smartphone.

"Responsive" describes many Oregon wine people to the challenges posed by vineyard management and, later, making wine. But this characteristic might be better termed "reactionary," with practical rather than ideological overtones. It then follows that an Oregonian who is passionate about wine country—as two tandem nouns—is also conservative, again not ideologically but in the sense of seeking balance and harmony sustainable via intelligent use of resources, including the experience and wisdom of others who have trod, or continue to tread, similar paths.

In sum, the Oregon wine industry evolved its practices in contradiction to the force of the demand that produced industrial winemaking in California. My own marketing experience in the industry beginning forty years ago suggests that the Golden State was quite ahead of the nation in wine production, even before the world noticed its output and quality. So, Oregon had the benefit of standing on another's shoulders, even though it historically had been making wine too. Preserving the differences while incorporating accumulated wisdom seems the best way to ensure that Oregon wine keeps its pluck and also its respect for the land and the attention it requires.

CRAZY FOR PLENITUDE

In his 2007 book on Marco Polo, author Laurence Bergreen claimed that the thirteenth-century wanderer approached things not with the "goal-oriented, scientific" determination of an explorer. Rather, the extravagant merchant of Venice observed and reported firsthand, supplementing the tales with hearsay and testimony. This admixture has stood the test of centuries for its entertainment value and its overall accuracy.

Obsessions with goals, directions, commands and litmus test proofs are the confining mantras of the corporate state and, in no small measure, the wine industry. The fantastical, the awestruck need not apply. Of course, readers by now will find my sympathies more in line with Marco Polo, egregiousness notwithstanding, than Alfred P. Sloan or Henry Clay Frick.

In 1936, Arthur O. Lovejoy published a book called *The Great Chain of Being*, required reading for most of its eighty-year run for anyone studying Renaissance literature. It is a worthy tome on what is called the "history of ideas." One idea is plenitude—that is, the superabundance of all things made by God, which seems an impulse driven to fill every self-storage unit in the universe to capacity. It is a good book, and it calls attention, if not always explicitly, to the human revolution instigated by the introduction to Europe of movable type by Gutenberg around 1450.

Plenitude manifests itself not only by the remarkable rise of literacy but also by the commercial stimulus the book trade sustained. In England, still the land of our mother tongue despite options on automated phone systems, the idea of plenitude spilled over into writing, from drama to verse to narrative and tendentious prose, to all manner of fanciful expression. It was steroid language and at its best gave us our finest writer, himself funny, melancholy, prolix and as exuberant or violent as the subject at hand required. Earlier in this book, I drew readers' attention to Dick Ponzi's wine press since it replicates the device Gutenberg used to alter perception and move information by reframing the accepted use of the press, which was for making wine. A good engineer is also an artist.

So, the abundant potential of the West, though spurred by the rush for mineral wealth, had to begin with the promise of plenty. Indeed, the stories related about the far reaches of the continent advertised both cheap land and its potential for productive farms. More than its neighbor states, Oregon wine lands are managed within a very palpable and oft-visible variety of mutually sustaining agriculture. One soon comes to appreciate the farm-to-table and vine-to-table proximities.

How far our wine knowledge and taste memory have developed in the past half century can be measured in the range of grapes grown to produce single varietals based on such fruit newly introduced or brought out from assemblages to stand on their respective two feet.

The economics that drive winemaking often recommend making wine blends. A perusal of wine shop shelves in tasting rooms and other retail outlets—both brick-and-mortar and virtual—reveals many blends. They can be afterthoughts or, like Phelps's Insignia, an ensign hoisted each year as the bearer of traditions coming from a particular place.

Why drink blends? They are fun and quirky. The culinary equivalent is *le pot-au-feu*, the cauldron on the back burner that absorbs different items from diverse places to make anew. But the blend offers more as it helps the vineyard manager and winemaker to assess potential, to make Henry Luce's future calculus.

For the consumer, the advantages stand out. The wine may contain various grapes that combine to pleasant effect. I think of Troon's Druid's Fluid red blend or a Riesling made with Grüner Veltliner or a Sauvignon Blanc augmented by 15 percent Chardonnay so as to create something fresh and unpredictable. These are often opportunistic wines made with fruit suddenly more available and economically viable to produce. Consumers win because the varietals, if newly tried this way, may recommend themselves for other blends or freestanding wines. It is like building a fourplex or a single-family home. The purposes of shelter are served.

Some of my favorite varietal adventurers include Byron Dooley of Seven of Hearts in Carlton, Dave Rasmussen of Purple Cow in McMinnville and the Hip Chicks who do wine in Portland. Jacksonville and Roseburg produce perhaps 75 varietals on their lands, allowing visitors to traverse plenitudinous wines sporting grapes you have not heard about.

A skier considers the invitation of a Naked Winery billboard. *Courtesy of Naked Winery.*

Sometimes I feel as if I'm on the set with Colin Clive in the 1931 horror classic *Frankenstein*, where the mad doctor is campy and over the top because all of what is possible is also apparently grand fun. To these I would further add Naked Winery in Hood River, with its little prurient jokes attached to an

Catnip to oenophiles. *Courtesy of Naked Winery.*

army of different varietals, and Enso in Portland city limits. The kid with a new chemistry set is out there in the winery, all flashing eyes and floating hair.

Here are some of the oddball varietals you can find, chosen almost at random. We have, for instance, Chateau Lorane Marechal Foch from the vines near Medford. Once an intense varietal used for blending, and left to ripen overmuch by a bit, it produces a throaty wine with a full range of black cherry notes riding a long finish to an oak obligato. Well, that is winespeak at its worst, but the wine is great for an outdoor picnic.

Olson of TeSóAria sources another French émigré called Abouriou, which as a single varietal offers up a kind of half-chocolate and half-earthy rendition of what this *vin de pays* component demonstrates when asked to take a solo bow. Dave Rasmussen farms around Newberg, home of his winery, from fifteen acres in neighboring Banks. The new operation assumes the Kristin Hill Winery property, with an updated tasting room and nineteen recently acquired acres of white varietals to add to the present properties. Combination blends seem an instinctive response to possible outcomes canistered in oak for various lengths of time.

Rasmussen has a loyal cellar club. "They always want the new thing. They want to try out varietals that they have heard about in passing but not tasted.

I love figuring out how these usually unfamiliar grapes will do in my Oregon landscape." Like Olson, this is a vintner interested in the corresponding ways grapes behave in an Oregon terroir no matter their origins or provenance. As in Lovejoy's book, correspondences give significance to the overbearing stuff of Creation. So much so that Rasmussen has started a second label, Vintyr, to accentuate the blend of uncanny varietals, enlisting, among others, Dick Erath, who still likes to tinker in the cellar.

Like Rasmussen, Dooley has two labels—Luminous Hills is devoted to Pinot Noir and Seven of Hearts to the thirty varietals under his care. "I spent two years figuring out where to purchase land in the Yamhill-Carlton AVA that would support my obsession with all of these grapes of differing temperament," he said. "I love the challenge of assemblage. Blends intrigue me because they express the various possibilities of different grapes."

Dooley came out of California, and like many refugees, he thinks that for all of their many successes, California wines even when beautifully made lack "soul." Oregon is different, he pointed out. "We can go from one planet to another in stepping from one block to another in the same vineyard." His signature Ice Princess, a take on Eiswein, is shaping up at present writing with Viognier because it is such a rich and expressive fruit. The last one was made from other varietals. I love the chances to approach the same kind of wine with completely distinct varietals. It is great fun, even when others flee from the prospect of herding so many cats.

Imagine for a moment the twenty minutes of Act 2 of Puccini's *La Bohème*. Set before Café Momus, it epitomizes depicting a festive crowd without a wasted gesture or note. It is like a winemaker staging a blend of grapes. Now imagine Picasso's *Absinthe Drinker*, where no crowds or marching bands show up. It resembles a maker of wine like Ken Wright, who focuses on several varietals to acclaim for Pinot Noir or Chardonnay only, along with making each a rare and splendid thing. Both the bustle and the introspection rendered in music and on a canvas are fed by infinite variety.

If we're going to swallow all that artisanal stuff on wine labels, we may as well approach what it suggests through other arts when we savor the stuff in our glass. And so plenitude may be less crazy than it lets on.

We are not alone in making connections to other art—the Millers' tasting room in PDX is a gallery and music venue. At Tisaetum at Newberg in the Ribbon Ridge AVA, proprietor and winemaker James Frey adorns the tasting room with his canvases. A beaucoup-bucks health industry exit led his family happily ensconced in a tony, horse-trailed Orange County McMansion to seventeen beautiful acres in Oregon. His kids found life without Ferraris more amenable, so the Freys made a happy transition. The wine displays it. Here is a place where Riesling gets its due, as do blends, Chardonnay and Pinot Noir. Here are Californians who skipped out and left techno-glamor for Oregon dirt.

The neighboring seventeen acres in this ten-square-mile AVA is utopia, named for Thomas More's popular eponymous satire. *Utopos* in Greek means "nowhere." Erasmus Desiderius, More's Renaissance humanist buddy, was a Dutch cleric who was the Don Rickles of his day—in Latin. Perhaps the proprietor and winemaker, a happy exile from Silicon Valley, is proudly a Netherlander by heritage, and his contrasting styles of wines made in many respects like those of his neighbor celebrate the delicious contrasts of Oregon's plenitude.

THE TRADITION AT WORK

When England and France fought their hundred-year war that started eight centuries ago, the vines around the mouth of the Gironde were fields of contention. Trade went on between these nations even as monarchs and popes argued about who got the corner offices. Even then, France was the leading wine exporter in the known world, and its résumé stretched well back to antiquity. The tradition ran more deeply than roots reaching from the vines.

In our nanosecond culture, it appears that "tradition" establishes itself as an act of will rather than of time. I contend that hype managed to drive California wine prices beyond propriety while driving the wines away from the traditions that first made them so bold and honest.

What about Oregon? If readers follow along with my take, Oregon winemaking at a certain level intentionally departs from traditions and seeks to clear a path to assert an individual persona. But should we not also ask whether a nontraditional pose is itself a tradition of sorts? And if we answer in the affirmative, should we not also ask what kind of traditions will best serve the reputation of Oregon winemaking and allow the industry and its customers the ability to sustain and support these?

No single answer suffices. Nancy Ponzi, who was here when the industry began in earnest a half century ago, thinks the "tradition," if any, exists in its absence. "We make wine differently from how people did over the centuries," she said. "The technological changes are numerous." What she believes has gone missing is the "collaborative nature" of the business, the sense of camaraderie that she, husband Dick and family became accustomed to sharing with other wine pioneer families. "I think those days are gone," she noted, the change a consequence of success and also, with the proliferation of Oregon wineries, a result of having "too many cowboys" trying to make wine—an expression of money leading good sense.

David Barringer, former CEO of Naked Winery in Hood River (the winery was acquired by winemaker Peter Schneider and a group of private investors in December 2017), contended that the tradition in Oregon steers people to a "natural welcoming" requiring no pretense but rather a sense of adventurous curiosity. The "naked" part, past the teases, strips wine drinking to just the pleasure of the moment, he said. "I do think our tradition is tied to our sense of sustaining our environment as much as keeping our markets growing." The dynamic turns on the social aspects of drinking wine, he added, but focuses, for example, on packaging: "We have placed considerable effort on coming up with wine containers that are easy to ship, easy to open and readily accessible."

Drink easy, the wines seem to say, and the recyclable poly containers skip the reverential address of corks. A screw cap is not a nudge but a statement of intent to remove obstacles from the experiences wine offers. His company is not alone in taking the rites of wine away from people wearing dinner jackets. Oregonians like outdoor activities, and this may explain their perverse pleasure in living in a state where rain falls often. The Naked Winery portfolio is extensive, and it is no stranger to the campground, the patio or the verge. Perhaps this tradition offers a tip of the fig leaf to our primordial, Edenic forebears.

Two additions contrast the preceding. Dick Ponzi remarked during a recent telephone chat that the "tradition" is found in making the choice to grow and produce a difficult varietal in a difficult if multifaceted environment, such as Pinot Noir in the north-central Willamette Valley. "We wanted the challenge and took it up," he said, adding that the more proto-California terroirs of southern Oregon are less exacting, even as the wines are good to drink. "There are two Oregon wine countries that divide us in the north from our colleagues in the south. I think they have an easier time of it."

Surely, varietals in the measurably different AVAs of southern Oregon attest to vines of another stripe. A visitor to the farm at Cowhorn is in for a treat, but the feel of the place—a working farm that also plants vines—conveys more than different wines. Plenitude with a vengeance.

At last, Jason Lett summed up this tradition as a work in progress. "We are collaborators. I am continually astounded to know my fellow winemakers will provide advice and more if asked. We all have a stake in this industry in Oregon." He continued, "We aren't complacent, either. When we explore clones that we can best suit to our terroir, we take the matter very seriously and work through the implications surrounding what will become our wines. We are proactive." After a pause, he added, "You know, I am often accused of having too much fun for a winemaker."

At Eyrie Winery at the Granary District at McMinnville, one finds Jason Lett, winemaker and proprietor, holding up a street sign with Doc Wilson and the author, trying to hold himself in one place. *Doc Wilson Collection, Jereld R. Nicholson Library, Linfield College, McMinnville, Oregon. Courtesy of Doc Wilson, 2015.*

Well, are you? After another pause (here is, after all, a legatee to the founders of Oregon's repute and its wine industry): "Yes. A lot of fun."

Traditions take shape, I think, around the diversity of the landscape and its terroir across the state, with some nice stories surrounding them. For example, Jesus Guillén, the winemaker for White Rose, also has his own Guillén family brand. Guillén was a kid whose family immigrated to *El Norte* as seasonal workers in vineyards. He caught the bug, and his attainments are works in progress, an all-American Dream. Try the 2011 Alexis Pinot Noir if you can still find this small-output gem.

Of the now eighteen Oregon AVAs at this writing, I am most impressed by the variety of the three growing areas stretching along the Columbia River from Hood River in the Gorge through the Valley and on to Walla Walla on its Oregon side. There are two states astride this mighty flow, so much a part of our Manifest Destiny that you can taste it. Geologically and geographically, this scenery is tops, and the varietals aspire to express the rugged beauty of the landscape. This is a Thomas Cole painting writ in vines.

Even more than in the dominant Willamette Valley, the visitor along the big river will experience place in all of its guises. It will take some doing to get the culinary scene to match the wine, a facet of Willamette Valley that already enjoys farm-to-table proximity for pairings.

At last, it comes down to an intersection of the private truths of taste memory and the places of origin. If we can identify something we can surmise as traditions of the wine in Oregon, perhaps we need look no further than our reflection in the glass as the wine, catching the light, smiles at us like the liquid La Gioconda.

PERSPECTIVES: THE FIRES AND AFTER

As we near production on this book, the Eagle Creek fires in Oregon and the Napa/Sonoma wildfires in California have been put down. Nature reminds men and women that when the gods grow angry, no amount of good publicity does more than a used cigar butt, especially since national and local television coverage of these events as they happened distorted impressions to a great degree. (Readers, please forgive this anachronistic intrusion, but I think these recent events illustrate the oft-fragile balance between commerce and nature.)

Suffice it to say, the industry will come back and with an even better feel that we are stewards of land rather than its slave drivers. The lessons of biodynamic and sustainable farming with which Oregon winemakers and growers have led their compeers derives from a family and small farm ethos. This example will not be lost on our Golden State neighbors.

California overcame a *phylloxera* plague in the 1880s. It survived Prohibition a half century later. The fires, we hope, will stem the impulse to overplant vines in a compressed topography. Perhaps, too, given the rallied forces engaged in fire control, some newfound collegiality will stick, too.

California's agricultural footprint looks like Tom Hanks standing in one left behind by Godzilla. The heritage of settlement was a succession on Spanish land grants of great size. The agriculture lent itself to mega-farms, and this spilled over into its wine cultivation. This, surely, marks the signal distinction between the two states. Oregon lives out its dreams on a smaller scale.

Ed Fus, winemaker, heard from other Oregon vintners about plans to create an emergency contingent to coordinate resources in the event of a natural catastrophe such as what attacked Napa and Sonoma Counties. The example of what has occurred in that state's worst wild fire disaster has prompted in short order the recognition that the unthinkable can occur. Within ten days of these events, one gleans how Oregon's approach to land stewardship is a future calculation. And it is a natural evolution of farming still human in its proportions.

For whatever emotional and financial damage these fires of 2017 caused, both in California and Oregon, we might find something of a silver lining after the smoke clears, as Communications Director of the Oregon Wine Board Sally Murdoch observed:

> While many of us across the state are optimistic to see how the wines will taste in bottle, the Oregon Wine Board was absolutely blown away by the generosity of Oregon winemakers helping other winemakers. Not only here, helping one another with information-sharing and webinars and lending one another equipment and labor, but also Oregonians turned around and sent money and even offered jobs to displaced Californian laborers when the Napa and Sonoma fires began (such as Jim Bernau of Willamette Valley Vineyards offering jobs, housing and food for cellar workers who had lost theirs in the fires). Specifically, Oregon winemakers answered the call to assist colleagues when Pierre Zreik, Sue Horstmann and Denise Seroyer recruited talents from seventy Oregon wineries and a dozen restaurants to offer a fall afternoon of food and fine wine at the Allison Inn & Spa. Four hundred wine lovers turned out, and the proceeds topped $35,000. A few weeks later, wineries from the Umpqua and Willamette Valleys joined their counterparts from Washington and California in support of a San Francisco Chefs Gala that brought in $750,000 for relief efforts.
>
> So, one of the biggest things the fires taught us is how generously big-hearted the spirit of the Oregon wine community is.
>
> Thanks,
> Sally

———— ✺ ————

CHAPTER 18

A POSTCARD FROM OENOTRIA

As anyone who has ever ordered a pizza at a local Italian restaurant probably knows, the country of Italy appears on placemats or menus as a great boot, poised to kick the soccer ball called Sicily through the goalposts once known as the Pillars of Hercules. We know the area as Gibraltar today.

What may not be known very well is that the toe of the boot was anciently known as Oenotria—literally, "the land of grapes," as in oenophile. The people of this land, with some modification of the place name, settled in the Latium near Rome and, other than for some burial art and Pottery Barn seconds, were called Etruscans and were soon absorbed by history and museum display cabinets.

Why any consummation of Oregon wine lore would hang around places like Capri, Naples or Sorrento is a powerful lesson in the story of migrations. Recorded history is a story about people who settle lands that they make arable and productive through agriculture and trade on the one hand and, on the other, brave if cruel brigands and marauders who take away and despoil such settlements for their own aggrandizement with the requisite pillage and rape that occur in the wake of slaughter and tumult.

The toe of the boot is a marker on the trail of viticulture and wine consumption. The origins of winemaking we trace to Shiraz, now in modern Iran, which once owned a civilization known as Persia. Indeed, under its great emperor, Cyrus, the counselors of state undertook decisions only when sufficiently lubricated with wine. (Today, the theocrats appear to drink only Kool-Aid.)

Judy Erdman and Doc with Ken Wright, owner and winemaker at Ken Wright Winery. *Courtesy of Doc Wilson.*

The techniques of vine tending, harvesting, storing and enjoying wine were inevitable outcomes of this knowledge. It translated well to Mesopotamia and the inner valleys of the Holy Land, traveled into Greece and onto islands floating on the Middle Sea prior to landing on that big toe. From here, the migration went north and then west with the Roman legions. We can guess that by the time of the Council of Nicaea in AD 325, the wine bug was well established in France, Spain, along the Rhine and across the fertile lands from the Bosphorus to the westward-facing shores of Portugal.

No conquistador set sail from Lisbon or Cadiz without wine and without, in short time, vines to plant as Christendom went on its mission to save heathen souls through the usual pillage and rape, slaughter and tumult. The migration continued. Italy, at once so suited to viticulture and so enmeshed in the machinations of the great con game called organized religion, marks a high point in the migration, and its influence, though haphazard at times, has continued without diminution.

Wine knowledge and custom continued to circumnavigate the globe as if Ferdinand Magellan were the besotted Bacchus in the Pastoral Symphony segment of Walt Disney's 1940 *Fantasia*. The pilgrims landing in what became the Massachusetts Bay Colony crossed the Atlantic on a wine transport called *Mayflower*. Whether or not they inhaled the fumes, the lands that became the original colonies were importers and then makers of spirits and wines in the nascent nation. Indeed, the men who argued the merits of independence in the Philadelphia summer of 1776 were sustained by barrels of Madeira wine.

Thomas Jefferson failed with his wine crop in Virginia colony, but this ill fortune didn't prevent his going broke in large measure from purchasing books and wine from Europe. Drink agreed with our third president; he bought Louisiana territory from Napoleon and then sent Lewis and Clark west to traverse the Oregon Trail in 1804–6. This spurred, in short order, the migration of viticulture.

William Cobbett didn't even have to leave the East Coast. This on-the-lam Parliamentary radical spent more than one year farming wine grapes on Long Island. Abundant land encouraged farm settlements farther west.

Thomas Lynch of Ohio solved a grain surplus problem for farmers by making whiskey. He grew rich. The forebears of Nick Longworth, drunken son-in-law to Theodore Roosevelt and longtime Speaker of the House, were descended from an entrepreneurial lawyer who made the Ohio River like the Theingau or the Moselle. Indeed, the largest AVAs in the continental United States are in flyover country.

Westward migration had brought to California and to the Northwest wine technology and the appetite for its consumption by the mid-nineteenth century. The first commercial winemaker in Oregon territory opened his barrels in 1859, but the Civil War killed his Jacksonville business soon enough. Nonetheless, the West opened by way of transcontinental expansion on the one hand, as well as via the Franciscan Junípero Serra, who was to Pacific-area wine what John Chapman was to apples. Serra founded missions from the San Diego area to the peninsula at what is now the modern San Francisco, all equipped with vineyards, thus migrating different traditions of viticulture up the coast. The rendezvous was propitious.

This perspective seems necessary as the global commercial ecosystem extended to South America, to Oceania, to southern Africa and, as if to complete the great circle, to the recent planting of vines in the remoteness of China's Gobi Desert. The bones of the Huns, Mongols, Seljuks and Tatars have long turned to powder and sand where now the Cabernet vines sun themselves. Here the barbarian hordes once perfected their slaughter and tumult skills. Now descendants of these bloodlines tend Cabernet grapes.

For good measure, the Jacksonville winery is open for business once again. It appears wine cultivation can survive mullahs and tyrants; it also can find its way to embellish the qualities of life. But can Oregon's wine industry survive success?

Let us excuse my CliffsNotes romp through human movement and attendant misery. As Will Durant wrote early in *Our Oriental Heritage* in 1935, all history that isn't guesswork is prejudice. But the contours in the tale ring true.

We may admire or deplore the scientific caste system inspired by certain influential critics and marketers to produce an international style of winemaking driven by celebrity and fashion. However, no doubt remains that money for the global expansion of wine trade follows the pattern of old conquering hordes, but without the pillage and tumult.

Indeed, much produced has created a kind of urtext grape, a varietal so cultivated and uniform that the nuances are lost in a kind of Oeno-Esperanto. What works for Coke and Pepsi does not translate into wineglasses.

The greater challenge producers and consumers face involves retaining the qualities of varietals specific to one area so the traditions extend and the wines improve through experience. For the moment, the shoals of Oregon seem poised to avoid being inundated by the tides of fashion—well, perhaps.

Doc and Dick Erath. *Courtesy of Doc Wilson.*

The author and Brad McLeroy (Ayres). *Courtesy of Doc Wilson.*

The Oregon wine industry did not quite exist when Richard Sommer planted Pinot Noir and other varietals near Roseburg in 1961. The pioneers who celebrated fifty years of winemaking did not just open a chain of dry cleaners. They changed the face of the state and its commercial ecosystem. Preserving the spirit that motivated these pioneers is essential to ensuring that the industry does not merely prosper but manifests its potential. Wine is a totem of Oregon identity that can be sullied by hype and corporate greed. It has happened before and not very long ago or far away.

Wine is a natural resource at its most essential; we must care for its land like Greenpeace enthusiasts care for the sea, but without the confrontational and infantile rhetoric.

So, can you guess the message on the address side of our postcard from Oenotria?

"Don't blow it."

CHAPTER 19

EVERYTHING WEARS DOWN

HOW THE STORY ENDS, OR, THE THREE PRINCIPLES MY COUSIN TOLD ME

Success is American manna. We seek it, and once attained, we begin to feel guilty about it. On the other hand, *schadenfreude* is not a varietal—it is the pleasure we experience when we watch someone's success tank.

Imagine a plot to poison vines in Burgundy in a dippy attempt at extortion. This occurred in 2010. Although inept, the intended crime elicited giggles of *schadenfreude* because the intended shakedown victim was the prized Romanée-Conti, the most expensive wine in the world. So, class envy joined general antipathy to things French, with their Gauloises and easy afternoon assignations, their unpronounceable entrées and their Vichy water.

The sheer size and success of California wine, especially high-profile celebrity wines from Napa and Sonoma Valleys, can outrun their value. This is a mistake often abetted by the wine trade and critics. The market distends, the consumer takes a beating and the brand is sullied and otherwise dissipated. Success can lead to unintended outcomes. Fashionability does not protect reputation or ensure value. That message is implicit in the postcard from Oenotria.

Wine knowledge is a goal post or target constantly on the move. Against this motion I offer three principles enumerated by my cousin a half century ago that remind us that nothing will stand still:

- Everything wears down.
- For every function, there is an equal and opposite malfunction.
- Where a void exists, a bureaucracy shall come to fill it.

Jim Prosser of J.K. Carriere Winery, whom we encountered early on in this book, reminds us that vines and a career in winemaking are a good run if they last forty years. The bump in the road is overdue for Oregon's wine industry; the widening acceptance of the wines runs the risk of losing the determination and resourcefulness of the founders and, with it, the collegiality among the vintners and, most of all, the inviolate character of lands encroached on or put to other use.

A happy ending will not be accidental. It will require visionary leadership to build on what has come before. To the extent we can hold some perspective, three strategies come to mind. To the extent this book does anyone a good turn, the first strategy is at hand: read about wine, talk about wine and drink considerable quantities of wine.

The second is succession and succession planning. I will relate the cautionary Mondavi tale as part of my State of the Vineyard message and reflect on how this American viticultural pioneer handled the challenge.

The third strategy derives from the second and implicitly from the pleasures of the first: the conservancy. This is a nimbus floating above the wine country; it seems to portend treating wine less as an extension of human appetite than as a natural resource developed to improve attitudes, or as Ben Franklin put it, to express a divine intent to make mankind happy. Alas, the wearing down is already happening.

THE WHITE WHALE IN THE VINEYARD

When newbies visit Oregon intent on winery visits, I recommend that their voyage to the Willamette Valley wine country along SR99 end at Chehalem. Its tasting room is presently located strategically on the city-bound side of the state route, just prior to leaving Newberg. On one recent trek, I saw a young group emerge from a very large Lincoln limousine. This land beast was all white. It was as if Moby-Dick had tired of sea chases and plowed along country roads instead. The group wanted to drink, and the beast they commanded allowed this to occur without risk.

It was a day trip, one said to me, and it would be a better day if they were not hauled into a tank because they sampled too much wine. The concession, however, points to something else beyond imposed prudence: the field is becoming crowded and the demography changing.

"We have noticed the change in our business," Carol Thomas of Wine Tours Northwest observed. "The customers are younger, drink lots of craft beer and spirits as well as wine. They're loyal to Oregon. They are out to have fun more than to study wines. And they tip very well." Times change. The new avatar tourist is conditioned to becoming a savvy if less concentrated consumer of the experience. The wine roads are something to do. That is what one of the young group suggested. The main theme isn't broadening knowledge of the wine, but a form of being entertained. Wine is an amusement.

Another wine friend and tour director, Larry Walters, demurs a little by pointing out that his oeno-tour trade comes mostly from outside the state, via Portland hotels and their concierges. "Most of them come to buy wine that they have already decided to sample." They are less interested in the experience of Oregon wine country than adding to their cellars, Walters pointed out. The impetus appears to be acquisition more than activity where the demographic tends to more established people, though not necessarily far older. "They are international travelers—plenty of Asian guests," Walters noted. My associate Doc Wilson has more than once come upon tour customers waving wine scores and insisting on visiting only the places with top ratings from third parties, buddies or the media. Readers might guess my response to such simplistic criteria.

What is yet lacking on the Oregon wine roads are mile-long lines of tour buses disgorging crowds of locust-like density that descend on tasting rooms, swirling and swallowing in a maelstrom of chatter and picture taking.

We have not yet attained the voracious intensity of Napa Valley on a promotional weekend. However, it will happen in time. To overcome the vulgarities of the free wine crowd, the same people who wait hours for a gimme hat from an arena or a plastic cup with a team logo to stuff between car seats, California tasting rooms have hiked the cost of tastings at wineries to fees upward of seventy-five dollars. This seems a great way to put off people who might actually want to learn something about wine culture. The fees in Oregon, based only on circumstantial observation, are less prohibitive—with a few exceptions, fees are waived when the visitors purchase wine. Crowd control remains an issue for many wineries and their visitors.

The whale appears to indicate two other factors. If wine is entertainment, it is no longer a natural resource, a food product or an indicator of shared cultural value. Wine tasting is simply like going to a club with shrubbery. And clubs rarely endure.

The new visitor, the millennial, a creature of social media, relies on peer acceptance. Holly Nuss, a Napa-based public relations expert, told me not to be fooled by the demographic. "These people graze. Their interest is in variety of experience, whether beer, wine or crafted spirits. They're passing through to enjoy the moment with a group of friends rather than to learn something. They have the will to spend money, but the exchange is ephemeral."

This book has dealt with wine-tasting practice as a means of expression, in terms of how winemakers handle varietals and how we verbalize our preferences and responses. A wired community paradoxically can be manipulated by the sheer density and immediacy of information. Therefore, one is likely to be chasing after moving goal posts. If wine teaches us anything, it is patience. "Hotter than hot, newer than new," the old song goes, but that mindset doesn't encourage or appreciate taste memory or the *genius loci*.

Market studies summarized in 2015 by *Wine Spectator*, a sometime reliable conduit outside its ratings of individual wines, reported that the millennial group, age twenty-one to thirty-eight, accounted for more than 40 percent of domestic wine consumption—much of it from non-California producers like Oregon and Chile. The eclecticism inspires, but the lack of depth or focus in this mammoth slice of the grape makes forecasting patterns an elusive proposition. This wanderlust may be a function of market diversity and saturation; the boomers trail them slightly but are more acclimated to California wine. Why? Because at the time these older folks picked up the wine threat, their experience was limited to mostly California choices, from marijuana mouthwash to prestige wineries.

Wine exploration is not speed dating. Start by accepting with grace that wine is a food product far more than an alcohol-delivery system, a point pioneer David Adelsheim made earlier. Wine is meant to share, and responses of one's compeers can extend one's own take on a wine. Furthermore, wine encourages meal taking. The pairing inquiry taps into collective traditions of the table. This resonance affirms living. It just doesn't come off the same way with a soft drink and a Saran-wrapped salad from the convenience store.

It seems to me that adventurous millennials in their drive-by drinking excursions more than most miss the essence of the place. Whether hip to a vibe or just cruising, the white whale should discourage our national predilection to cram as much into an interval than possibly gives the time spent coherent value.

In fairness to millennials, we might posit that their entertainment ebullience may mellow into a more considered view of wine as something more than exchanging Facebook photos and posts. It takes effort to learn something about wine, as the topic is so prolix. However, as long as wine touring is just another segmentation of the amusement dollar, the responses and sensibilities will remain superficial. This reinforces number rankings rather than taste memory and context. In turn, if this mode persists, winemakers will be forced to commodify their efforts, so everything will tend to "EZ to drink" clichés of varietals. This will erode the fragile balance of artisanal vintnering to purely commercial imperatives.

Finally, vintage and taste memory conflate to produce a palimpsest with multiple layers of narrative. A library wine tasting is something like Scheherazade doling out her fantastic tale bit by bit over 1,001 nights. The details, impressions and memories accrue. Terroir is narrative by elements, a kind of song of the earth.

We might consider the library tasting something rare. It is. When we experience a vertical tasting—a succession of wines over a number of years—we experience something else. It can suggest an evolution of style or different winemakers or getting past a very challenging year. But it can also become tricky.

As Jim Bernau of Willamette Valley Vineyards told me, "A vertical tasting can be very misleading. You have the vintage years all lined up, but each year may be represented by bottles with relative differences in the bottle time, or laying up. So, the net result is a kind of ambiguity or elusiveness you wanted to work around by having a vertical tasting in the first place."

Dick Shea, the well-respected grower with more than two hundred acres and twenty-two eager winery customers who line up for his Pinot Noir fruit, contends as well that a vertical flight may "fool our palates" for the same reason. We agree that horizontal tastings—wines across a single year from different producers—may tell us more. But verticals are surely worth our participation.

Since wine tasting rooms usually offer current inventory, you taste a range of different varietals and vintages for sale. The stuff of a meaningful horizontal or vertical flight comes with winemaker dinners from time to time, but mostly when enthusiasts and geeks put them on privately. So, one path to a more comprehensive taste memory is to make new friends who own too much wine. Restaurant-placed exclusive wine dinners wheel in some big-

Jim Bernau inspecting the take. *Courtesy of Willamette Valley Vineyards.*

gun winemaker or "expert" and serve a meal paired to wines that cost too much while being constrained by the format of the event. They all start to feel the same. Go with the geeks, where the spirit is more of a potluck or a barn raising.

And—pay close attention here—the value is found less in the cost of the tasting than in what the land and the fruit reveal in concert with the winemakers. Ahab, go back to your boat.

PERSPECTIVES

Although I take all news from "studies" heard in the media with a Dead Sea of Salt, some items get through the filters.

A recent "Pour" column in the *New York Times* ran a story about a marijuana farmer and processor in the McMinnville AVA who has irritated his vineyard-tending neighbors. The pot man is as welcome as a herpes rash on a bridesmaid. The wine people fear introduction of alien chemistry in their biodynamic rows. They're not comfortable, either, with the kind of people who are bud buddies. It's our own Willamette Valley culture war.

Fear of the unknown is quite a human trait, part of our adrenal defenses. So, what's this really about? Answer: demography and fashion. (It's really about class assignments and, above all, property values.)

Here is the way I see it. Full disclosure: I inhaled. I never liked pot. I also really did not have sex with *that woman.* I think decriminalizing marijuana is okay if it helps reverse all the crimes carried on beneath the flag of affirmative action. But that part won't happen because all the progressive states have eased the ban on the bud. It's cool. I think it makes people even dumber than they were prior to toking up. But the bandits who run state governments see marijuana sales as a good way to raise money they heretofore squandered on things like tent cities, asylum for killers and, above all, pension plans owned by municipal and state employees. That's hard to overcome.

The beneficial use of dope is considered swell, just like fortune telling, astrology and burning of heretics.

The demography comes into account like this: The population of wine-buying publics is paced by millennials (36 percent), with baby boomers (27 percent) and Gen-Xers (25 percent) rounding out the field. (I guess that leaves 12 percent for Baby Snooks and Granny.) Note that these numbers differ from earlier citations as these are for California only rather than gross domestic sales.

Given the social habits of the leading group, wine producers will soon find themselves in trouble. The "progressive" way of life is easy on making judgments about personal responsibility or values, especially other people's responsibilities and values. Wine is an amusement, a label to wear outside, and it is "cool." But it is, despite the buzz, a very modest way to deconstruct reality. Pot works better.

Dopers and stoners ingest or inhale their naturally grown weeds in order to skew reality—not as by-product but as the main point. Stoners don't pair food with weed, as a rule. They toke up to get the munchies. So, when the munch crunch happens, what do stoners prefer? So says a study I ran into on the same day as the "Pour" column:

- 43 percent go to McDonald's
- 19 percent head off to Taco Bell
- 17 percent hit Burger King

Shareholders may smile, but what happens at the winery?

Bud is a plant. So is *vitis viniferas*. But the active ingredients in the former don't in themselves lend much to other foods other than a scarf-and-barf event. True, we can overdo wine consumption and gorge ourselves on Salmon Mousse. But wine as food is very different because it already is food; it does not require a secret dipping sauce that comes packed inside a recycled paper container imprinted with a smiley face.

The whole experience of marijuana is to elevate one above or escape from experience. So the fast-food numbers once again attack the traditions of meals eaten at tables rather than the back seat of a Beemer. Read the panegyric to the gathering at the close of *The Boys Up North* and you will understand what lacks. And there's little call for thoughtful wine pairing, for conversation and for community. Marijuana is like brain poison ivy designed to put people somehow "beyond their own heads." It is a solipsism looking for an exit in the wrong stairwell. Its use manifests fear of unknown proportions with respect to wine education and commerce.

At last, as described earlier in the story of Prohibition, it comes down to logistics and money. My libertarian self argues that no substances ought to be controlled. We as a nation face other challenges. But my revenue-gathering self says that the licensing of marijuana use improves its product, and such sales fill tax coffers. Free money to politicians is like heroin for junkies.

Put that into your pipe…etc.

CHAPTER 20

SUCCESSION SURVIVAL GUIDE PART I

INSTITUTIONAL MEMORY WITHOUT LOSING YOUR MIND

Succession is the fulcrum that balances the warring forces of enterprise and tradition. This book occurs at a time when Oregon wine founders are still on the premises, so how they move from center stage to the wings constitutes the best part of the act. By contrast, the succession story at Robert Mondavi Winery in Oakville, California, has the gravitas of Shakespearean history plays, with their focus on inheritance, patrimony and traitors to the cause, real or imagined.

In his article "The Fall of the House of Mondavi" (*San Francisco Magazine*, 2005), Paul Chutkow does not mimic Poe's Gothic title for nothing. Chutkow had a long and pleasant association with Robert Mondavi, founder of the eponymous winery in 1966. This piece appeared shortly before the closing of the sale of the winery to Constellation following a public family feud not surprisingly set off by a 1993 public offering engineered by Wall Street *goniffs* at Goldman Sachs.

I am sure many people who liked Mondavi wines purchased shares for romantic reasons, as well as an opportunity to be part of a pretty sure bet, given the stature of the firm. At first, they were happy, as the ticker clocked in at over $50 after an IPO price of $13.50. The promoters at Goldman Sachs came up with a two-tier stock program that precluded the public from acquiring voting shares. That power remained with the family in its extended sense. It is as if a person returns to a childhood home only to see that the old and secure memory was replaced by a massage parlor. Sentiment is not a realistic way to measure the merits of an investment any

Susan Sokol Blosser and Bill Blosser look over plans during the construction of their new tasting room. Their son, Alex, and the family dog are also present. *Courtesy of Sokol Blosser Winery and Susan Sokol Blosser.*

more than expecting the old neighborhood to remain the same. Both are not good ideas.

When I dined with Bob Mondavi in Kapalua, Hawaii, in 1988, the man was a robust seventy-five years old. He was amiable, but one look at his hands suggested a kind of tough elegance—after all, he once famously punched his brother. The rift caused him to leave the family business at Charles Krug Winery (inspiring a name change at Krug to C.K. Mondavi, complete with name infringement litigation). By this time, Robert, the older brother, had begun his legendary run. Not the least of the internecine rancor derived from the senior brother's globe-hopping and immense drive; the younger brother, Peter, concerned with wine production, was of a more sedentary disposition. It's the stuff of Willy Loman as well as the Lancastrians and the Yorkists. (At this writing, Peter Mondavi passed on, age 101, as if to recommend a sedentary life. His son Marc owns a winery called Divining Rod and has found new work looking for groundwater with his, natch, divining rod. Sometimes California drought brings surprising benefits.)

Bob Mondavi did not put on airs. He didn't need to. He was the visionary and the patriarch who found the sleepy confines of Napa Valley containing twenty-five wineries and turned it by his drive and business acumen into a tourist megalith with nearly five hundred wineries by the time of his death at ninety-four. He promulgated wine education for consumers and producers, putting millions to fund his ideas. "Wine is a food," he told me as we enjoyed Maui's seductive air. He saw his wines as part of the ritual at a table where people connect—a fine notion.

The man paid lip service to succession, although he proved far more adept at defining a mission for his company and its industry. He simply did not know how to turn over the reins of global operations to his children. They were often left disappointed by their father's responses to their ideas and the wine they produced. The elegance and suppleness of the great early vintages of Mondavi wines were indeed lacking for a time in the Monica Lewinsky era, which coincided with the IPO and the maturity of other wineries, both in California and elsewhere.

The wines lost their institutional memory; what replaced it was rancor about the boardroom table. Should the premium line take precedence, or ought, as son Michael proposed, the company to focus on its value wines? Depending on your point of view, it is how to vertically integrate a product line within a large company. On a grander scale, General Motors would jettison neither Chevrolet nameplates nor Cadillac, but it lost little sleep when the time came to jettison Pontiac and Oldsmobile. Brand equity means something to the devices we ride around in, and it matters for wine. "You're putting my wine in your body," Robert Mondavi said to me, "and it is my reputation you're drinking. It has to be good."

But with all the public money that grew a $115 million operation into something closer to $650 million, sheer liquidity does not auger automatic success. So the flagship premium wines took a palpable hit, as if those big hands now had liver spots.

Even Robert M. Parker, the Alpha Critic, noticed the fall in 1998–99 vintages. When the institutional memory is erased or ignored, the quality of the wine and its characteristic advantages go into the witness protection program. This happened to Mondavi, and it occurred because the winery took imprudent business practices to Wall Street for a fix that produced even greater imprudence—this time splayed on the front pages of respected newspapers.

When Constellation forked over $1.36 billion in 2005 for the winery holdings, the patriarchy and the often-shunted heirs made oodles of cash, plenty enough to blaze new paths in the wine lands.

Constellation owners are wine people, too, so the change was smoother than if some Silicon Valley software gazillionaire wanted to purchase a lifestyle, complete with seasonal workers who never came up to the big house. But the damage is done. The wine properties have to be seasoned with experience and tradition by the people who know the land because it has been in the family for generations. That is what Robert Mondavi grasped intellectually and what explains his joint ventures with the Chadwicks in Chile and the Rothschilds in France. But one has to let go at some point, and this admirable man did not have the moxie to trust his children until their fractious interactions spurred a lot of harebrained projects that roasted a golden goose. The only promising part of this tale is that in time, someone will stumble on restoring the institutional memory enough to think it's new. And so it shall be. Memories are priceless. All that cash will have to go to something else.

No one wished to run afoul of the old man. He knew that his approach over a long and accomplished life would help to map experience and instill traditions for coming generations. But he didn't factor in his fallible if durable flesh until his controlling nature clouded the vision he so wanted to become his legacy. All of the marketing and PR can play the notes set down on this particular score, but it will not be the same. And that is Napa Valley's loss and our loss.

One sees examples of how it might be done. For example, Wynne Peterson-Nedry is winemaker at Chehalem, where she collaborates with her father, winery founder Harry Peterson-Nedry. Ken Wright, of Ken Wright Cellars in Carlton, can drive a few miles to Purple Hands Winery, where son Cody owns and runs the place. Kim Kramer is winemaker at the eponymous Gaston winery run by her parents, Trudy and Keith, along with a few dogs. It must be in the water they seem to miss in California not so far down the road—Oregonians prefer collaboration as a rule to confrontation.

By way of contrast in a few other wine companies, we might look to the Ponzi daughters and legatees at Sherwood, Oregon. The new visitor center and winery facility scream success and elicit an impression that if Frank Lloyd Wright built a winery, it would look like Ponzi, so respected for its take on Pinot Noir. Family dynamics and places of origin are fuzzy things, but the Ponzi clan emigrated some generations ago from a more maritime place in Italy, and when Dick and Nancy Ponzi settled in Oregon from California, where Dick was a mechanical engineer in the Walt Disney entertainment galaxy, the etiology was of a different species than that of the Mondavi clan, which evolved from a grocery in a mining town and shipped wine grapes to Italians living in the upper Midwest during Prohibition. The differences are not only in origin and generation but also in temperament. The Ponzis are amiable; Mondavi *père* was a commanding presence and knew it.

In the same year as the aforementioned IPO, the scion of the Ponzi family turned the operations of the place over to his girls. Neither Nancy nor Dick Ponzi affect the life and cultural force of their Napa Valley precursors, but they had enough good sense to listen to nature—sustainable farming—and to their intuition that their daughters could handle this.

So, the Ponzis affect a less contentious group of strong personalities leavened with the notion that excellence need not also be an exercise in bloodletting. Luisa Ponzi possesses considerable international experience

From left to right: The author, Dick and Nancy Ponzi and Doc. *Courtesy of Doc Wilson.*

and repute as winemaker, and she exudes a great deal of personal charm. "When Luisa started making the wines," her father told me, "I would look in on her and ask, 'Anything you need to ask me?' and the reply was, 'No thanks, Dad.' After a few gentle rebuffs, I got the message that she knew her stuff." On the commercial side of the enterprise, Maria has taken on the management of marketing sales.

The Ponzi family is not made of shrinking violets. However, the cultural and historical context of being wine pioneers in Oregon has not left the deep lines that Robert Mondavi earned during his brilliant career. The Ponzi Vineyard helps to set a benchmark for Oregon, and this book has gone out of its way to differentiate it from California, despite the enormous example the Golden State offers to other places.

Readers recall the second chapter and its celebration of Willamette Valley's founding families, the Pinot Noir pioneers. Excepting Charles Coury and David Lett, the people who advanced a vision are still here to see their children take up the business of making and selling world-class wines. By general contrast, California's wine pioneers have in time faded into the hills, with some notable exceptions. The winemakers there move from place to place the way relief pitchers move from one team to another after the All-Star break. Properties change hands and are associated with very big numbers. California craves notoriety; Oregon coddles collegiality. The difference is profound, and I would suggest that the sheer size of the wine population in California makes it less stable and more volatile. Too much of its finest output became lost in the glut of options, from "Two-Buck Chuck" to Harlan or Hughes family wine. One can book excursions to Napa and Sonoma yet be harder pressed to visit Lodi. One might miss the Bennett Valley AVA while looking for its marvelous Jemrose or Mayacamas.

If I were to suggest the major difference other than scale and size between the wine roads of Oregon and those of California, I would think it far easier in Oregon to smell the flowers—that is, to remain cognizant of the land supporting the enterprise. It is not a surefire reason to produce good wine, but I think it contributes mightily to pleasures of wines made in Oregon. We call it context. The land is the wine, and the wine inspirits the land.

Susan Sokol Blosser was so interested in succession that she wrote a book called *Letting Go*, about releasing control of a going concern that happened to be a pioneering wine company. As she explained, she decided in 2005 that she wanted to create a scenario that would allow her to move away from the daily operations of a winery. She hired a consultant familiar with transition strategies, and as they became acquainted with the nuances of stepping aside, they put into place a definite plan. This was not a cabal effort either. Susan's daughter and son—the inheritors—knew they were not nominally involved as beneficiaries of a trust but rather participants in it. The process took two years to develop, and in 2008, Sokol Blosser let her children take the "test drive." After they became accustomed to the feel of running a substantial Oregon winery, and after considerable debriefing, the transition went into effect, with Sokol Blosser retaining her boardroom presence but acting more as advisor, as this was consonant with her personal goals. Psychotherapists who like gender case studies might find the qualities intrinsic to the Ponzi and Sokol Blosser families as markedly distinct as Mars is to Venus when set next to the Mondavi family dynamics, allowing for the generational difference of the founders. Indeed, the Mondavi heirs are closer generationally to Sokol Blosser and Ponzi. Robert Mondavi endowed concert halls, learning programs and opera houses. He needed monuments as if his contribution to American wine was not sufficient. Perhaps this driven man could never escape from the passing lane on life's interstate.

In the lobby of the Ponzi Winery is a small wine cask fitted with a screw press, the same improvisation Johannes Gutenberg used when he engineered movable type for printing around 1450. The press made

Dick and Nancy Ponzi's first wine back in the 1960s. That is the scale of the Oregon wine adventure. You will not encounter this in Oakville, California, where the totems are grand and the memory is a bit fuzzy. But there's an opera house in Napa.

Let's leave the soap opera, however, for reruns on cable late at night. An undeniable influx of capital has found its way to Oregon for quite a while. The Alpha Critic's nephew, Jared Etzel, has a beautiful new tasting center for Domaine Roy on Worden Hill Road in Dundee—the Rodeo Drive of the Willamette Valley. His brother has joined father Mike at Beaux Frères, where the Alpha Critic uncle straddles the website like the Colossus at Rhodes. The wines do justice to the visitor center. This is the kind of structure serious money can produce. It has the most modern of local grandeur that would have seemed out of place ten years ago. We cannot detour the money that chooses to follow fashion. We can only seek to keep Croesus from ruining the landscape.

The conclusion one can draw: the eclectic wineries of Oregon can benefit from the influx of capital. But also, as we see next, they may not.

CHAPTER 21

SUCCESSION SURVIVAL GUIDE PART II

DO THIS BUT NOT THAT

Mark Freund likes Oregon wine very much. In fact, he heads north several times annually to enjoy it, traveling from Napa Valley, where he directs Silicon Valley Bank's wine division, a component of this highly regarded, innovative financial institution.

The bank boasts more than 320 winery clients, and its annual "State of the Wine Industry" report sources its analysis from more that 650 companies and maven consultants. Readers can find the report easily online.

The 2015 overview estimates that 70 percent of winery owners surveyed say they would happily sell their interest in their wineries. Even if this number is half true, it's plenty of grapes to crush. There is only one problem with the report, and it is as old as the battles Andrew Jackson, our eighth president, fought with the Bank of the United States, which he closed down: the antipathy between bankers and farmers. It doesn't take a Wharton MBA to recognize Silicon Valley Bank's report is a "selling" document.

The team at Silicon Valley Bank doesn't care if you sell elderberry wine to Thursday night bingo ladies with blue hair insofar as they have plenty of green in their totes. As Freund told me during a phone interview in October 2015, "If you are selling premium wine, we want your business. And if your business cannot perform profitably in the present economy, there is something wrong with how you're operating." Fair enough? Sure—and if you make only value wines for the broader market, SVB is likely to pass. So the novice wine drinkers with limited funds can fend for themselves. The free market is free before it's fair.

But there is something radically wrong with this picture, like those kiddie puzzles that put tires on the dog's feet or fish fins on the pussycat.

Jim Bernau, the founder and CEO of Willamette Valley Vineyards in Turner, told this writer, "Wineries don't conform to the bankers' view of the world with its quarterlies. Wine [business] represents a long-term commitment. Bankers and their investors want to make money and winemakers want to make their wine."

We ought to recall that Silicon Valley Bank established its wine division in 1994 as relaxed banking regulations were being phased into practice. Freund recalled that his company entered the sector as Bank of America and Wells Fargo slithered out, seeing more ready return on real residential and commercial property financing than on servicing loans for vineyards, farm equipment and inventory as it rested in oak barrels. Silicon Valley Bank calculated that it could fill the void neatly and did so.

However, the banking scenario is not simply concerned about equipment loans, checking accounts and processing credit card sales. It is about the endgame: the transaction that ultimately separates founders from what they founded by outright sale, merger or even public offering. The bonuses and perks for leveraging such a deal are obscene. The compensation for overseeing the deal sets into motion other priorities that have little to do with residual sugar or canopy trimming.

Recent history provides the mother of succession mishaps, as narrated in the previous chapter.

Touching on this tale twice should suggest that the legacy of a fine family and its mission only demonstrate that money—a neutral commodity—powers destinies unsought or unintended. The man who created a legacy ultimately could not find the exit in time enough for his heirs to take over.

Readers can return to my opening pages, which described the fiftieth anniversary of Pinot Noir planting in the Willamette Valley as celebrated by the actors in this now long-running show. It is no mistake that Adelsheim, the Campbells of Elk Cove, Eyrie, Ponzi and Sokol Blosser have all made succession successful and that, along the way, some even worked with Freund's bank.

Recalling the event and the tale from Napa, Bernau quipped, "Well, those of us around early in the Valley are moving toward stepping aside." He added, "I think we are a more collaborative lot," alluding to the far more familiar names from the California wine industry.

Willamette Valley Vineyards took a different tack than the iconic Mondavi brand. The Oakville mission-style plant opened in 1966. Thirty years passed before the company went to the public market to raise money, and it did so because it needed it.

Bernau followed contrary advice. Early in the life of the company, he intended to obtain public money but without the strings attached by going down a path strewn with bank loans. "We wanted investors willing to hold their shares for a long time," he said. "And we wanted them to get in or out without our being in the middle of that decision or its being carried out. Above all, we wanted to make our wine without the oversight of people whose interests were only about returns on their dollars. They liked the idea of owning winery shares but ignored our priorities because they don't work the property or make the wine." He added that as an equity holding, wine keeps its own counsel.

I consider the path taken by Bernau a major factor in the improvement of his company's wine over the years; the team of winemakers and growers has achieved output of consistently quality wine, often with a good story to distinguish one property from another. The net result is focus and an evolving institutional memory. Just ask to see the winery's library.

The difference is profound in these respective scenarios. The current preferred stock offering occurred the day of our interview, and they're voting shares—for everyone. Bernau's more substantial holdings from previous raises are placed in trust, so that their legatees will be able to manage the winery's future activities and operations with the assurance they can plan and act decisively. The business model contains an element of Zen.

Bernau recalled a trip he made with fellow winemakers to Burgundy, only to be berated by the host, who said that American winemakers meddle too much with their product. "Have the courage to do nothing," said that Burgundian.

Paradoxically, by bringing in the public at various stages of Willamette Valley Vineyards' evolution as an enterprise with its own commercial ecology, the company has not only cultivated 645 acres in Oregon country but also established a succession path with the exits marked clearly so no one will stumble off the stage when that moment arrives.

When the current Adelsheim winemaker, David Paige, came to Oregon in 2001, he left a successful tenure at Jekel in Monterey, California, where he had similarly made wine for the previous decade. "The big money from institutions totally altered the nature of the wine industry there," he told me. "By the time I started, there were few wineries, and when I came

Wayne Bailey, winegrower, Youngberg Hill Vineyards, McMinnville. *Courtesy of Carl Giavanti.*

north, that landscape was crowded with new people wanting to try their hand as producers."

The market appreciates competition, as the rising tide lifts all boats. But a flood tide might drown us in wine geared to some suits' idea of what makes wine good rather than the artisans who put their inspiration and labor into actually making the wine. We can anticipate many me-too wines that are nice to drink and easy to forget.

Market penetration should not also mean saturation, as the consumer can become confused by seeming endless choices that are, indeed, Hobson's choices. Serious money does not guarantee anything but larger outputs. The scale of winemaking suffers when ROI is set by disengaged third parties with more love for the idea of wine than the idea that wine is integral to a larger economic and social ecology.

We in Oregon are blessed still to have people like the Baileys at Youngberg Hill at the edge of McMinnville, the Kramers at their eponymous Yamhill winery, Vicki and Don Hagge at Vidon and Mike and Drenda Bayliss at Ghost Hill—these are people farming grapes whose affinity for land has its value expressed in nature rather than on the Multiple Listing Service as dirt to sell. Bayliss said, "My grandfather built this old house on these acres, and we intend to keep them in the family." Herein lies a source of continuity that, if promises remain fulfilled, will allow Oregon to continue setting precedents and nurturing traditions unique to this part of Planet Wine.

If Ghost Hill summons the past, Vidon heads where no man has gone before. Proprietor Don Hagge started as a winemaker in 1999 at age sixty-nine; he signs his letters and e-mail as "farmer, physicist, winemaker." As others do, he combines the scientific with the artisanal aspects of winemaking. The result is a mix of insouciance and technique that marks the personality of Oregon winemaking. To wit, from their web welcome mat: As a scientist and inventor, Hagge is constantly innovating to achieve the ultimate in quality, consistency and efficiency. He built his own proprietary argon gas wine preservation tap system for his tasting room that protects the wine from oxygen and extends the usable life of a bottle for up to two weeks. This

Above: Vidon Vineyard & Winery in Newberg. *Courtesy of Carl Giavanti.*

Left: Dr. Don Hagge of Vidon Vineyard, barrel sampling at Newberg Winery. *Courtesy of Carl Giavanti.*

dramatically reduces waste but also allows the winery to offer visitors tastings of even micro-production bottlings. In addition, Hagge uses no corks on Vidon Vineyard wine, preferring sterile Vinoseal glass closures to avoid the risk of cork taint and pre-oxidation. Not surprisingly, perhaps, he has also designed and built a unique bottling line for these closures using pneumatic pressure to insert them and a space-age heat gun to secure the capsule.

Indeed. Welcome to Oregon. Beam me up.

PERSPECTIVES

The year 2017 poses an existential threat no less severe than the outbreaks of *phylloxera* or of false morality such as Prohibition caused. The fact that wildfires are not just for casebooks will have an enduring effect on land use and safety beyond what means existed until now.

Despite the horrific circumstances in the West, it might be worthwhile to uncover some of the less frightening occurrences.

Janice Fletcher's www.planetcheese.com is for those delights we often pair with wine. When the fires erupted, Fletcher's Napa Valley classes were bumped. It left her with ten pounds of really excellent cheeses in her refrigerator. She decided to donate the cheese to the temporary shelter network established to deal with evacuees and displaced persons. "Sorry," said the center official, "we cannot take perishable items as donations." Clearly, the perishable persons and property out in the fires didn't strike any of officialdom as absurd or ironic.

It gets better. Fletcher tried the main fire and rescue agency next. The policeman on watch also politely demurred on the cheese. "We cannot accept this. We have our own caterer."

Fletcher to her public: "That's so Napa."

We hope the ten pounds of cheese found a good home.

CHAPTER 22

CONSERVANCY, NOT BUREAUCRACY

A ll enterprises operate through networks. When networks work well, people are prized for their collaborative and their singular skills. When networks perform less well, arbiters of such things may blame cronyism or nepotism. These old stories repeat in the mature and evolving industries as well. Oregon's wine industry appears quite well wired. Even in transition, the interplay of people with talent seems to show up in time, despite inevitable speed bumps or detours.

For many, "networking" is all about a Chamber of Commerce mixer. There you hope to find business or love or somebody who can fix your roof. These rubber chicken feasts have since gone viral through social media. People with so little better to make of their time put photos of food plated in restaurants or collect galleries of wine labels off bottles with names they're afraid to pronounce. O brave new world that hath such creatures in it!

Pardon the snark. Readers should re-frame the idea of networks. Coming into focus are paths of exchange and resources that constitute part of the ongoing process rather than being the point itself. The following passages demonstrate the way these phenomena can occur in the Oregon wine business. They provide a timely instance of how traditions grow or even may continue. Networks are as old as the race—the Asian spice road, the Columbian exchange and the opening of the West are all examples of networking. Basic material and technological changes accompany or emerge in these activities and occur *sub rosa*, like the processes running behind the applications open on a computer desktop.

SeVein Managing Partners at the Pambrun groundbreaking. *Left to right*: Marty Clubb of L'ecole no. 41, Norm McKibben of Pepper Bridge Winery and Amavi Cellars, WVV winery director Christine Collier, Chris Figgins of Leonetti Cellars and Figgins Family Wines and WVV founder Jim Bernau. *Courtesy of Andrea Johnson Photography*.

Several of the cooler tales to come out of Oregon wine lands are Alit Wines (formerly Witness Tree) Vineyard and Ghost Hill Cellars. Both make very good wine.

Eric Hamacher has a pretty nice network. He is husband to Luisa Ponzi, connecting his credentials to a pioneering Oregon clan. When his friends at Ghost Hill, the Baylisses, asked Eric to pinch-hit as ghostly winemaker when the regular winemaker went on active duty in Romania for the USAF during the 2015 harvest, he grabbed his bat. Hamacher has plenty on the ball. He co-founded with Rhone-centric Andrew Rich the Carlton Winemakers Studio. The Studio makes a fine day trip objective, especially when a release party gathers current tenants using this facility to make and market an array of wines. The Studio illustrates one aspect of the wine country; the tales a bit up yonder in Willamette Valley illustrate something else.

But all of these scenarios have something in common: instincts to help out paired with healthy self-interest.

The ghost at Ghost Hill once had a body and a horse. Thieves relieved him of both, as well as the bag of gold he had sluiced out of a local stream. Needless to add, said ghost wanders the hills above the property in the Yamhill-Carlton AVA looking for that stolen stash. The 240-acre plot is highly desirable, for its fruit is very good. But the Bayliss family won't sell. The house has been here for more than a century, Mike Bayliss said. "We keep making wine to keep the land."

It will be a sad time when the vineyard and the winery become ghosts, so the mission at hand and for the future demands keeping both on the books, with the original families overseeing the vines and crafting the wine. Bad guys murdered the old prospector and killed his horse to keep anyone from being led to the scene. They wore black hats. Fashions wane. Now they smile that Rotary Club smile and keep a stiletto concealed in their Armani suits. Same creeps. Can't steal the gold? Steal the land. Let us not bear witness to a mindless spoliation of Oregon's wine land.

Winemaker Eric Hamacher (*left*) with owners Mike and Drenda Bayliss of Ghost Hill Cellars in Carlton. *Courtesy of Carl Giavanti.*

When last at the old house, Bayliss poured his Hamacher pinch-hit Pinot, not yet released. "We have labels to print," said Drenda Bayliss. "We'll have to sell more of what's here now so we can pay for these labels."

Silence descended over the dining room, which pinch-hit for the tasting room on that afternoon. It came home at once. Land of value, wine of quality and no way to get the wine into the market to tell the story. This, in microcosm, explains the situation faced by small producers. The margins belie the glamor of the lifestyle holding on for dear life. I hear Sal (Abe Vigoda) telling Tom Hagen (Robert Duvall), "Tell Mike it was only business. I always liked him…."

So, like Sal, some wineries one day aren't there anymore. Happily, Ghost Hill didn't go for a ride.

We must note the tree that is the Alit Wines (formerly "Witness Tree," aka the Shroud of Turin or, for that matter, Madonna's missing etiquette manual) has been offering settlers a place to consummate deals perhaps ten years before Oregon joined the Union as a free state (1859). Seeing it from the eponymous tasting room, bare branches set against the March sky, makes it a perfect metaphor for the vulnerability of the state's original wine history and traditions.

Alit demonstrates both the down and upside of such flux. The Witness Tree founders came from the Midwestern United States and settle in wine country. Their children were vines, and their extended family was the wine club. Sans progeny, when the husband passed away in 2014, his widow, seventy-nine years old as I write, decided to move on. There were no heirs— only a good story about a tree.

Enter Portland (and thus local) money. They purchased the prime asset, the vineyard, and moved the public face of Alit to Dundee center, at a tasting room resembling a postmodern service station. It could hardly be better noticed.

Oh, well wasn't Chapter 24 here? Had they marketed a wine called Fire and Flood to note the primary geologic events that shaped the soils in the Dundee Hills? Weren't these the same people who shared a storefront in old town Newberg *as* Fire and Flood? And who was Chapter 24? Professor Moriarty? And who also shared that space as a separate wine company? Sherlock Holmes?

The wandering wines became a new brand, adding the challenge of identity and product recognition as some travelers continue to hunt for the Witness Tree. This is beginning to resemble a stage farce, like Michael Frayn's *Noises Off.*

Well, this appears to be all downhill. No heirs, no more wines from Witness Tree after 2015. And a widow hanging up her tastevin.

Dissolve from Tree. Fade in Dundee Hills central intersection.

Mark Terlov was once president of Evening Land wines, which operates its tasting room adjacent to the Ponzi Bistro and its contiguous wine bar. Argyle is across the highway, if one can call it that. A few doors away is the postmodern garage.

Terlov is a conceptual dude. He partnered in Fire and Flood and then Chapter 24. A passion for microbes informed these wine brands along with the eons of geologic events that went into making $60 bottles of wine—pretty good wine, too. "So Napa," one might start to think. There were happily aborted plans to produce a labor-intensive Pinot Noir that would tip the wallet at $300 per bottle. (Now that was *really* Napa.)

Terlov then moved the pea right under our noses. He conceived "Alit" that shines a little light on pricing transparency for a bottle of good Oregon Pinot Noir. Bean counters of the world unite! We have nothing to lose but our markups and pass-throughs! Terlov's financial partners come from senior residence properties and software technology. Being so Oregon, they are together trying out the new pricing model that eschews overcharging customers for estate-grown wines. The initial Pinot Noir draws fruit from both the original Witness Tree land and the vines in the Dundee Hills surrounding their newly acquired Black Walnut Inn. The market's hidden hand has yet to reveal itself.

Terlov made Alit a direct-to-consumer commodity. No wholesale. All costs revealed. A $60 bottle of wine really costs $27.45. So that's the cost to consumers. Will it work?

Americans want $60 bottles of wine they can boast about having paid $27.65 for. They probably would prefer paying $13.86 for a wine under $28 but won't brag about it. Overcharging is as American as Manifest Destiny if you can boast to your friends.

What most interests me in the tales of these six degrees of wine lore and sales strategies drills down to one fact: the wines are quality. They're well-made wines highlighting differences while avoiding me-too pratfalls. But are they memorable? Is the tradition sacrificed on the altar of novelty? I pose the question not as a pejorative; I recommend wine explorers rely on their own standards.

The net reaction I had to all of these aliases and networked etiologies indicates that the collaborative spirit inhabits the way we come to Oregon wine now. Like the stage farce, the enterprise introduces recycled concepts and the recycled people who regroup to make another wine. We need a racing form to track the changes.

Reviewing these rapid costume changes suggests a risk (little institutional memory) but also an upside (pushing envelopes to make something stick—coherent, demonstrable and, ultimately, intuitive). The grapes at Witness Tree went into Alit; so did the fruit from the Dundee Hills' (see above) Black Walnut Inn. Often good fruit is simply awaiting the next winemaker. The network is alive and well, if unseen.

That intuition gives the Cote d'Or its ways of doing things over decades that can navigate the shoals of change. Here the nexus of mutual admiration occurs between the Old World and the New. An evolving grid of custom and methods reinvigorates the traditional ones. The French houses arrived in Oregon to make wine in Oregon. To appreciate and emulate the Burgundy producers is not, strictly speaking, flatteries of imitation. It's decoding the grapes here to make wines that are Oregon wines.

Success at each end brings rewards. How the industry handles this boon will light the time to come. Or not.

When something is worth preserving, we cannot assume the next fellow will do the job. This section considers a proposition built on one governing principle that distinguishes Oregon's wine culture: it is collegiate and cooperative. There is something in the air and water that keeps the wine industry from becoming noisy, frantic, self-centered and overdecorated, as Alison Lurie once described the women of southern California. At the same time, generations pass, and not everyone wants to farm grapes or make wine. The foresight that since 1973 has produced a series of inhibitions to untrammeled growth pushing outbound from cities to suburbs has allowed Oregon to preserve much good wine-producing land, both attractive and beneficent. Still, success breeds money, and money has no conscience. It is, as H.L. Hunt said, "just a way to keep score."

Rolling hills and happy vales make for nice views from the back deck. But yielding to the temptation to put people into places fit for grapes is a poor way to manage land use. Development is a form of consumption, not a creation of resources. Humans make more noise than birds, they eat more than bears and they cannot seem to stay too long in one place without driving someplace else only to discover they're bored. They also forget.

Industries grow as a benefit of expanding networks that also turn on themselves; the collaborative gene resides in this commercial DNA. The gyre augments and accelerates change and innovation. When this balance is sustainable, we foster long-term qualitative improvements. They create change; they also weather it. Each AVA, given the right drivers, will generate institutional memories that are linked by approach and method from one block to another. It's going to eventually show in your glass of wine.

Readers may wish to Google "Willamette Valley growth restrictions," as did your author. Plenty of items relate to this topic query, and most are university or government based. This means the studies often begin with an agenda or desired result. Regulations placed in order to curtail sprawl can, in time, be modified by the efforts of lobbyists who count on public apathy that over time clouds the original motivations creating these very same controls. It's not just that "you can't go home again." It is that beautiful vines appear to have been swallowed by beige façades and pretty neon signage. Walk down Third Street in McMinnville, heart of an AVA. The old look is going away, and I pray to retain Faye and the corny signage of the Blue Moon Café (a tavern with breakfast).

A 2015 growth plan for Portland anticipates 1.4 million more citizens over twenty years and the need for eighty thousand housing units. This eastward push will also encroach on agricultural land if not compromised to reduce negative impacts.

No Luddite am I; however, it is easy to notice the encroachments on the *mise-en-scène* by bland Babbittry—me-too wine expressed in storefronts. A Snooth post dated September 15, 2016, asked readers to distinguish "industrial" wines made for "entertainment" from artisanal wines made for more serious drinkers, with the understanding that the common denominators in the former are its vast tonnage and the absence of distinction beyond pleasant diversion. The very topic bespeaks the paradox in wine industry marketing: to become noticed, wine has to become all but invisible. It needs to help while the time away rather than help to define place and varietal. So, the imperative denudes the individuality as it seeks to broaden appeal. In the landscape, this pressure puts the emphasis on output and not unique characteristics. One

The finest retro dining counter in the Northwest—Blue Moon Café at McMinnville, complete with bloody Mary. *Courtesy of Jonathan Potkin.*

can follow the trail to vineyards prized for bulk rather than soul. It is the threshold we have wanted to avoid.

An indivisible correspondence exists between the Oregon wine industry and the land that produces the grapes. As obvious as the point seems, it nonetheless gets lost in the jumble of many visitors who search for pretty views and free wine. How do we maintain the shield wall of the tiny amoeba of the commercial ecosystem when it floats among so many predators, not the least of which is changing demography and fashion? Can you believe Kendall Jackson suits who have purchased more than 1,300 acres of vines in Oregon when they say they will *not change anything*? Hey, were you born under a rock?

I asked Plato, the old aristocrat, author of the *Republic*. Make no mistake: Plato has great press. Most think he is a progressive, a Greek LaFolette. Well, really his Utopian vision is a society run by highly intelligent rich men. And in his long excursuses, I found a little riff on farming—one of the sustaining components of his republic. He said that landholders should not own giant farms and that after fourfold capital appreciation, the state should buy the farmer out. Along the way, the landholder has paid into a sinking fund. Fast-forward to the present. With a new mediating entity, the republic has organized drainage, built canals, improved roads and generally handled infrastructure to the mutual benefit of the parties. Then a new farmer comes along and the cycle reboots. It inspires.

So, says I, what advantages does Plato offer to Oregon twenty-three centuries after he floated his idea? Well, accruing wealth by four times on property is not terrible. And having a built-in buyer avoids speculators. And infrastructure attains a level that sustains the farming. Because the parcels of land are relatively small, the wealth gets spread around without the mega-concentrations of lucre we encounter in contemporary media so deferential to lots of zeros when great wealth gets to fritter itself away on trivia—or football teams with players who don't stand up when the band strikes up the national anthem. The farmer builds value by production, and the land is protected in its activities from the radicals, the reformers and the people who don't work.

When, in turn, the local and state agencies quickly forget that their people serve the general population and not the other way around, it's not too long before the sewer planners are telling winemakers what to make.

The whole point is that enterprise and property are protected from the great unwashed masses and experts who respectively crave space to play and lands to "transform." Typically, such talent expands opportunities for coercion by compliance applied by "experts." They're as likely to invent obstacles as to contribute useful practices. Mother Nature doesn't always wish to have a makeover.

Historically, the Greeks of the Golden Age were as fractious as they were freedom-loving. The republic suggested a social blueprint that contained the violent upheavals while creating the illusion of managed freedom. Is there something for us today to apply by this example?

My attention was drawn to Plato by that four-fold ROI, and it came secondhand. But untrammeled growth and devaluation of real property are no less significant in twenty-first-century Oregon than in Athens in the late fifth century BC.

We witness changes in our surroundings each time we tool around the wine roads. We discover the pavement has smoothed, a new wine palace has replaced a stand of trees and a fence with a family wine name unassumingly tacked to it has become a halogen-bright monument. These observations represent a kind of progress even as they give the sense of some falling off, some sacrifice of a more forgiving, more informal approach to growing grapes and making wine. Ken Wright, hosting a dinner shortly after showing up on the cover of the May 31, 2015 issue of *Wine Spectator*, retreated from the Douglas MacArthur pose that didn't seem to suit him. "It's really simple. It comes down to the grape," he said, before proceeding to describe how to encourage the roots to travel deep beyond the surface soil and into the rock beneath. It is another example of wine Zen.

The best wine expresses connection to a place and the people who nurture the land and make the wine. I think this is how we begin to resolve a lost chord. It remains for me that feeling of bringing the boat home, where experience and memory themselves become a recurring experience and memory. When the novelist Vladimir Nabokov was asked how he wrote, he said he was like a magician performing one trick while explaining another to his audience—seamless.

I began with a notion to find a language to write about drinking wine, and the search became, as such a topic might, about something more and something else. A glass of wine catches the light; it is all anticipation. And simultaneously, it tells a story about its places of origin, of the artisans who made it and about the year and the conditions that promoted its survival from bud break to harvest. The moment is evanescent; the descriptions we seek attempt to clarify something already in the past. So, I wonder, is it the wine itself or its associations that stir me? The wine supports and provides reason for conviviality, hospitality and the rituals of the table. Remove these constituents and we have a fermented food product. When we subtract the ceremony, as Richard II laments in Shakespeare's play, what remains? Are the words sufficient?

It rather appears the wine represents and occupies a moment. But it also embodies its past and, by proper storage, anticipates a piece of the future.

In a commercial ecosystem, the wine in the glass helps to validate larger concerns that run across varied disciplines. Winemaking is one facet of agriculture; raising cabbage or carrots are others. Each makes demands on the land beneath and around. It seems to me worth ensuring that the land stays viable and its purposes preserved.

A conservancy extends the growth legislation put into effect more than forty years ago by the fortunate accident of having winemakers cognizant of their potential legacy. The restrictions on sprawl would not be easily implemented or preserved at a later time. The will found opportunity and the opportunity found support. This kind of vision would today be sullied by real estate speculators, public school districts, self-proclaimed environmentalists and, above all, a brace of lawyers filing counter-motions.

This chapter is not the place to argue the particulars of a conservancy. I am not a policy wonk. But if readers wish to learn some of my inspiration, I direct them to Tony Hiss and his 1990 book *The Experience of Place*, as it lays out the thought behind the Peconic plan on Long Island at the time Oregon wine people wanted to ensure a future. Oregon's visionary allocation of agricultural land originated at the right time, and despite pressure to overrun vine rows with condos, the front has held—more or less. In addition to Hiss, as if to remind us that according to plan isn't necessarily as planned, I urge readers to look at Thomas Sowell's 2008 *Economic Facts and Fallacies*. Both books will suggest how conservancy works in ways to limit the metastases of government bureaucracy while fulfilling intent for common good.

Visitors to Long Island's North Fork will experience an integration of agriculture, aquaculture and viticulture that in a small area seems to reflect the larger bounty of these commercial ecosystems in Oregon and in the Northwest.

Bottom line: make wine country a free-enterprise state park run in trust for growers and winemakers.

So the story goes on, ending or no. And still in the distance, the rows of vines soldier up the slope where the land kisses the blue-framed billowed clouds.

The stand of trees suggests a modest proposal: Could we keep, so to speak, the wine country in the family? Could the collegial nature of Oregon

From left to right: Richard Dean, Dick Erath, chef Phillippe Boulot and Jean-Luc Deguines pose at the Erath Vineyards twenty-fifth anniversary celebration at the Mark Hotel, New York City. *Erath Winery Collection, Jereld R. Nicholson Library, Linfield College, McMinnville, Oregon. Donated by Dick Erath, 2012.*

winemakers extend to creating conservancies comparable to state parks? Since the government is at local, state and federal levels already involved in the industry as alcohol and agriculture, what might prevent—other than polymorphous perversity—the people who built the wine industry from continuing operations, as generations pass from the scene by attrition or commercial incentive? In other words, rather than allow the wine lands to disappear, as many did in southern California to the white shoe elastic belt car dealer lizards east of Los Angeles, might a conservancy help to protect good grape acres and inoculate them from rampant growth and progress that offer little benefit? Could these conservancies provide the testing grounds for new farming and viticulture that, by keeping things in perspective, protect the endangered species *Homo vinifera*? I would think this program could make a difference and avoid the Napa Nuclear Option.

Taste memory and place memory interweave. Stories from the Oregon wine country become part of your story. I think that's a nice touch. Or, as the Alit Wines formula supposes, each time we decode a grape we encode another.

Consolidating his holdings would suggest to some entrepreneurs that Dick Erath is done doing wine. No way—he just has freedom to putter with other wine projects, to collaborate and enjoy the *eminence grise* stature and still make a barrel of wine or two, like Bill Fuller or Jim Maresh or Don Hagge or Susan Sokol Blosser. Their activities and interests diverge, but they each remain connected to the industry they helped to build.

PERSPECTIVES

Context explains the wines' relationships to the land bearing the fruit. And what is the land about?

Ken Wright drilled into the dark places to which the vine roots explore like Orpheus in the Underworld. That helps to frame the following, a piece of knowledgeable sales puffery from Elk Cove Winery in Gaston appearing online over the signature of Adam Campbell, who long ago succeeded his parents' stewardship of 360 planted acres in the northwest Willamette Valley.

Campbell, as does Wright, finds the linchpin encompassing terroir, that slip-sliding wine belch of a word, to what I call context. It embraces the air, light, soil and moisture—the Four Elements of the ancients. The fifth element is context. It keeps these four magical things spinning like a juggler's plates on *The Ed Sullivan Show*.

Somewhere between those precarious plates, we advance and reconstruct taste memory. We decode grapes. Take it away, Adam…

Oregon has a wild geology shaped by volcanoes and floods, winds and time. This varied geology is one reason why the Northern Willamette Valley is an excellent area for growing grapevines. Today, the three dominant soil types for growing Pinot Noir in our region are Willakenzie, Laurelwood and Jory. It took us decades, but we now grow Estate Vineyards on each of these three soil types:

- *Willakenzie/marine sediment—Our Winery Estate (La Bohème, Roosevelt), Mount Richmond & Goodrich Vineyards*
- *Laurelwood/windblown silt—Our Five Mountain & Windhill Vineyards*

- *Jory/volcanic clay—Our Clay Court Vineyard*

Curious how soil affects wine? Our Soil Trilogy is a great way to experience three wines made with the same varietal, by the same winemaker from grapes grown on each of the three primary soil types here in the Willamette Valley. Cheers!

What's underfoot, indeed, are thousands more stories in the wines and the places their vines inhabit. Some appear on maps as seen throughout this book. Some appear in pictures collected over decades. But most simply arrive in the wine in our glass. Once Campbell has booked the sale, and we have drained the glass, what's left? Taste memory and a new story to come.

EPILOGUE

On any afternoon near harvest in Oregon's wine country, you notice the light and its relation to the land. It has clarity, indeed. But the light is not aggressive, thus making it less intense than sun-drenched places like Napa Valley's productive floor. The difference, of course, is place. The angle of the sun in its climb and path is determined by the curvature of the earth. So, the more diffused sun in the Northwest feels different from that shining down the road, and the variation becomes more pronounced the farther one travels through California as far as Baja.

We might say the sunshine over Oregon wine country is never in your face. So, bearing this genuine perceptual variation, we can conclude that my snapshot of the whole place is differently illuminated. I think it alters the personality of the context and the behaviors of the state's winemakers. They're knowledgeable, of course, but they preserve an openness and humility that allows them to take less seriously their now far-reaching esteem in the present world wine scene.

Writing about Oregon wine demands a sympathy for stories both weird and wonderful. And I would offer that the views from country lanes amid the orchards and vines provide the gloss on any reasonable attempt to describe the virtues of the wines made here.

Decoding is an effort to "disambiguate," as Wikipedians do so well, in order to come up with something plausible to support taste memory. This seems to me a big job, a continuing labor, thoroughly out of reach—but just.

Above and opposite: Landscape at Elk Cove Winery. *Courtesy of Jonathan Potkin.*

The angle of the sun makes people do little things well. When Ken Wright began to build his own brand, he sold futures by recording the names of purchasers on a yellow legal pad. Now sanctified in the wine media, he still uses that pad. It is a small but good sign. Keep aware of what brought you notice early on, before the tides of fashion swamped the rows like a late spring flood.

America is populated by tourist attractions that attempt to replicate the past, like Old Tucson, Colonial Williamsburg and every ersatz Disney Main Street. The effects run from authentic to vulgar; the attraction remains in the attempt to capture a lost time. So it seems that the Oregon wine scene still has the advantage of its earlier history at hand. The challenge of success is to retain the spirit of what brought the accolades and recognition about. Thus, timing is crucial to ensure the best of what has passed remains alive by example.

The sunlight shines down on a recurring series of activities that produce wines, and the continuation of these cycles are the fount of local habits of doing and seeing things. It's as if a diamond road sign warned "Go Slow. Tradition at Work."

I suggest that readers consider wineries like TeSóAria and Mosier. One uses an ouroboros as its logo, the serpent swallowing its own tail—an ancient symbol of renewal. The second uses the Ptolemaic symbol of the analemma, the sideways infinity loop used to track the sun's path in relation to the land below. Each winery acknowledges the recurring seasonal rhythm of planting and tending vines.

My private analogue is the Portland Streetcar system. Its main route on the west bank of the Willamette River begins—or ends—in front of my apartment, itself part of the waterfront. Fred, nearly the most senior motorman in the transit system (save for one), learned a while ago about this book and would sometimes ask of its progress from the public address system in the cab of the streetcar. What other city has a transit system whose pilots are interested in wine books?

The correspondence between the analemma and the ouroboros in relation to the loop of the streetcar reassures me. Here am I, living atop the main viticultural valley of the state, being constantly reminded of and participating in the life of the wine industry.

Its basic story tells of the durability and proliferation of the vine for purposes of winemaking, as well as all the pleasures and rituals to accompany a glass of Oregon wine still close to its nearly contemporary origins.

Portland Streetcar is a metaphor for the recurring miracles of Oregon wine culture, and it can put its travelers in proximity to urban wineries. *Courtesy of Sergio Ortiz.*

Wine gets its meaning from lore, not from score. If I have provided some utility to readers, it comes from re-framing the argument to empower a person to get to the basis of his or her preferences and escape the deer-in-the-headlights effect of a wine list longer than the Talmud or a retail shelf display with more red caps than the College of Cardinals.

The drilling down herein falls into the broader scattershots of the narrative. Wines, like Mozart's operas, never cease to reveal while never revealing completely their divine mysteries.

Oregon still has room for the catholicity of the Carlton Winemakers Studio, where Andrew Rich presents some takes on Euro-pretense in wines that would please the Avignon popes. It also has Naked Winery of Hood River, where the sex jokes prompted one cellar club member to arrive for his pickup attired only in a bath towel. It has the august Domaine Drouhin, which acquired its Dundee property with a high purpose and centuries-old Burgundian lineage and has done credit to both. And at last we have winemakers who have adopted ancient symbols to remind us that wine can be a little recurring miracle, but as brief as a season—the bird flight through the Norse mead hall.

Ouroboros, the serpent that swallows its own tail, is an ancient symbol of recurrence or renewal. Brooks Winery in Salem and TeSóAria of Roseberg use the symbol in their operations, drawing on its relation to the harvest cycle—and because they think it's cool.

The Book of Fred reminds us that our great southern neighbor has lost some of its oenological innocence on the way to becoming the nation's most dominant wine producer. Oregon, by contrast, is significant, but on a far smaller scale; thus its humaneness, its respect for the land and all of its quirks and myriad variations.

To illustrate the point, visit a working farm and winery like Big Table in northern Willamette Valley or Brooks at Salem or Cowhorn at Jacksonville. The horns of cattle are used in making fertilizer and nutrients using this remnant of said cattle, an external sinus, as a vessel to put into the dirt to mojo that soil. It's an instance of ancient bio-dynamism. What's in the horn? Don't ask. But it is ethical and it works.

The land is more than marketing palaver; it manifests a recurring cycle of creation, corruption and transformation. If there's a ground bass to this music in vineyards, I think this is it—ever changing and self-renewing, just like the route of the streetcar.

The Book of Fred is a commentary, though hardly specific, on the contrary motions the spiral dancing suggests. Each vintage year is a triumphant reprise of the basic rhythm in Creation, with its five-point cycle of bud break, flowering, clustering, maturation and harvest transformed into wine through other subsequent processes orchestrated by humans from start to end. And then the dance begins anew. Thus another vintage commences its story in the longer narrative of anticipation, commercial ecology and the unrecorded incidents of pleasure and discovery as wine makes its first impression on us. To survive, we must also weigh what is worth preservation.

I think the most interesting sparkling wine in the state comes out of the Columbia Gorge, with its two state constituents and its vineyards ranging from just inches above the river and upland over one thousand feet. This is terroir with attitude. Analemma is the producer, and its name and logo come from Ptolemy in the proto-classical study of astronomic phenomena. The symbol appears as a sideways sign for infinity and mimics the variation of arc in the path of the sun.

Left: Analemma logo. *Courtesy of Analemma Wines.*

Middle: Analemma vista. *Courtesy of Kenji Sugahara.*

Bottom: Analemma harvest. *Courtesy of Analemma Wines.*

You need not write about wines professionally to have a point of view. Remember, in the end, taste memory will guide you more reliably than expert opinion. Finally, recall the timing of this book in light of the current history of Oregon wine country, a compound of nouns where "country" is apt to disappear under the crush of the overpasses, the apartment parks and the encroachments of other commerce. To save the land you need to own the land, if only in a gustatory and spiritual way. Success can easily go off the rails.

Consider the benefits of wine, about which it is just as easily puffed up as claiming you were at Anzio or Woodstock or Ground Zero. Your acquired wine narratives will get better in the telling, for you're helping to celebrate and extend a great Oregon natural resource. As T.S. Eliot penned somewhere, all significant truths are private truths. Good wine is just a stab at such a fleeting truth.

When asked to provide "rules" for Oregon wine appreciation, an endeavor that entails drinking some wine, I usually demur. But since we're about to take the exit ramp, I offer these:

- Small output wineries (e.g., 1,500 to 7,500 cases) get close to best showcasing or exposing the winemaker's affection for and skill with the grapes.
- Sample older vintages with current vintages. Celebrity chef Anthony Bourdain in his 2001 *A Cook's Tour* reminded us that taste is all about memory and context. This holds true for wine as in obtaining the differing aspects of one varietal or so from one place.
- Try to focus on wines sourced from the land immediate to it; that is, from the farm beyond the fence.
- Consider wines in terms of body—light, medium and heavy— to establish your preferences. A Rosé of Pinot Noir will be very light most likely, and more than a few Pinot Noirs are also classified as light. I think many are more made to medium. You can work the perceptions of body by drinking an array of wines.
- Pay attention to texture. As in food, so much more reveals the quality of wine than its layers. Texture is how we arrive at harmony in a glass.
- Value exuberance in wines you drink. The characteristic is more than excitement, enthusiasm or cheerfulness, as we

noted earlier. When you pop a cork and pour some wine, the anticipation will meet *joie de vivre*. As with class, you will know it when you open the bottle.

Also, ignore these points wherever you find wines you enjoy.

Timing matters, as we pointed out in our own cook's tour in the prologue. So recall, please, that the aforementioned suggestions serve to help appreciate not only the wine but the styles and traditions in the making. It's about the wine; it's not about you, your scores, your iPhone. Allow the story in the wine a chance to unfold, to reveal some of its mysteries and much of its place.

It has been said of Nietzsche that he looked into the abyss and it looked back. I believe it satisfactory for winemakers to push and also have their grapes push back. The wines we most remember come out of such *frisson*. After so many wines with words in tow, I am reminded that we should at last decode the grape—a message in a bottle. "Tradition is to the group as memory is to the individual." So said Pope Benedict XIV to Voltaire in a post-mortem dialogue. So there it is, *n'est-ce pas*? (If the Durants could make this bit up, I can steal it.)

Don't miss the ride. All aboard!

A Final Perspective

The moral for the stories told, messages in a bottle or two, have a bipolar pull. On the one hand is the reality of fire. What occurred in Oregon's hills and forested lands also happened in California's wine country counties with more destructive force. The responses to the disasters were prompt and sincere. However, the unthinkable happened. The communities of growers and vintners, as well as those who support them, cannot ignore concomitant risks that tag along with expanding markets. We cannot prevent biblical disasters; we can only expect to mitigate them, and such amelioration begins in the storied vineyards. Vigilance has a commercial and spiritual payday.

On the other side of the pole comes Eric Asimov's "Pour" column from the *New York Times*. He spent some time in north Yamhill-Carlton AVA and came away with this impression that

I think captures the esteem for Oregon wines I have presented throughout. It is a good place to end my song:

> [A]fter spending 10 days here in late July, visiting winemakers, tasting an awful lot of bottles and, incidentally, speaking at the International Pinot Noir Celebration, I can't help but conclude that Oregon is right now the single most exciting winemaking area in the United States.

I could hardly say it better.

———————※———————

A WINERY LISTING

I spoke of this list as an exclusive one—by which I mean sorting out the wines we in the editorial prerogative have tried on site, at private homes, at eateries and at the wineries and shops. I reckon these account for nearly 30 percent of what's out there, or a bit less counting wines made across the Columbia Valley in Washington State.

I remind readers that as much of Manhattan Island looks west into another state, so on a grander scale do Oregon and Washington stare at each other, one with many fruit-forward and big-spirited wines and the other with wines of earthy and supple character. The proximity makes including the wines up there complementary to those down here. At last, I have provided the map location for wineries listed. Omissions do not signify any more than we still have much quaffing to anticipate.

Enjoy the bounty surrounding you. I apologize for any errors or transpositions despite many proofs. This book was written to serve readers and acknowledge the hundreds of men and women whose efforts have changed the Oregon wine scene for the better. And neither you nor I could have done any of this without California. Thank you all.

Abacela Winery	Roseburg	OR
Abiqua Wind Vineyard	Scott Mills	OR
Adea Wine Company	Gaston	OR
Adelsheim Vineyard	Newberg	OR
Agate Ridge Vineyard	Eagle Point	OR
Airlie Winery	Monmouth	OR
Alloro Vineyard	Sherwood	OR
Amavi Cellars	Walla Walla	WA
Amity Vineyards	Amity	OR
Analemma Wines	Mosier	OR
Anam Cara	Carlton	OR
Anderson Family Wines	Newberg	OR
Andrew Rich Wines	Carlton	OR
Angel Vine	Carlton	OR
Ankeny Vineyard	Salem	OR
Anne Amie Vineyards	Carlton	OR
Antica Terra	Dundee	OR
Apolloni Vineyards	Forest Grove	OR
Aramenta Cellars	Newberg	OR
Archery Summit	Dayton	OR
Argyle Winery	Dundee	OR
Artem Wine Company	Carlton	OR
Arterberry Maresh	Dundee	OR
Artisinal Wine Cellars	Newberg	OR

Ashland Vineyards	Ashland	OR
A to Z Wineworks	Newberg	OR
August Cellars	Newberg	OR
Augustino Estate and Vineyard	O'Brien	OR
Aurora Vines/Aguila Vineyard	Talent	OR
Authentique Wine Cellars	Amity	OR
Awen Winecraft	Medford	OR
Ayoub Cellars	Dundee	OR
Ayres	Newberg	OR
Bacchanalia	Salem	OR
Barrister Cellars	Spokane	WA
Bartholemew Cellars Seattle	Seattle	WA
Beaux Freres	Newberg	OR
Beckham Estates Vineyards	Sherwood	OR
Bella Vida	Dundee	OR
Belle Fiore Winery	Monroe	OR
Benton Lane	Monroe	OR
Beresan Winery	Walla Walla	WA
Bergevin Lane Winery	Walla Walla	WA
Bergstrom Wines	Newberg	OR
Bethel Heights Vineyard	Salem	OR
Big Table Farm	Gaston	OR
Black Walnut Inn & Vineyard	Dundee	OR
Blakesly Estates Winery	Sherwood	OR

A Blooming Hill Vineyard	Cornelius	OR
Bobo Wines	Talent	OR
Boedeker Wines	Portland	OR
Bow & Arrow	Portland	OR
Brandborg Vineyard and Winery	Elkton	OR
Bridgeview Cellars	Cave Junction	OR
Brigadoon Wine Co.	Junction City	OR
Brittain Vineyards	McMinnville	OR
Broadley Winery	Monroe	OR
Brooks Winery	Amity	OR
Browne Family Vineyards	Walla Walla	WA
Burner Wines	Dundee	OR
Burnt Bridge Cellars	Vancouver	WA
Cadaretta (Middleton Family Wines)	Walla Walla	WA
Cameron Winery	Dundee	OR
Campbell Lane Winery	West Linn	OR
Cana's Feast Winery	Carlton	OR
Canoe Ridge Vineyard	Walla Walla	WA
Canvasback Wine	Walla Walla	WA
Capitello Winery	Eugene	OR
Caprio Cellars	Walla Walla	WA
Carabella	Wilsonville	OR
Carlton Cellars	Carlton	OR
Carlton Winemakers studio	Carlton	OR

Cascade Cliffs	Hood River	OR
Cathedral Ridge Winery	Hood River	OR
Catman Cellars	Tigard	OR
Cerulean Wine	Hood River	OR
Champoeg Wine Cellars	Aurora	OR
Chapter 24 (Alit Wines)	Dundee	OR
Chateau Bianca	Dallas	OR
Chateau Lorane	Lorane	OR
Chehalem	Newberg	OR
Christom	Salem	OR
Cinq Cellars	Redmond	OR
Clay Pigeon Wines	Newberg	OR
Cliff Creek Cellars	Gold Hill	OR
Coelho Winery	Amity	OR
Coeur de Terre Vineyard	McMinnville	OR
Coleman Vineyards	McMinnville	OR
Colene Clemens	Newberg	OR
Col Solare	Benton City	WA
Columbia Gorge Wine Growers' Association	Hood River	OR
Cooper Winery	Benton City	WA
Cor Cellars	Lyle	WA
Cots De Voe	Red Mountain	
Cowhorn Farms and Vineyard	Jacksonville	OR
Crater Lake Cellars	Shady Cove	OR

Cristom Cellars	Salem	OR
Crowley Wines	Newberg	OR
Cubanisimo Vineyards	Salem	OR
Daisy Creek Vineyard	Jacksonville	OR
Dana Campbell Vineyards	Ashland	OR
DANCIN Vineyards	Medford	OR
Dauntless Wine Company	Cornelius	OR
David Hill Vineyards & Winery	Forest Grove	OR
Deer Creek Vineyards	Selma	OR
Delfino Vineyards	Roseburg	OR
Del Rio Vineyards	Gold Hill	OR
Denison Winery	McMinnville	OR
De Ponte Cellars	Dayton	OR
Deuce Cellars	Walla Walla	WA
Division Wine Company	Portland	OR
Division Wines	Portland	OR
Dobbes Family Estate	Dundee	OR
Domaine Drouhin Oregon	Dayton	OR
Domaine Roi et Fils	Dundee	OR
Domaine Serene	Dayton	OR
Domaine Trouvere	Dundee	OR
Dominio IV Wines	McMinnville	OR
Dowsett Winery	Touchet	WA
Dragonfly Time Vineyards	Medford	OR

Duck Pond Cellars	Dundee	OR
Dumas Winery	Walla Walla	WA
Dunham Cellars	Walla Walla	WA
EdenVale Winery	Medford	OR
Elizabeth Chambers Cellar	McMinnville	OR
Elk Cove Vineyards	Gaston	OR
Enso Winery and Tasting Lounge	Portland	OR
Eola Hills Wine Cellars	Rickreall	OR
Erath	Dundee	OR
Ermisch Family Cellars	Bend	OR
Evening Land	Salem	OR
Evesham Wood	Salem	OR
The Eyrie Vineyards	McMinnville	OR
Fences	Medford	OR
Fidelitas Red Mountain	Woodinville	WA
Figgins Family Wine Estates	Walla Walla	WA
Fire and Flood	Dundee	OR
Firesteed	Rickreall	OR
Five Star Cellars, Inc.	Walla Walla	WA
Flying Dutchman Winery	Newport	OR
Flying Trout	Milton-Freewater	OR
Folin Cellars	Gold Hill	OR
Foris Vineyards	Cave Junction	OR

Foundry Vineyards	Walla Walla	WA
The Four Graces	Dundee	OR
Fox Family Wines	Newberg	OR
Freed Estate Winery	Winston	OR
Gamache Vinters	Prosser	WA
Ghost Hill Cellars	Carlton	OR
Gilbert Cellars	Yakima	WA
Gino Cuneo Winery	Walla Walla	WA
Girardet Wineyards	Roseburg	OR
Gramercy Cellars	Walla Walla	WA
Granville Wines	Dundee	OR
Great Wine Buys	Portland	OR
Grizzly Peak Winery	Ashland	OR
Guillen Family Wines	Dayton	OR
Guzzo Family Vineyard	Grants Pass	OR
Hamacher Wines	Carlton	OR
Harry & David Vineyards	Medford	OR
Hawkins Cellars	Dundee	OR
Hawks View Cellars	Sherwood	OR
Hedges Family Estate	Benton City	WA
Helioterra Wines	Portland	OR
Hellgate Cellars	Grants Pass	OR
Henry Earl Estates	Walla Walla	WA
Henry Estate Winery	Umpqua	OR

Hillcrest Winery	Roseburg	OR
Hip Chicks Do Wine	Portland	OR
Honeywood Winery	Salem	OR
Hood Crest Winery	Hood River	OR
Hood River Vineyards and Winery	Hood River	OR
Huett Cellars	Corvallis	OR
Illahe Vineyards	Dallas	OR
Iris Vineyards	Cottage Grove	OR
Irvine & Roberts Vineyards	Ashland	OR
Jacob Williams	Wishram	WA
J. Albin Wines	Hillsboro	OR
Jan Marc Wine Cellars	Portland	OR
Jasper Sisco Wines	Portland	OR
Jaxon Vineyards	Medford	OR
J Christopher Wines	Newberg	OR
J.K. Carriere Wines	Newberg	OR
John Groschau Winery	Salem	OR
Jones of Washington	Quincy	OR
J. Scott Winery	Eugene	OR
JWrigley	Sheridan	OR
Ken Wright Cellars	Carlton	OR
King Estate	Eugene	OR
Kiona Vineyards	Benton City	WA
Kitzke Cellars	Walla Walla	WA

Kramer Vineyards	Gaston	OR
Kriselle Cellars	White City	OR
Lachini Vineyards	Newberg	OR
Lagana Cellars	Walla Walla	WA
Lange Estate Winery & Vineyard	Dundee	OR
Laurel Ridge Winery	Carlton	OR
Lavelle Winery	Veneta	OR
Leah Jørgensen Cellars	Portland	OR
L'Ecole No. 41 Winery	Lowden	WA
Ledger David Cellars	Central Point	OR
Left Coast Cellars	Rickreall	OR
Lemelson Vineyards	Carlton	OR
Lenne Vineyards	Yamhill	OR
Lewman Vineyard	Salem	OR
Lily Rose	Roseburg	OR
Liner & Elsen Wine Merchants	Portland	OR
Llahe	Rickreall	OR
Lobo Hills	Seattle	WA
Long Shadows Distinguished Wineries and Vineyards	Woodinville	WA
Long Walk Vineyard	Ashland	OR
Love and Squalor	McMinnville	OR
Lumos Wine Co.	Philomath	OR
Maine Roi et Fils	Dundee	OR

Maison Bleue Family Winery	Walla Walla	WA
Marchesi Vineyards & Winery	Hood River	OR
Marcus Goodfellow/Matello	McMinnville	OR
Marigold Wine Bar	Portland	OR
Mark Ryan Winery	Woodinville	OR
MarshAnne Landing Winery	Oakland	OR
Maysara Winery & Momatzi Vineyard	McMinnville	OR
McMenamins Edgefield Winery	Troutdale	OR
Meier Family	Helvetia	OR
Melrose Wineyards	Roseburg	OR
Memaloose Wines	Lyle	WA
Merrill Cellars	Bend	OR
Methven	Dayton	OR
Misty Oaks Vineyards	Oakland	OR
Montinore Estate	Forest Grove	OR
Moulton Family Wines	Applegate	OR
Mount Tabor Wines	Portland	OR
Mustard Seed Cellar	Roseburg	OR
Mystic Wines	Amity	OR
Naked Winery	Hood River	OR
Namaste Vineyards	Dallas	OR
Natalie's Estate	Newberg	OR
Native Sun Wines @ Purple Star Winery	Benton City	WA
Nehalem Bay Winery	Nehalem	OR

Newberg Winery Association	Newberg	OR
Noble Estate	Eugene	OR
Noble Pig Winery	McMinnville	OR
North Willamette Vintners Association	Gaston	OR
Nota Bene Wines	Seattle	WA
The Old Portland Wine Bar	Portland	OR
Oregon Wine Board	Portland	OR
Oregon Wine Reserve	Lake Oswego	OR
Oregon Wines on Broadway	Portland	OR
Oswego Hills Winery	Lake Oswego	OR
Owen Roe	St. Paul	OR
Panther Creek Cellars	Dundee	OR
Patricia Green Cellars	Newberg	OR
Patton Valley Vineyard	Gaston	OR
Pebblestone Cellars	Medford	OR
Penner Ash Wine Cellars	Newberg	OR
Pepperbridge	Walla Walla	WA
Pheasantbrook Vineyards	Eagle Point	OR
Pheasant Valley	Hood River	OR
Phelps Creek Vineyards	Hood River	OR
The Pines Winery	Hood River	OR
Plaisance Ranch	Williams	OR
Platt Anderson Cellars	Ashland	OR
Plum Hill Vineyards	Gaston	OR

Poco Colina Gelardi Vineyard	Cheshire	OR
Ponzi Vineyards	Sherwood	OR
Prince Hill Vineyards	Dundee	OR
Prive Vineyards	Newberg	OR
Pudding River	Salem	OR
Purple Cow Vineyards	Newberg	OR
Purple Hands Vineyards	Dundee	OR
Quady North	Jacksonville	OR
Quest Vineyards	Dundee	OR
Rainsong Vineyard	Cheshire	OR
Rainstorm Wines	Silverton/ Umpqua	OR
Rallison Cellars	Sherwood	OR
Raptor Ridge Winery	Newberg	OR
Raylee Wines	Corvallis	OR
Redhawk Vineyard	Salem	OR
Red Lily Vineyards	Jacksonville	OR
Remy Wines	McMinnville	OR
Reustle-Prayer Rock Vineyards	Umpqua	OR
Rex Hill	Newberg	OR
Ribbon Ridge Vineyards	Newberg	OR
Robert Ramsey Vineyards	Woodinville	WA
Roco Winery	Newberg	OR
Roots Wine Company	Gaston	OR

RoxyAnn Winery	Medford	OR
R. Stuart & Co. Winery and Wine Bar	McMinnville	OR
Saffron Fields winery	Yamhill	OR
Sarver Winery	Veneta	OR
Saviah Cellars	Walla Walla	WA
Schmidt Family Vineyards	Grants Pass	OR
SchöneTal Cellars	McMinnville	OR
Schultz Winery	Grants Pass	OR
Scott Paul Wines	Carlton	OR
Season Cellars	Roseburg	OR
Secret Squirrel	Walla Walla	WA
Senzia	Portland	OR
Sequitur	Newberg	OR
Serra Vineyards	Grants Pass	OR
Seven Bridges Winery	Portland	OR
Seven of Hearts/Luminous Hills	Carlton	OR
Seven Sails Wines	Portland	OR
SE Wine Collective	Portland	OR
Shea Vineyards	Carlton	OR
Silvan Ridge Winery	Eugene	OR
Simple Machine	Talent	OR
Sineann	St. Paul	OR
Sip D'Vine	Portland	OR
Skylight Cellars	Walla Walla	WA

Slagle Creek Vineyards	Grants Pass	OR
Sokol Blosser Winery	Dundee	OR
Solena	Carlton	OR
Soloro Vineyards	Grants Pass	OR
Soter Vineyards	Carlton	OR
Southern Oregon Wine Association	(See Website)	
South Stage Cellars	Jacksonville	OR
Spangler Vineyards	Roseburg	OR
Springhouse Cellar	Hood River	WA
Spring Valley Vineyard	Walla Walla	OR
Stag Hollow	Yamhill	OR
Stangeland Vineyards	Salem	OR
Stave & Stone Wine Estates	Hood River	OR
Steelhead Run Vineyards	Applegate	OR
St. Innocent	Salem	OR
St. Josefs	Canby	OR
Stoller Family Estate	Dayton	OR
Stone Griffon Vineyards	Carlton	OR
Stony Mountain	McMinnville	OR
Sweet Cheeks Winery and Vineyard	Eugene	OR
Symnington Family Estates	Shoreline	WA
Syncline Winery	Lyle	WA
Tebri Winery	Eugene	OR
Terra Blanca Winery & Estate Vineyard	Benton City	WA

Terra Vina Wines	Wilsonville	OR
Tertulia	Walla Walla	WA
TeSóAria	Roseburg	OR
Tetrahedron Wines	Lyle	WA
Teutomic Wine Company	Portland	OR
30 Brix Winery	Central Point	OR
Thistle	Dundee	OR
Torii Mor	Dundee	OR
Trisaetum Winery	Newberg	OR
Troon Vineyard	Grants Pass	OR
Tyee Wine Cellars	Corvallis	OR
Urban Crush	Portland	OR
Utopia Winery	Newberg	OR
Valcan Cellars	Corvallis	OR
Valley View Winery	Jacksonville	OR
Van Duzer Vineyards	Dallas	OR
Vidon Wines	Newberg	OR
Viento Wines	Hood River	OR
Vino on 28th	Portland	OR
Viola Wines	Portland	OR
Vista Hills Vineyards	Dayton	OR
Vitis Ridge	Silverton	OR
VX Vineyards (Vercingetorix)	Newberg	OR
Walla Walla Vinters	Walla Walla	WA

Walla Walla Visitors Bureau	Walla Walla	WA
The Walls	Walla Walla	WA
Walter Scott Winery	Salem	OR
Weisinger Family Winery	Ashland	OR
Welsh Famiy Wines	Portland	OR
Westrey Wines	McMinnville	OR
White Rose Estates	Dayton	OR
White Salmon Vineyard	Underwood	WA
Whitetail Ridge Vineyard	Roseburg	OR
Whoa Nelly	Salem	OR
Wild Rose	Winston	OR
WillaKenzie Estate	Yamhill	OR
Willamette Valley Vineyards	Turner	OR
Willful Wine Company	Portland	OR
Winderlea Vineyard & Winery	Dundee	OR
Witness Tree	Salem	OR
Woodstock Wine	Portland	OR
Woodward Canyon Winery	Lowden	WA
Wooldridge Creek	Grants Pass	OR
Wy'East Wineyards	Hood River	OR
Yamhill Valley Vineyards	McMinnville	OR
Youngberg Hill Vineyards	McMinnville	OR
Zerba Cellars	Milton-Freewater	OR
Z'IVO Wines	McMinnville	OR

ADDITIONAL PORTLAND-AREA WINERIES

Avalon Wine Inc.
The Bar at PAFW (formerly Bardot)
Blackbird Wine Shop
Cellar Door
The Civic Taproom and Bottle Shop
CorksCru Wine Merchants
Devil's Den
Division Wines
E&R Wine Shop Inc.
1856 Beer Wine Cider
ENSO Winery
Europa Wine Merchant
45th Parallel Wines
Great Wine Buys
King Boulevard Liquor
Liner & Elsen Wine Merchants
Made in Oregon Store(s)
Mitchell Wine Group
Mom and Pop Wine Shop
Mt. Tabor Fine Wines
Orange Line Wines
Oregon Wines on Broadway
Pairings Portland Wine Shop & Bar
Park Avenue Fine Wines
Pearl Specialty Market & Spirits
The Portland Bottle Shop—Sandwiches
    Wine & Beer
Portland Wine Bar & Winery Tasting Room
Portland Wine Merchants
Red Slate Wine Company
Sec Wines
Sip D'Vine
Thelonious Wines
Vinopolis, LLC
The Wine Cellar
Woodstock Wine & Deli

AN OREGON WINE STORY

This ran 12/14 in the Oregon Wine Press *and has done the rounds because its subject carries stacks of stapled duplicates in the trunk of his car. It is an Oregon wine story, so I append it for your enjoyment. Do not miss the punchline. Doc and I really believe it happened as written. Jake's Famous Crawfish endures post-Doc, and a copy of the original OWP story was posted between the kitchen and the dining room for perusals and, later, for darts.*

DOC WILSON HANGS UP HIS TASTE BUT STAYS IN THE GAME

The restaurant scene is, if anything, ever in flux. Concepts morph into trends and trends into fashions and then, like Atlantis, sink out of sight. So, any establishment that can mark its duration in double or triple digits must be commended. Such survival marks some of Portland's noted destinations, like Dan and Louie's, Huber's and Jake's.

When these arrived on the scene, a long distance phone call went from one room in Alexander Graham Bell's house to the next room. Or, "Kaiser" meant the bellicose German emperor, not a dinner roll. Picasso hadn't picked up a paint brush; indeed, Van Gogh had need for two earmuffs. So, too, venerable eateries can survive only if their personnel are stable and nearly as consistent as the food quality.

Doc Wilson spent 32 years treading the rows between the tables at Jake's Famous. Oregon did not own an AVA when he started there. On a mid-September Sunday night this year Doc served 23 of his closest friends who brought an array of very reputable older vintages to the party. Early on in the sitting, the GM made it clear to most everyone in the restaurant and probably to several taxis coming down NW Stark that Doc Wilson had made the scene a little brighter for a long, long time. I know this because I was at that table.

Doc and I met a few years ago, but he wasn't there. In my trips prior to moving to Portland, I had a ritual. PDX to Jake's Famous. There I downed two martinis and a dozen oysters on the shell. Writing an account of Oregon's wine industry, I wanted nourishment for the task. "If you're writing a book about Oregon wine," Pete the barkeep told me, "you need to know Doc Wilson." And leaving a card, I thought little more of the discussion until a month later, the telephone rang. It was Doc Wilson, resonant baritone brimming with agreeable savvy. If the delivery doesn't convince you this guy knows his grapes, the enthusiasm will. These are not unheard of characteristics for a person selling wine in Gastric Guerrilla Theaters that are upscale and take their menu and wine list seriously—but just so.

The resulting cuvée in Doc's case comes across immediately. It becomes even more agreeable because Wilson has a sense of play that makes the wine lore more than useful. He makes it a helluva lot of fun.

So, on behalf of OWP, I caught up to him to secure his take on the Oregon wine industry and his career as one of its best liked advocates. As usual, Doc did not require much of a prompt. Nor did he lack for words. One expects a crossword puzzle fanatic to be valuable. And the spirit of the game translates to Wilson's take on Oregon's wine industry, too.

FROM SECOND BASEMAN PROSPECT TO WINE MAVEN

Wilson is a native of the northwest and attended Queen Anne High School in Seattle. He aspired to pro sports, particularly baseball and football. He got close enough to the national pastime to realize it wasn't in the cards. Inducted into the U.S. Army, he spent his tour in Vietnam as a medic— hence the sobriquet "Doc." He was twice wounded and spent two decades in the Reserves. Along the way to Jake's he will tell you that he was in the garlic industry. Did he roast it? Did he make wreaths for peasants in Transylvania? I leave it to readers.

What did finally happen was Jake's Famous Crawfish, by then owned by Bill McCormick and Doug Schmick of the eponymous restaurant combine. Ron Day, the fish house GM at that time, was introduced to Doc as the new guy. It turns out both were stationed at Fort Randolph in San Antonio prior to shipping out to the Far East. Both were medics and both served in the same division. Small world? Doc seems to make friends who never quite leave the room.

Doc like many locals knew enough about beer and wine to notice that the restaurant already had a separate Oregon wine list with 14 items. It intrigued him enough to pursue the subject in greater depth. It led to visits of wineries on behalf of Jake's to Napa and Sonoma counties, Walla Walla, and the recently planted vineyards of Willamette Valley. Though this assignment was not in the initial job offer, it soon evolved that Doc was the go-to guy in the wine sales the restaurant generated.

DOC DECODES THE GRAPE

Wilson over time became a major-league schmoozer. Given our association, I assert we shared similar, though not identical tastes in wine. But his palate, like his distinctive presence, is not innate. "People are not born with great palates. The appreciation of the wines we drink occurs over time because we drink them."

Then why do so many people stare like deer in the headlights when a wine list comes tableside? "Wine is part of daily custom in France, Italy, and much of Europe. Children drink wine diluted with water from an early age. Here wine is a rite of passage and a forbidden fruit so we cultivate a kind of ignorance to satisfy a weird sense of propriety. In America, despite our consumption and production, we're still playing catch up."

When Wilson started working at Jake's Famous Crawfish, the list was dominated by wines from other places. Oregon had perhaps two dozen producers. Now there are 720. He then directs his attention to the foodie media.

The awareness of Oregon's potential was brandished by the media magazines because of the greatness of the '83 and '85 vintages. With the coming of Domaine Drouhin to Oregon in 1987 gave a certain legitimacy and validity to Oregon to grow great wine, especially Pinot Noir. Ironically in 1987 the first IPNC or International Pinot Noir Festival was started, showcasing not only Oregon Pinot but Pinot from around the world. 27 years later it's more a worldwide forum for the Pinot Noir grape. It celebrates Oregon winemaking.

Wilson adds that the notoriety has exerted upward pressure on prices, but not to absurd levels. He sees the big picture on value in relation to both Old and New World wines: "Most of Oregon's exceptional wines are in the 30-50 dollar price range. With a good vintage Pinot with good acids well balanced with fruit and tannins will last just as long as their higher priced Cabernets from California where the vintages are almost essentially the same."

He offsets the state's wine further by its range and versatility. All wines are Wilson's friends. His best friends are local. His home cellar bears this out; nonetheless, his assertions of virtue derive from presenting wines to "guests"—customers who wonder what to order with their meals.

"The wines of Oregon pair with a larger range of foods like seafood, chicken and pork. They are still a great value because of this versatility. Pairing Pinot Gris with Dungeness crab, oysters and other shellfish is a natural. Pinot Noir does well with Pork, chicken and Salmon, where the acidity of the pinot cleans the palate of first bite of the oily fish so the next bite is clearly enjoyed especially if the Salmon is topped with a light Buerre Rouge sauce."

Once the kingdom of Austro-German varietals, the rush to plant Pinot Noir resulted in uprooting the traditionally planted vines. This was too exuberant and ill-advised. Once more, "Riesling is being resurrected in Oregon with award wines from Trisaetum and Chehalem. Cheeses, fruit and nuts on a bright summer day partner with the lighter alcohol Rieslings."

After a pause, he looks past these recent developments of the industry in the state.

"Please don't forget Chardonnay. The buttery oaky Chards from down South are not common in Oregon. With the use of the Dijon clone, the grapes ripen on average two weeks earlier and give tropical fruit flavors. Most Oregon chards are made with an emphasis on the fruit. Some do a stainless steel chard and a partial male-lactic one that give more body without being flavored by wood tannins." This preference born of experience finds its way into the patter of wine tours Wilson has conducted for visitors to the state for years.

Longevity has its privileges. Wilson is known as the "Kevin Bacon of the Oregon Wine Industry," a tip of the cap to the film *Six Degrees of Separation*.

Test this anecdote when you're in a tasting room. As this anecdote suffices. "Two years ago I learned that some of my friends had gone into a tasting room and had mentioned my name. The person in the tasting room had been in the Oregon wine industry for a number of years, said to them, "You mean Doc, the Kevin Bacon of the Oregon Wine Industry?" Obviously referring to the movie about six degrees of separation, meaning that my name was known in wine circles. I thought it was very funny.

Any regrets or tasks left incomplete? "32 years at Jakes and the only regret is that the education, the wine seminars and tastings that I did for my fellow employees couldn't have had a wider sweep with the McCormick and Schmick Empire."

The bottom line over time has set different priorities. "The greatest markup in any restaurant is hard liquor, followed by food and lastly by wine. So there wasn't a great emphasis on wine and thus wine education was usually put out last or on the back burner until it was necessary, was selling a great product, seafood from the Northwest as well as wine. Now I'm still selling the Northwest by taking people on local wine tours and showing them why we live in such a great part of the USA." He looks at his Mickey Mouse watch that asserts the insouciance that comes with any encounter with Doc.

Doc served his country; he has served its area wines. And the Kevin Bacon business? I took my first meal at Jake's Famous Crawfish in 1984. I ordered salmon and asked for a Pinot Noir suggestion. Now many years later, when I recall the enthusiastic fellow who made that pairing and popped the cork, I pause and ask the reader…guess who?

A BIBLIOGRAPHIC NOTE

The film writer Joanna Dovalis is by day a marriage and family counselor. Like your author, she is fascinated with Carl Jung, whose *mythopoesis* is as story-filled as wine glasses contain lore. She is one of a few friends, like the barkeep Kurt Fritzler, whose taste in contemporary fiction I can abide. She also cannot imagine a person becoming physically aroused while assembling citations, like end notes or works referenced.

Well, I admit that in the past, when my vision was not impaired, a jolly time awaited me as I arrived at the bibliography. This, however, is a bibliographic note, and it is brief. The wine listing earlier covers more than those described throughout, which, nonetheless, were imbibed in the writing and are, for the most part, imbued with the spirit of Oregon.

The wineries' details can be found online, so readers can plot their own courses. The list is representative rather than exclusive (drink or else!) or exhaustive; new brands and wineries sprout like toadstools on the forest floor. Thus, it is broadly imagined as a starting place. As said variously, the list offers some convenience but is not a buyer's guide.

I would hope that readers toss this book into their vehicles when setting out into the country. A measure of usefulness will be revealed by wrinkled pages and glass rings. A resource has to be worked.

Bottle shops and wine managers in restaurants can help direct your trek into taste memory and will have connections to share with you. Associations such as the Oregon Wine Board or the Columbia Gorge Winegrowers Association are representative of how even the modestly determined wine pilgrim can trek Planet Wine. Ask them for referrals.

SOME FURTHER READING

C.S. Lewis is best known to millions as the Narnia cycle author. But his day job as literary critic and historian is how he earned his chops. One book, titled *Studies in Words*, appeared as a compilation of a series of lectures published by Cambridge University Press in 1960. The entire argument for describing rather than evaluating things comes right out of Lewis.

The age of discovery fascinates me. David Boyle's *Toward the Setting Sun: Columbus, Cabot, Vespucci, and the Race for America* is demonstration of how capital's search for markets and resources helps ideas and people to migrate. Other works, such as Jared Diamond's 1997 *Guns, Germs, and Steel* and Kevin Starr's *Golden Gate*, also help to explain migrations of technology and, in the latter, how the Nob Hill swells got their Napa Valley wine into the cellar before the permanent crossing was opened in 1937.

Readers need to visit the late Kevin Starr's seven-volume history of California. The pages on the beginnings of the Napa Valley, among the other places of agricultural abundance, represent a great story well told. Without the influences of California winemaking and vine tending, the Oregon wine industry would have had no blowback to move ahead. The other side of this translation can be found in Samuel Eliot Morrison's multivolume study of Columbus and his great contribution to the advance of civilization, just as we now in some quarters seek to deconstruct it. From his second voyage, begun in 1493, grapevines came with the ships sailing under the Spanish flag, thus beginning a Pacific Coast migration of vine tending and winemaking.

The most interesting books of discovery narrations, and also the most Oregon-specific, focus on the 1804–6 Lewis and Clark expedition. One little book traces for sleeping bag–bearing campers and acorn kissers the traverse of the entire journey, from akimbo St. Louis to Astoria. You will sense the wonder in natural surroundings observed without earbuds or mind-altering drugs. My idea of camping is about as roughing-it as the Fairmont Grand Del Mar in San Diego. (Thank you, Claire.) The 2003 book by Elizabeth Grossman is *Adventures Along the Lewis and Clark Trail*. It reinforces all those qualities that present-day academia and popular culture distort with their tiresome platitudes about victimhood, conveniently overlooking the freeman or Indian scout—*femme sauvage*—who were integral to that party of North American explorers. You will quickly gain plenty of new respect for the wilderness that today is the Stoler Family Winery or the wetlands south of Astoria.

Terry Teachout's biography of H.L. Mencken, *The Skeptic*, provides wonderful invective against Prohibition from the man himself. More to the point, even noted *inter alia*, is Paul Johnson's *The Birth of the Modern* and *Modern Times*, and a splendid corrective to Marxist claptrap, such as that penned by my one-time government professor, is Johnson's *A History of the American People*. Each of these books shows how idealism applied to social progress spawns unintended and ugly consequences.

I also point readers to *Wine and War* by Don and Petie Kladstrup, *Ardent Spirits* by John Kobler and *Blood and Wine* by Ellen Hawkes, the last about the incredible success of the Gallo wine family and its forceful presence in the nation's wine culture. *The Great Gatsby* owns the best-ever summer cocktail party appearing in a Prohibition-era novel (1925).

James Joyce's "The Dead" appears as the last story in his *Dubliners*. It is the finest short fiction in the English language. It not only tells a sad tale inside the frame tale of a Christmas dinner given by two maiden aunts, but it is also a literary *tour de force* in its parodies of other writers, most notably Dickens and Flaubert. The dinner scene itself, the core of the parody and the main action of the story, is also a superb depiction of food and wine. To learn what can be done with words as opposed to mindless scores on table matter makes the utility here as valuable as the greatness of the piece.

All writing owes something to the titans of Renaissance drama and verse. It more recently must acknowledge Raymond Chandler, where prolixity vies with savage economy—dead men are heavier than broken hearts—and so brings to writing the vivacity of the mighty line of old. His pulp fiction and his seven novels are guilty pleasures to admire for their craft, like artisnal winemaking. If you love-hate L.A. like this writer, you will love following Philip Marlowe into every dive and ritzy bar that exists in the febrile soul of this great alcoholic author. Try your next gin gimlet by adding a dash of bitters. Chandler apparently did, often.

Reading preferences, though subjective, do lead by example. Thus, I share some of mine. One can go on with William and Ariel Durant's eleven-volume *Story of Civilization*, published between 1935 and 1975, and especially John Julius Norwich's *Absolute Monarchs: A History of the Papacy*, where wine flows all over the place and has all but nothing to do with the Sacrament. The Rhone-style wines produced in the American West, you will learn from Lord Norwich, owe oblations to Pope John XXII, who knew how to live it up (and lived past ninety). Equally debonair and informative are the same writer's books about Byzantium and Venice. Lord Norwich is a spinner of tales replete with grace and humor. John Berendt's *The City of Falling Angels*, published in 2006, offers another wicked take on *la Serenissima*. I can depend on these works, as I can on Tony Hiss's *The Experience of Place*, to get to the marrow of terroir, an unfortunate though still useful metaphor.

Should you wish to hear what desperation sounds like when drink is not legal in a big, proud country run by prigs, find the Columbia Records release of *The Original Sound of the 20s*. You will erase your hip-hop collection. You ain't got anything on those early desperate, lively days of a near century ago.

For regular wine news, I follow winefolly.com, lot18.com, snooth.com, sipnorthwest.com and oregonwinepress.com. I have been writing for the last for about three years as this book was under construction. These sites have the temerity to sell stuff, so get over your undergraduate disdain for people who, as the British upper crust say, are in trade. Information, good and questionable, moves at the pace of money. *Caveat emptor*—you can benefit from knowledge others have labored to assemble.

Anyone who wants to know about writing on food and wine should locate the essays of Anthony Burgess, published shortly after he passed in 1996. Then there are biographies of James Beard and Julia Child, not to mention their fine cookbooks, *American Cookery* and *Mastering the Art of French Cooking*, respectively—the latter is to the American kitchen what the long-playing record was to American music listening. And both arrived around the time I arrived on Planet Wine.

Several other writers deserve mention for different reasons. M.F.K. Fisher writes of table customs and matters with exemplary refinement and keenness. Calvin Trillin has written deliciously about American food and dining habits with sheer exuberance.

Tender at the Bone is Ruth Reichl's first autobiographic excursion and defends its claim on your time. In addition to being a strong writer, Reichl's also a real baker with restaurant kitchen experience. I refer, though, to her experience with the author and winemaker Kermit Lynch on the first trip she made to Burgundy. I will not parse the story. You should read it.

Understanding how Oregon Pinot Noir, for instance, is not French Pinot Noir is amply explained in the 2014 book by Maximillian Potter, *Shadows in the Vineyard*, a shabby story but wonderfully informed and well told. Pinot Noir is our go-to wine, and its iterations are manifold. To wit, I sampled a 2014 Resonance from Louis Jadot, one of the Burgundy wine companies settled in our state. Yes, it first seemed like a gruff Burgundy. But it transmuted in my glass, opening its aromas and flavors into an Oregon wine. It reaffirmed my pleasure of noting that French winemakers coming here bring their lineage and traditions here but make Oregon wine. And it's good.

Finally, you can discover Katherine Cole's summary of Oregon wine history on the Oregon Wine Board website. And, then, too, there is Paul Pintarich's *The Boys Up North*, still a good read after a generation. Francis Robinson and others still provide for those able to lift it a wonderful resource guide to wine pretty much everywhere.

Robin Goldstein, very smart (if you count Harvard date stamping important), is a gadfly in the way Ralph Nader is not, as he possesses a wicked sense of play. He snookered one of the best-known wine consumer pubs with a phony wine list for a phony restaurant—and won. He wrote the 2008 *The Wine Trials*, based on this simple, butter-would-melt-in-my-mouth question: Why do people like cheap wine more than costly wine? A man of such temerity and mischief may even be able to live down degrees from Harvard and Yale. Don't take my word for this, but Goldstein redirects the argument about what constitutes "good wine." See for yourself.

The library of taste memory begins in your glass. So imagine the earlier wine list as not just rows of wine grapes but as a great cellar stocked for your consideration and regard. Think of it as your very best term paper magically metamorphosed into your glass. Happy quaffing.

INDEX